The Legacies of
Sr. Madeleva Wolff, CSC

The Legacies of Sr. Madeleva Wolff, CSC

Edited by Jessica Coblentz
and Susan Mancino

Paulist Press
New York / Mahwah, NJ

Cover image: Painting of Sr. Madeleva Wolff by Alex Ann Allen, commissioned by Saint Mary's College in 2021. Used by permission of the artist. All rights reserved.
Cover design by Sharyn Banks
Book design by Lynn Else

Library of Congress Cataloging-in-Publication Data
Names: Coblentz, Jessica editor | Mancino, Susan editor
Title: The legacies of Sr. Madeleva Wolff, CSC / edited by Jessica Coblentz and Susan Mancino.
Description: Mahwah, NJ: Paulist Press, [2026] | Includes bibliographical references. | Summary: "A collection of essays about the life and influence of Sr. Madeleva Wolff, CSC, who, when the president of St. Mary's College, South Bend, Indiana, began the first program of graduate theological studies where women could enroll"—Provided by publisher.
Identifiers: LCCN 2025034397 (print) | LCCN 2025034398 (ebook) | ISBN 9780809157327 paperback | ISBN 9780809189007 ebook
Subjects: LCSH: M. Madeleva (Mary Madeleva), Sister, 1887-1964 | Saint Mary's College (Notre Dame, Ind.)—Presidents | Women Christian educators—United States | Women in higher education—United States | LCGFT: Biographies
Classification: LCC LD4821.S2417 M235 2026 (print) | LCC LD4821.S2417 (ebook)
LC record available at https://lccn.loc.gov/2025034397
LC ebook record available at https://lccn.loc.gov/2025034398

ISBN 978-0-8091-5732-7 (paperback)
ISBN 978-0-8091-8900-7 (ebook)

Published by Paulist Press
997 Macarthur Boulevard
Mahwah, NJ 07430
www.paulistpress.com

Printed and bound in the
United States of America

CONTENTS

Preface

During the summer of 2021, Saint Mary's College in Notre Dame, Indiana, commissioned a new portrait of Sr. Mary Madeleva Wolff, CSC (1887–1964), its third president and an influential figure in American Catholic religious life, poetry, theological education, and women's higher education. Among the elegant portraits of the revered nun that already hung on walls around the campus, this one stood out in size, color, and the prominence of its placement. At seven feet wide and five feet high, it featured Madeleva's confident visage surrounded by the wide, fanned coif once worn by the Sisters of the Holy Cross.[1] This grayscale depiction of Madeleva in habit stood out against a magnificent backdrop of color: Halos of yellows, oranges, and blues encircled her face and radiated outward on the canvas. To the left of her face, one bright swirl swept over the front of her habit, as if enveloping her in light. You will recognize the image from the cover of this volume.

The college displayed it in the bustling Reignbeaux Lounge, a spacious, wood-paneled meeting place inside the campus's central administrative and residential building. This is where prospective students meet with the Office of Admissions and begin their campus tours; where current students frequently study and host club gatherings; and where faculty line up each May to begin their procession to the college graduation, which takes place just outside its doors. All this activity was to be overseen by the prominent image of a poised Madeleva, wearing a modest grin and a sparkle in her eyes.

The portrait's creator was Alex Ann Allen, a young local artist whose giant murals grace the sides of buildings all around the surrounding city of South Bend. During the last decade, her art brought vibrant color to the sometimes bleak landscape of the former factory town, and that brought her local notoriety—so much so that locals who stood before the Madeleva commission would likely recognize it as Allen's creation. Her rendering of the famed nun was thus a bridge between the city and the campus as well as a symbol of the newness that was emerging and transforming these communities for good.

When students returned to campus in fall 2021, the new portrait of Madeleva was a hit by several measures. The portrait was replicated on stickers that students plastered on laptops and water bottles. Some hung posters of the image in their dorm rooms. Some faculty framed prints to display in their offices. What was once an ordinary corner in Reignbeaux Lounge became a destination for campus visitors, curious to glimpse this new addition to the campus's impressive art collection.

But then, a few months later, the portrait was gone.

News about the removal of the painting spread through campus in whispers. Why was it taken down? Was it simply relocated? But where? Where was it? Rumors suggested that, for all the love and enthusiasm generated by the new piece, Madeleva's portrait also had some vocal critics. People heard complaints about Madeleva's smile, about the contemporary feel of the painting, about its departure from others' memories of her. Whatever the criticisms, they were convincing enough that the college took the painting down, where it stayed hidden away for many months. As of early 2025, the portrait of Madeleva has been hung again, now in the third-floor hallway of the campus's Moreau Center for the Arts. Amid a few faculty offices, classrooms, and art studios, this corner of campus sees little traffic. Relatively few see this expansive, vibrant image of Madeleva now save those who seek it out like pilgrims.

Art is evocative; Sr. Madeleva believed this more than most. That a painting of a woman religious more than sixty years gone elicited these extremes of affection and distaste is unexpected, however. Its mixed reception captures the unique and enduring importance of Sr. Madeleva. It also shows how contested her image and legacy remain among those who care about her. Yet there has been relatively little academic reflection and deliberation concerning Madeleva's life and legacy even as she remains a notable figure in the history of U.S. Catholic women religious. And when discussions of her life appear in print or surface in the popular piety of the communities to which she belonged, accounts of her legacy vary a great deal. Some memorializations cast her as a wise spiritual mother whose insights should be mined for religious life today. Others know her as a unifying persona or mascot for the institutions she spearheaded. Still others venerate her as a kind of martyr who sacrificed her personal talents and interests for worthy religious causes. But was Sr. Madeleva a mother, a mascot, a martyr—or some other? How does her life and legacy appear to us today? What do these legacies tell us about the communities that continue to commemorate her? And what can Madeleva's legacies teach us about navigating contemporary realities?

Who Was Sr. Madeleva Wolff, CSC?

Before turning to Madeleva's many legacies, it is fitting to begin with her history. Born on May 24, 1887, she was baptized "Mary Evaline" under the care of her parents, August and Lucy Wolff. August, a Lutheran born to a single mother in Pomerania, and Lucy, an ardent Catholic and the daughter of Prussian immigrants, raised their three children in the Catholic community of Cumberland, Wisconsin, a small, rural lumber town where August ran a harness shop. Mary Evaline, called "Eva," was the family's only daughter and the middle child between an older brother, Fred, and a younger brother, Vern. Following a public school education where the precocious Eva excelled, she followed Fred to the University of Wisconsin in 1905. It was rare at the time for women to attend university, and Eva enjoyed her year there with her brother, recalling her vibrant social life and pride in her long chestnut hair. Eva nevertheless found herself wanting "more" than the life this institution afforded.[2] After seeing an advertisement for Saint Mary's College in a literary magazine during the summer following her first year at university, she transferred to the all-women's "convent school" in Notre Dame, Indiana.

Eva's year at the University of Wisconsin had cultivated her curiosity for studies in English, which flourished during her time at Saint Mary's under the mentorship of Sr. Rita Heffernan, CSC. With an anecdote telling of the future poet's rebellious personality, biographer Gail Porter Mandell recounts an early interaction between Eva and her mentor:

> Asked by her new teacher to write a lyric poem as a class assignment, Eva announced, "But I cannot write poetry." Sister Rita was unmoved. "And I don't know what to write about," she added. Sister Rita advised her that perhaps giving thought to the subject might solve the problem.[3]

Eva rose to the occasion, and by the close of her sophomore year, she was publishing poetry in the college's literary magazine and had declared an English major.

Along with her interests in poetry and literature flourished Eva's commitment to her Catholic faith. During junior year, she rose early to attend Mass with the nuns and receive communion—a daily practice uncommon among laypersons of the era. She also prayed for knowledge of her vocation, and in the summer following that junior year, she was accepted to the postulancy of the Congregation of the Sisters of the Holy Cross. As her classmates embarked on their senior year at Saint Mary's in fall 1908, Eva entered religious life. Though this decision was a difficult departure from the expectations of her beloved family and her friends at the school, it was but another step along the same path that had brought her to Saint Mary's—that search for something "more" for her life.

Following an abbreviated postulancy of three months, the young Eva entered the novitiate. As was customary of the time, her community bestowed upon her a new name: She would henceforth be Sr. Mary Madeleva Wolff, CSC. With this new name came new work: In addition to her ongoing religious formation, Madeleva took on service to the congregation's ministries beginning with an assignment to teach English at Saint Mary's Academy, the sisters' secondary school. With her transition from novice to scholastic in 1910, she additionally took on the instruction of several English classes at the college and eventually courses in philosophy and scripture as well as the oversight of various student activities. Never mind that the young novice had not yet finished her own bachelor's degree; Madeleva would serve where she was needed—a commitment she carried through the rest of her life.

In August 1919, the congregation called upon Madeleva's obedience again when on short notice it instructed her to relinquish her duties at Saint Mary's to move to the mission territory of Ogden, Utah, where she would serve as principal of the community's boarding school, Sacred Heart Academy. After two years of exhausting leadership at the academy, Madeleva's already fragile health deteriorated further, prompting a summer of "rest" in California. Though Madeleva hardly rested during that summer of 1921, it was a refreshing change of scenery that occasioned a visit to the University of California at Berkeley, where she gathered information about their doctoral program in English. In the summer of 1922, she received permission to begin graduate work at

Berkeley—a continuation of the master's level studies she began at Notre Dame after finishing her bachelor's degree while teaching full-time at Saint Mary's. To the delight of her Berkeley professors and to her own surprise, Madeleva excelled, prompting the congregation to reassign her that fall to Holy Rosary Academy in Woodland, California—about a three-hour train ride from Berkeley—where she would teach and serve as principal while pursuing her doctorate in English.

By the time she finished her doctoral studies in 1925, much had unfolded: She had continued to succeed as a top student—"one of the three best" in the whole university, one professor declared. Her first collection of poetry, *Knight's Errant*, had won high praise. She had also acquired multiple book contracts for her work on religious themes in English literature. Rather than remaining in the ivory tower, however, she left the Berkeley hills for the mountains of Ogden, Utah, where once again she was assigned as principal and teacher of the sisters' Sacred Heart Academy. Her tenure there was brief because of a new, surprising assignment from her congregation: She was to establish a college in Salt Lake City. Saint Mary's-of-the-Wasatch was established on September 9, 1926, with Sr. Madeleva as its dean—a title later revised to "president."

In May 1933 after seven years at Saint Mary's-of-the-Wasatch and an increasingly disagreeable relationship with the convent community there, the leadership of Madeleva's congregation pledged financial support to send her and a companion abroad for a yearlong sabbatical of sorts: She would study at Oxford and explore educational possibilities for members of the congregation. From August 27, 1933, to July 1934, she did just that, albeit not according to her original plans. When her companion Sr. Verda Clare became ill and needed a warmer climate to recuperate, Madeleva's Oxford studies were cut short—after only one month. She accompanied her companion to a convent in Hyeres in the south of France. Her plans thwarted, Madeleva nevertheless flourished during the remainder of her trip. Upon Verda Clare's recovery, they enjoyed several excursions, including a trip to Egypt and the Holy Land at the invitation of a priest they met. Thomas O'Grady's chapter in this volume recounts another trip to visit with the renowned poet William Butler Yeats in Ireland. Such happy encounters with well-connected and influential people were not only a mark of her trip—which included new friendships with English literary greats C. S. Lewis, J. R. R. Tolkien, and G. K. Chesterton—but a regular feature of her life before and after.

A brilliant, charming, and captivating person, Madeleva was ever a desired interlocutor and social companion.

After her year of adventure abroad, Madeleva returned to the United States with some reluctance, and aptly so in view of what awaited her. Fighting within the congregation in the United States had left morale at a low while the state of affairs at the college she founded in Wasatch worsened. Saint Mary's College in Notre Dame, too, was hurting financially, and the search for a new president for the college was underway. Just two days after her arrival to Indiana, where Madeleva expected to work for the next year, she learned that, contrary to her request and the assurances of her superiors, *she* had been assigned to serve as Saint Mary's third president. Madeleva called the assignment a "disaster."[4] Not only was she still haunted by the failures of her administrative post in Utah, but she also knew that the prestigious administrative post meant her longings for a more contemplative and prayerful life would go unmet.

Despite her own reservations, in the fall of 1934 Madeleva assumed the presidency with gusto and wasted no time innovating. She instituted new student government structures, loosened many of the strict rules governing student life, reimagined the curriculum, and welcomed prestigious visitors and new faculty members to campus. Though entrenched in the life of the college and its founding congregation in Notre Dame, Madeleva prioritized travel to conferences and speaking events in the name of strengthening the college's image. Her travels accomplished that while also sustaining her notoriety as a poet and scholar—a vocation she continued to identify with and share with students, as we learn in Eva Hooker's personal and poetic chapter in this volume. Madeleva's esteemed academic reputation endured despite how the demands of her administrative post once again limited her ability to write and teach.

Though there was hardly a time during her twenty-seven-year tenure as president when Madeleva was not scheming something new for the college, some of her efforts stand out as prophetic for their time and especially meritorious for their lasting legacy at and beyond the college. She transformed the campus landscape, overseeing the fundraising and construction of several campus buildings: In 1939, she built Riedinger House, a space of active learning for students in the domestic science program, at seven-eighths scale in response to the financial pressures of the Depression. In 1957, *Life* magazine featured Madeleva and the newly built Moreau Center for the Arts (completed in 1956).[5] She also built Haggar College Center (in 1941), Havican Hall (in 1947), and the Science Hall (in 1954). As Sally Geislar explores in her chapter, Madeleva also transformed the campus grounds with seedlings she herself often planted and, in 1954, recruited the college's first master gardener, Joe Bonadies, to flourish the campus's lush grounds.

Madeleva applied her knowledge of and passion for the medieval university to modern, interdisciplinary curriculum development. In 1935, she brought together sisters at the college and some of the leading minds in liberal learning at the time to develop and implement the "Trivium in College Composition and Reading" that would serve as the core of the college's curriculum for the next twenty-five years. Sister Miriam Joseph authored a textbook for the curriculum that helped other colleges adopt and adapt this liberal arts curriculum as well; its popularity is evident in its publication through five editions.[6] As a demonstration of her continued interest in the Christian foundations of modern education, Madeleva later helped to found the Program in Christian Culture, which offered Saint Mary's students a more in-depth study of Christianity's influence on Western cultural and intellectual traditions.

In 1941, Madeleva issued a unilateral decision to integrate the college and refused debate with any objectors. Saint Mary's thus welcomed its first Black students before most other residential private colleges and universities. In the face of outrage and predictions of ominous consequences for the college as a result of this decision, Madeleva declared: "For years I had been waiting for this question. I knew only one answer, the right one. If it emptied the school, we would enroll Negro girls in residence."[7]

Madeleva continued to expand educational opportunities for women through the founding of the School of Sacred Theology at Saint Mary's, which serves as the focus of Sandra Yocum's contribution to this volume. Like so many initiatives from Madeleva and her congregation, the school was a response to an obvious yet unmet need in the Church. Though in 1939 the National Catholic Educational Association had affirmed the importance of teaching theology in Catholic schools, colleges, and universities—including those owned and staffed by women religious—most opportunities for advanced theological training were confined to seminaries and thus reserved de facto for male clerics and clerics in training. There was simply no opportunity in the United States for laypersons, including women religious, to attain graduate theological training in a full-time program that matched the rigor and priorities of the seminary education clergy received. After other Catholic universities declined Madeleva's solicitation to open graduate programs in theology for laypeople, Madeleva decided to start one such program at Saint Mary's. With the approval of Pope Pius XII, the School of Sacred Theology was formally established in 1944. Two years later, Saint Mary's became the first women's college in the United States to offer an undergraduate degree in theology.

These accomplishments were part of Madeleva's broader contributions to Catholic higher education and religious life, as Margaret Eletta Guider, OSF, documents in her chapter in this book. Having experienced firsthand the burdens of being thrown into a classroom without adequate professional preparation, Madeleva harnessed her leadership in the National Catholic Educational Association to advance the Sister Formation Movement, which championed a standardized program of professional preparation for women in religious life. Beginning in 1949, Madeleva's contributions helped to transform the formation programs of the Sisters of the Holy Cross and of women's religious communities across the United States.

Amid this busy career, she maintained correspondence with famous and influential people, including Mortimer Alder, G. K. Chesterton, Theodore M. Hesburgh, CSC, Helen Hayes, Conrad Hilton, members of the Kennedy family, Benjamin Lehman, C. S. Lewis, Clare Boothe Luce, Jacques Maritain, Thomas Merton, and Edith Wharton, among others. Through these communications, which fueled the importance of Madeleva's voice among her contemporaries, she regularly coordinated educational opportunities, public relations, fundraising efforts, and guest lectures made available to students. This correspondence continued into her retirement, which began in 1961; in fact, Madeleva received a personal note from President John F. Kennedy at the time of her retirement.[8]

Released from her presidential post, she distanced herself from the daily administrative tasks of the college but continued writing and traveling for speaking engagements. On a trip to Boston in July 1964, Madeleva needed surgery to remove her gall bladder. Following a successful surgery and optimistic prognosis, she experienced a rare complication that led to her sudden and unexpected passing on July 25, 1964. "Sister Mary Madeleva, a leading Roman Catholic educator, poet and the author of 70 books, died today in New England Baptist Hospital. She was 77 years old," announced her obituary in the *New York Times*. "Sister Madeleva achieved distinction and fame as president of St. Mary's College at South Bend, Ind., but her reputation as an educator was frequently overshadowed by her great outpouring of verse and essays. During her 27-year administration, St. Mary's was greatly developed and enlarged."[9]

Overview of the Volume

Although Sr. Madeleva is a revered and recognizable name among those who study U.S. Catholic history, comparably little research has been published on her across Catholic theology, spirituality, poetry and literature studies, and religious history. Writers and researchers who engage with Madeleva often do so within the context of their treatment of another topic, per Nick Ripatrazone's recent *The Habit of Poetry: The Literary Lives of Nuns in Mid-century America*.[10] A notable exception to this pattern is Gail Porter Mandell's much earlier biography of Sr. Madeleva, which remains often read and cited among Madeleva enthusiasts today.[11] By centering the figure of Madeleva and bringing interdisciplinary perspectives to her life and legacy, the current volume offers a needed supplement to these and other important treatments of the revered nun.

The volume's chapters explore the legacies that follow from the various and sometimes disparate roles Sr. Madeleva embodied in life and occupies in collective memory today. From October 3 to 5, 2024, the volume's authors first presented their essays during a conference on this topic hosted by the Center for the Study of Spirituality at Saint Mary's College, an event that marked the beginning of the esteemed center's fortieth-anniversary year. There, the authors responded to one another's contributions, and so did those in attendance that weekend: Sisters of the Holy Cross who knew Madeleva firsthand, longtime members of the college community who have seen her legacy evolve across the decades, current Saint Mary's students and alumnae with varying degrees of exposure to Madeleva's life and legacy, as well as a host of other interested participants. The rich conversation at the conference confirmed the relevance of this project and enriched the insights offered in the volume's chapters.

Hailing from various disciplines—theology, history, poetry, English literature, communication studies, and environmental studies—our authors provide greater depth and insight on many of the events mentioned in the brief history of Madeleva presented above. They also offer inventive perspectives on the rich and complex legacies of Sr. Madeleva. And while this collection does not capture a complete picture of Madeleva's contributions and legacies—no single volume can—the essays work from interdisciplinary perspectives and methodologies to signal Madeleva's multifaceted contributions to U.S. Catholicism, consecrated religious life, spirituality, literature, poetry, and Catholic and women's education. Together they demonstrate that her persona remains vibrant across broad-reaching communities.

The volume commences with a reflection from the foremost academic expert on Madeleva, Gail Porter Mandell, who recounts her writing of the 1997 biography of Madeleva that informs many of the volume's chapters. The subsequent essays are then divided into three parts, each of which addresses Madeleva's legacy as a woman religious, as a scholar and poet, and as an educator and administrator, respectively.

In addition to these organizing legacies, several themes emerge across the authors' explorations of Madeleva's legacies for our contemporary moment. First, through her personal spirituality and leadership in Catholic education and religious life, Madeleva regularly challenged perceptions of the stark division between the sacred and the secular. She instead articulated something much more vibrant—a belief that the secular holds paths to God and the sacred has something important to teach the world. These intersections are abundant in Madeleva's response to the "machine age," the space age, and hyperconsumerism. Her responses speak to questions of our present moment, too: How does one live as a religious person in a "post-Christian," secular world? Madeleva tells us: Find God everywhere. And what can Christianity, and religion in general, offer the secular world? Madeleva responds: A training for wonder as well as for God. This theme comes into focus in a special way in chapters from Margaret M. Gower, Daniel P. Horan, and David A. Clairmont.

Second, these essays display the value of retrieval and the risks of hagiography. Madeleva's broad contributions to U.S. Catholicism and women's education as well as her more localized achievements for the Congregation of the Sisters of the Holy Cross and Saint Mary's College were significant. The chapters in this volume recount Madeleva's establishment of the School of Sacred Theology, her advocacy for adequate educational preparation for women religious, her accomplishments as a poet, her keen leadership of the college during tumultuous times, and her thoughtful connections to leading intellects of her time. Retrieving and documenting these successes lend important insights into the value of her work and legacy for contemporary communities.

Simultaneously, these chapters bring a critical eye that discloses the risks of romantic hagiography. As Katie Ann-Marie Bugyis's chapter shows, for example, Madeleva's important scholarship on Chaucer left his anti-Semitism unaddressed, a concerning oversight that stands in tension with her commitments to ecumenism and interfaith relations. Susan Mancino's chapter points to the colonial origins of Madeleva's oft-cited promise of "discovery," inviting readers to examine its place in the collective memory of Saint Mary's College so it can be interpreted anew. Appreciating Madeleva's many path-breaking accomplishments across so many realms, Jessica Coblentz's chapter warns that memories of the nun's competence and accomplishments easily overshadow the physical, psychological, and spiritual costs of her work at a time when many women religious and other laborers still bear these unjust burdens. Paired together, the value of retrieving lessons from Madeleva's life as well as the risks of hagiography call us, first, to a clear-eyed look at Madeleva situated within the contexts of her historical moment and, second, to critical reflection on the contemporary implications of the legacies she leaves and the example she extends to the present.

As the volume editors, we were impressed by how the volume's wide-ranging essays came together. And like all good works of scholarship, the authors' analyses illuminate additional trajectories for future research in Madeleva studies. The chapter from the current president of Saint Mary's College, Katie Conboy, notes Madeleva's bold and righteous decision to racially integrate the college in 1943. Especially at a time when many Catholic colleges and universities are reckoning with their histories of racial injustice, there is more research to be done on this pivotal moment in the college's history in relation to the wider landscape of U.S. Catholic higher education.[12] Conboy's chapter also identifies the declining number of Catholic women's colleges in the United States, which far outpaces what Madeleva predicted as she envisioned the future of Catholic higher education. Contemporary shifts in social constructions of gender were also beyond the nun's purview, so much so that even today's moderate feminists will balk at some of Madeleva's comments on womanhood. How to view the remarkable strides Madeleva made as a woman and for women with the limited views of gender she espoused warrants further reflection. Madeleva's extensive correspondence with brilliant and influential contemporaries offers a huge number of possibilities for further academic exploration as well. We hope this interdisciplinary volume inspires researchers across the academy to take up these and many other trajectories for Madeleva research.

As we conclude this preface, we express our utmost gratitude to the volume's contributors, to Donna Crilly and the team at Paulist Press, and to the institutional sponsors who supported this volume through their financial support of our research: The Center for the Study of Spirituality, the Offices of the President and the Provost, the Center for Academic Innovation, and the Center for Women's Intercultural Leadership—all at Saint Mary's College; the International Thomas Merton Society for the 2022 Shannon Fellowship; and the Cushwa Center for the Study of American Catholicism at the University of Notre Dame, especially for the 2022 Mother Theodore Guerin Research Travel Grant.

Jessica Coblentz and Susan Mancino

Notes

1. It is customary in scholarship to use "Madeleva," her religious name, as a reference rather than her family name, Wolff.

2. Marjorie Hall Walsh, "Sister Madeleva: Lyric Poet" (master's thesis, Creighton University), 1–3.

3. Gail Porter Mandell, *Madeleva: A Biography* (Albany: State University of New York, 1997), 39.

4. Mandell, *Madeleva*, 144.

5. "Nun, President, and Poet," *Life*, June 10, 1957.

6. Mandell, *Madeleva*, 151.

7. Sister M. Madeleva, CSC, *My First Seventy Years* (New York: Macmillan, 1959), 98.

8. Mandell, *Madeleva*, 245.

9. "Sister Mary Madeleva, 77, Dies; President of St. Mary's College; Headed School in South Bend, Ind., for 27 Years—Poet and Author of 70 Books," *New York Times*, July 26, 1964, https://www.nytimes.com/1964/07/26/archives/sister-mary-madeleva-77-dies-president-of-st-marys-college-headed.html.

10. Nick Ripatrazone, *The Habit of Poetry: The Literary Lives of Nuns in Mid-century America* (Minneapolis: Fortress Press, 2023).

11. Mandell, *Madeleva.*

12. See, for example, Jeannine Hill Fletcher, *Grace of the Ghosts: A Theology of Institutional Reparation* (New York: Fordham University Press, 2025).

1

Writing *Madeleva: A Biography*

Gail Porter Mandell

In the late 1980s and through most of the decade that followed, I researched and wrote *Madeleva: A Biography*, the first full-length biography of Sister M. Madeleva Wolff, CSC.[1] As evidenced by obituaries in the *New York Times* and other national and international publications, she had become by the time of her death in 1964 "the most renowned nun in the world" thanks to widespread acclaim as a college president, scholar, poet, and spokesperson for Catholic higher education.[2] By the time I joined the faculty of Saint Mary's College in the 1970s, however, she was no longer in the spotlight. How had I, someone who had never met the woman, knew little about her, and had no thought of writing a biography of anyone, come to write hers? This will sound strange, as Madeleva died almost a decade before I set foot on the Saint Mary's College campus, but the only way I can explain it is that my subject chose me.

Meeting Madeleva

Early in the 1970s, Saint Mary's was in the process of merging with the nearby University of Notre Dame to form a coeducational university. After merger negotiations collapsed, Saint Mary's chose to remain a women's college, and I became the assistant to the academic dean, with a spacious office in Le Mans Hall and a smaller, adjoining office for my secretary. The arrangement resembled a suite; it included a full bath, a windowless alcove off my office, and a private terrace outside French doors. Thanks to an alumna who visited one afternoon, I discovered that my office had been Madeleva's bedroom after she retired from the presidency of the college. The alcove had been her anchorage, a place of meditation and prayer, and the terrace, her favorite spot for contemplating the beauty of the campus. The alum introduced me to the remarkable woman who had spent the last years of her life in the space I now occupied. As a result, I found, framed, and mounted a photo of Madeleva on the wall. I had the feeling that something of her spirit remained there, and I wanted to honor it. Before I returned to the faculty, I spent five more years in the place I came to think of as "our" room.

In my early years at the college, many remained who had known Madeleva personally, most of whom lauded her presidency as the "glory days" of the college. Under her leadership from 1934 to 1961, Saint Mary's became known as a center of Christian culture. She established innovative programs, most notably, the School of Sacred Theology, which for the first time allowed women and laymen to study full-time for graduate degrees in Catholic theology. She also instituted a modern version of the medieval Trivium of grammar, logic, and rhetoric for all first-year students and an interdisciplinary program in Christian Culture (later renamed Humanistic Studies), which Madeleva dubbed "the department deluxe."[3] She built a performing arts center where medieval mystery and miracle plays as well as operas and contemporary dramas were staged, featuring, among others, Broadway star Helen Hayes, a personal friend.

When I began working on the biography, almost twenty-five years after her death, Madeleva had faded from public memory, and her era, sometimes referred to as "The Golden Age of American Catholicism," had ended. The Catholic educational system and the religious congregations that allowed colleges like Saint Mary's to flourish were shrinking rapidly, with their histories and those who made them largely forgotten. On campus, the liberal arts building bore Madeleva's name, but few students, faculty, or staff knew anything about her or even who she was. One of the seminar rooms in which I taught contained memorabilia of the donor, an avid fan of Sister Madeleva's poetry who had endowed the building in her memory. A life-sized, spectral painting of Madeleva by artist Margo Hoff hung in the main corridor, with a large bronze emblem with her name and dates and an excerpt from one of her poems embedded in the floor at her feet. But I recall no other commemoration of her anywhere on campus. One afternoon, I overheard two students wondering if "that nun in the painting" was buried under the bronze seal.

That institutional forgetfulness began to change when Professor Keith Egan joined the faculty. In 1984, he founded the Center for Spirituality (now the Center for the Study of Spirituality), and the following year inaugurated the Madeleva Lecture Series. For the past forty years, it has showcased women theologians in an annual lecture that commemorates the School of Sacred Theology, regarded by many as Madeleva's crowning achievement.[4] As a result, the series—along with "The Madeleva Manifesto: A Message of Hope and Courage" dedicated to women in the Church that was composed and signed in 2000 by fifteen Madeleva lecturers—has been a lasting legacy, reviving and sustaining interest in both the School and the founder herself.[5]

Beginning the Biography

Not incidentally, the biography began with a knock on my office door and an invitation. It was mid-February 1987, and I had just been awarded a Lilly Foundation fellowship. After joining the full-time faculty, I designed a course called "Lives and Times" to introduce students to the study of culture through various forms of biography and autobiography. At the time, few if any academic programs offered such courses, and my fellowship proposal was to interview contemporary biographers about biography. When I opened my door that February afternoon, there stood Elena Malits, a Holy Cross sister and theology professor. She came with a proposal of her own. No one had yet written a book-length biography of Sister Madeleva, she informed me. "Why don't *you*?" I protested that my fellowship was to interview biographers, not to become one. Besides, I added, I knew very little about Madeleva. Nor did I know anything about nuns or life in a convent. Elena persisted: "Visit the college and convent archives. See what's there." I thanked her and for months ignored her invitation.

Then, just as the academic year ended and my yearlong sabbatical began, I had a dream. Madeleva and I were in bunk beds. I was in the bottom bunk, trying to fall asleep, but she kept talking, and as she talked, papers and handwritten notes came fluttering down from above. I awoke with no memory of what she said in the dream or what was written on the pages, but I felt compelled to visit the college archives. (Later, I realized that the dream and subsequent visit occurred the same week as the anniversary of Madeleva's one hundredth birthday!) In the archives, I found an extensive collection that included all of Madeleva's publications, more than twenty books of poems and essays, including her autobiography; a scrapbook from her college years with photographs of lovely young Mary Evaline Wolff; and scores of boxes filled with files containing Madeleva's personal and official correspondence, exchanged over many years with some of the most notable figures of the twentieth century: authors, scholars, actors, political and religious leaders.

One of the first files I happened on included letters Madeleva received over a span of years (ca. 1920–1934) from a Holy Cross priest who had taught her philosophy as a young sister. He later served as her spiritual advisor, hoping, in his words, "to make a mystic of her."[6] His language frequently employed erotic images and metaphors that suggested the biblical Song of Songs. However, some references were unmistakably personal, as in a letter dated June 11, 1929: "This is meant to be a love letter, with lots of kisses and hugging and tears of joyful reconciliation." How to interpret protestations of his "virginal love" for "my little sweetheart" and his assertion that she was, in his words, "one of those on whom I should be glad to spend my manhood"?[7] I was intrigued. Hooked, in fact.

Between trips to interview contemporary biographers during the year that followed, I returned to the college archives to read my way through the Madeleva letters and papers and all her printed publications, taking copious notes.[8] Members of the Sisters of the Holy Cross who had lived and worked with Madeleva were still alive, and with several sisters who were faculty colleagues acting as intermediaries, I began a series of interviews in person and by telephone with members of the congregation who had known Madeleva best. Fortuitously, I learned, other projects that focused on Madeleva were either underway or had been recently completed, among them several unpublished graduate theses that focused on aspects of Sister Madeleva's life and work, one on her poetry and another on her leadership.[9] Sister Maria Assunta Werner, CSC, was in the process of compiling a pictorial biography of Madeleva.[10]

When I contacted surviving members of the Wolff-Arntz family, I discovered that a family genealogy was close to completion.[11]

Often, my search seemed like a scavenger hunt, with clues planted along the way. For example, one of the fattest files in the Madeleva Collection contained scores of letters written to Madeleva over four decades by Benjamin Lehman, one of her professors at the University of California at Berkeley, where she earned her PhD in English in 1925. Many of Lehman's letters were replies to hers, which I feared no longer existed; that is, until I happened on a reference to his papers, housed in the archives at Berkeley. There, I discovered a hidden treasure: her half of the correspondence, more than eighty letters, most of them handwritten, dating from the mid-1920s through the early 1960s. At that point, I began to feel (and I am not a superstitious person) that Madeleva's spirit must be leading me ("prodding" might be a better word) where I needed to go.

At the same time, my research on the art of biography, along with the interviews I taped with seven biographers, proved an invaluable asset in writing Madeleva's life story. During my sabbatical year, I read dozens of biographies, from ancient texts to recently published works. Plutarch's *Lives* taught me to look for the detail that reveals character,[12] and Judith Thurman's *Isak Dinesen: The Life of a Storyteller* offered a master class in the seamless integration of a subject's life and work.[13] Moreover, I had the privilege of conversing with some of the most distinguished biographers of the modern era.[14] Particularly helpful to me was Michael Mott, author of the authorized biography of Thomas Merton, a famous writer and Trappist monk with whom Madeleva had an extensive correspondence. Mott's understanding of religious life and institutions, along with that of my husband, who spent several years in a Benedictine monastery, clarified for me crucial aspects of Madeleva's experience as a Holy Cross sister.

Before I fully committed myself to writing the biography, I contacted several of the sisters who themselves might wish to write a biography of Madeleva; all of them encouraged me to go ahead, with their blessing. I also obtained and received explicit permission from the Sisters of the Holy Cross and the college to consult and publish materials in the convent and college archives. Understandably, the leadership of the congregation was concerned that any biography of one of their members should be one they could approve, but I made clear that I would need the freedom to publish without censorship. Of course, the publication of any material exceeding fair use would require permission from the copyright holders themselves. Eventually, I did receive the necessary permissions, but doing so was not always easy. Who could grant permission to quote from Madeleva's published works? The convent? The college? Most of her publishers were no longer in business. And what about the thousands of letters to Madeleva stored in the archives from correspondents (who legally owned the copyrights), most of them long dead? Sister Miriam Cooney, CSC, a colleague who worked closely with Madeleva in her last years, offered encouragement, information, and advice; she even volunteered to intercede for me with members of the congregation, should I need it. When I finally put pen to paper, she read and critiqued the manuscript. I suspect that, thanks largely to her trust and support, the congregation generously contributed to and unconditionally supported the project.

Wanting to experience for myself the places that had shaped Madeleva's early life, I traveled to Wisconsin, where she spent her first twenty years. Of course, the place where Madeleva spent most of her adult life (first as a student, then as sister, teacher, and finally president) was Saint Mary's, a place I thought I knew until I began to discover its history. Much of what I learned came from conversations with those who had lived and worked at the convent and college for generations, many of whom I met for the first time. I also discovered several histories of the congregation and college and biographies of some of the early Sisters of the Holy Cross, most written by members of the congregation themselves. They helped me appreciate the extent to which many of Madeleva's educational ideals and innovations, such as the creation of the School of Sacred Theology, were inspired by those who came before her. Only after I delved into the historical accounts and learned something of Madeleva's lesser known but noteworthy predecessors—the women who had built the college of which I was now a part—only then did I discover it, validating T. S. Eliot's poignant claim in *Four Quartets*, "And the end of all our exploring / Will be to arrive where we started / And know the place for the first time."[15]

The writings of Madeleva herself were indispensable sources of information, among them her occasional diaries and her voluminous correspondence, of which as president she kept carbon copies. Most unusual for women of that era—and for any nun ever—was *My First Seventy Years*, her autobiography.[16] It offers a firsthand account of her early life and her religious vocation as well as her multifaceted achievements as a scholar, poet, essayist, and educator. However, warning the reader that the autobiography is not "the story of a nun on her prie-dieu," it reveals few of her religious experiences.[17] She admitted that much was omitted, promising a sequel that her sudden death made impossible. In truth, the autobiography was not her idea; she wrote it at the request of her publisher, who gave her a choice between a biography or writing the life herself. She wrote the autobiography by hand on yellow legal pads during a two-week stay in a sanatorium, making few revisions. Helpful as it was to me, her eventual biographer, in charting the events of her life and revealing something of her ideas and personality, Madeleva's narrative offers nothing of what she refers to as her "profoundest feelings." In her "Preface," she explains, "The silence of my text is all that I can tell you of these."[18]

Narrating a Life

Based on the sources available to me, I saw my task as biographer to develop a coherent narrative by answering as well as I could the journalistic five *W*s: WHO was Madeleva; WHAT did she do, think, feel; WHERE and WHEN did she do it; and WHY; along with the ultimate legacy question, "SO WHAT?" Like the novelist, I had to tell a good story—and I soon came to believe that Madeleva's life was indeed a good story to tell—but like the historian, I had a pact with truth. I often felt the tension caused by those competing obligations. What, and how much of what I learned, should be revealed? What right did I have to make public what Madeleva herself had not revealed when she told her own story? Such questions were complicated by her unexpected death. The sister who was her secretary and later became the college archivist assured me that Madeleva had gone through her files before her admission to the hospital, culling carefully, and that the files were preserved exactly as she left them. Nevertheless, sorting through the private papers of another person is disconcerting, especially if one intends to make them public.

What should I do, for example, with the information I received from a member of the Wolff family about the illegitimacy of Madeleva's father and the scandalous reputation of his mother, Madeleva's paternal grandmother? I had no evidence that Madeleva knew anything about this chapter in the family history. She makes no mention of it in her autobiography, but it seemed to me a plausible explanation for the choice of Mary Magdalene as her patron and namesake when she entered religious life. The Wolff family had no objection to my using the information, but I relegated the supposition about Madeleva's religious name, for which I had no proof, to an endnote.

Even more challenging than dealing with family secrets was interpreting Madeleva's complex, sometimes troubled relationships with those close to her, including members of her religious community. I puzzled as well over her intense, long-lasting friendships with three quite different men: Benjamin Lehman, her professor and mentor at Berkeley; Father Charles O'Donnell, CSC, a priest and poet who became president of Notre Dame; and Father Cornelius Hagerty, CSC, a priest and philosophy professor who taught Madeleva as a novice and later became her spiritual advisor. Perhaps the most challenging of all was comprehending the nature of Madeleva's spiritual and religious life, which she did her best to shield from public view. Were such private matters any of my business? In the end, I decided to follow Emily Dickinson's sage advice: "Tell all the truth, but tell it slant."[19] In other words, I told the truth as I saw it, in a nuanced way, suggesting rather than pontificating.

"Truth," however, can be exasperatingly elusive. I doubt that anyone can fathom the inner life of another; nevertheless, it was clear to me that someone with more knowledge of theology and spirituality would be better qualified than I was to understand and interpret this essential aspect of Madeleva's life. Her academic interest in theology was apparent. Like John Henry Newman, she saw theology as "queen of the sciences" and the "linchpin" of the curriculum of the Christian university.[20] When the School of Sacred Theology opened its doors, she herself attended classes regularly. Also well-documented was her fascination with mysticism and mystical writing. She began a scholarly study of Dame Gertrude More and wrote that she intended to pursue her interest in some of the other "lovely Middle English ladies," such as Dame Julian of Norwich.[21] In her letters, she often expressed a desire for a more contemplative life, writing that if she were to choose again, she would enter a Carmelite monastery.[22] She often emphasized the "imperative need of the interior life," which her administrative duties made difficult to satisfy.[23] Although she never wrote explicitly about mystical experiences she herself may have had, she consistently identified her poetry as prayer, and many of the poems contain mystical themes and language.[24]

Shortly before she entered the convent, Madeleva began writing poetry, and much of her early work was published in her first collection, *Knights Errant*, replete with Franciscan spirituality.[25] She wrote and published poetry throughout her life; her last collection, *A Child Asks for a Star*, appeared in 1964, the year of her death.[26] Although the number and quality of the poems diminished over time, I came to the conclusion that taken as a whole, they offer the best evidence available of her interior life, but it remains for others to explore her poetry in the context of the mystical writers who inspired it.

Intimately related to Madeleva's spirituality (and no less difficult to discern) was her relationship with Father Hagerty. Except for two extant letters written by her, which I found among his papers in the Provincial Archives at Notre Dame, his letters to her were all I had to go on; it was imperative that I do my best to understand the man who had written them. I discovered that the Wolff family knew him. Madeleva's niece recalled his visiting the Wolff family home several times during her childhood.[27] One of his letters to Madeleva mentioned a letter he had just received from her mother, Lucy, to whom he referred by her first name.[28] In the University of Notre Dame library, I discovered a privately printed personal account of his extensive canoe trips into the Great Lakes and down the Mississippi River. By his own admission, the trips were his way of subduing his emotions, which he described as "irascible and concupiscible."[29] The Holy Cross priests I interviewed remembered him as a fine teacher, if at times hotheaded and outspoken.

Stymied as I tried to interpret the relationship, I had a second Madeleva dream. Two figures whom I knew to be Madeleva and Hagerty faced each other in a doorway, she looking over his shoulder into rooms behind him, while he looked into interior rooms that were hers. Neither crossed the threshold that separated them. To put it simply, the dream conveyed to me an intimacy beyond the physical. In the biography, I decided to let the dream imagery speak for itself: "They met, as it were, face to face in a doorway through which neither passed but from which each could see into unentered rooms beyond."[30] The truth, told "slant"? Only much later, reading accounts of Jean Vanier, the founder of L'Arche, and other supposedly holy men accused of seducing women in the guise of spiritual direction, did I question my interpretation of events.[31] Based on the evidence I had, although I admit it can be construed in other ways, I stand by my interpretation as consistent with my sense of both individuals.

Sharing Madeleva's Story

In 1994, still in the process of writing the biography, I was asked to give the 1994 tenth-anniversary Madeleva Lecture on Madeleva's life and achievements. I found myself in the uncomfortable position of stealing my own thunder. My first draft of the lecture focused on writing the biography, but halfway through, I realized that what the occasion demanded and the audience expected was Madeleva's story itself. With a PowerPoint presentation of images of Madeleva through the years, I emphasized her roles as poet, scholar, educator, and nun. The lecture came at a time when the third wave of feminism was cresting. Young women were searching for feminine icons, and for Saint Mary's students, discovering one of our own satisfied a need to reclaim the past and look to the future as the new millennium approached. Student interest in Madeleva had recently grown, thanks in part to the SISTAR Program, funded by the Knight Foundation. A Humanistic Studies major, Moira Murphy, asked me to mentor her research proposal on Madeleva's year at Oxford. Together, we spent eight weeks on the project, which we presented to the college in the fall of 1991. Shortly after the Madeleva Lecture, three Humanistic Studies majors requested an independent study course on the biography, in page proofs at the time, which prepared them to design and team-teach an elective course on Madeleva's life and legacy, under my supervision. Some fifty Saint Mary's students enrolled in two sections of the one-credit-hour class, approved by the dean as "experimental." Thanks to the exposure, Madeleva was back on the campus radar, but unfortunately, not anywhere else.

Finding a publisher for the biography proved even more difficult than I expected. Assuming a Catholic press would be my best and maybe only option, I contacted the University of Notre Dame Press and received a quick invitation to submit the manuscript. A few weeks later, the editor telephoned to inform me that although the reviewer "enthusiastically" recommended publication, the press ran on a shoestring budget. Because biographies of religious figures were not selling, the press would need Saint Mary's to subsidize the cost of publication. I appreciated but rejected the offer, as well as a similar response from Paulist Press, which only two years earlier had published *Madeleva: One Woman's Life* as one of the Madeleva Lectures.[32] On the advice of a friend, I contacted the press at the State University of New York (SUNY) because of its interest in gender studies. SUNY unconditionally accepted the manuscript, which finally appeared in 1997 and is still in print. To my knowledge, the book remains one of only a handful of available biographies that record the contributions to church, country, and world of American women religious and their congregations. Theirs remains an untold story in our national history.

Madeleva's Ongoing Legacy

While Madeleva was never completely forgotten, as even a quick internet search makes clear, I was surprised by a request from *American Catholic Studies*, the journal of the American Catholic Historical Society, to commemorate the fiftieth anniversary of Madeleva's death with an essay on her legacy.[33] Any such undertaking seems to me to require a crystal ball. But at the time, I identified as her major achievements the foundation of the School of Sacred Theology and her role in the Sister Formation Movement, both of which elevated the status of women in the Church. Less recognized was her devotion to creating and practicing an "apostolate of beauty," which includes her poetry and the art she commissioned as well as the campus architecture and landscape she engendered.[34] A few years later, Thomas C. Fox, the editor emeritus of the *National Catholic Reporter*, argued that "Sr. Madeleva Wolff forever changed the face of Catholic theology" by admitting women to study of theology.[35] His extravagant claim once again brought Madeleva before the public eye. Over the years, various publications and lectures have similarly highlighted facets of her pioneering work, which include redefining and expanding the role of women in the Church and academy, leading the way in the racial integration of residential colleges and white religious congregations, and anticipating and enacting liturgical reform well in advance of Vatican II. These, as well as other aspects of Madeleva's legacy, all touched on in the biography, await further exploration, as does her apostolate, her ethic, of beauty.

In retrospect, what most appealed to me—and still does—about Madeleva's story is her quixotic attempt to reclaim and adapt ancient verities for her own time while simultaneously—without abandoning her religious faith or the institutions that shaped it—embracing the modern world. Like any life, Madeleva's multifaceted self and story reflect the world that shaped her and shine light on all she passes along to us.

Recently, I met Tess Hayes, a Saint Mary's undergraduate student who has just completed her senior comprehensive essay on Madeleva's spiritual practice of detachment, personified by the "relaxed grasp." For Tess, Madeleva is an "everyday saint," a fallible woman of faith, vision, and action whom Tess met on a wintry morning run through the nun's cemetery on campus, where she noticed Madeleva's name on a tombstone. Tess writes, "Finding her, a fire ignited inside of me."[36]

As the scholarly papers and topics in this edited volume suggest, there are many ways and places to "meet" Madeleva. Some find her through her poetry and other writings; some through what has been written about her and the lectures delivered in her name; and others through the places and spaces she created and those she occupied, including her last resting places: a bedroom (now an office) and a grave. Once you meet her, she sticks around.

Notes

1. Gail Porter Mandell, *Madeleva: A Biography* (Albany: State University of New York Press, 1997).

2. Barbara C. Jencks, "Jottings: Sister Madeleva," *The Southern Cross* 45, no. 7 (August 20, 1964): 4, https://gahistoricnewspapers.galileo.usg.edu/lccn/sn22185748/1964-08-20/ed-1/seq-4/print/image_564x817_from_0,0_to_6099,8828/.

3. Bruno P. Schlesinger, personal interview, March 20, 1995.

4. "Madeleva Lecture Series," Center for the Study of Spirituality, Saint Mary's College, https://www.saintmarys.edu/spiritual-life/center-for-spirituality/madeleva-lecture-series.

5. "Madeleva Manifesto," Center for the Study of Spirituality, Saint Mary's College, April 29, 2000, https://www.saintmarys.edu/mission-madeleva-manifesto.

6. Cornelius Hagerty to M. Madeleva Wolff, CSC, letter dated June 11, 1929, Sister Madeleva Collection, Box 5, Folder 62, Saint Mary's College Archives, Notre Dame, IN.

7. Hagerty to Madeleva, letter dated June 11, 1929.

8. These interviews were published in Gail Porter Mandell, *Life into Art: Conversations with Seven Contemporary Biographers* (Fayetteville: University of Arkansas Press, 1991).

9. Mary Ellen Klein, "Sister M. Madeleva Wolff, CSC: Saint Mary's College, Notre Dame, Indiana: A Study of Presidential Leader-

ship, 1934–1961" (PhD diss., Kent State University, 1983); Marjorie Walsh Hall Witherspoon, "Sister Madeleva, Lyric Poet" (master's thesis, Creighton University, 1962).

10. Maria Assunta Werner, CSC, *Madeleva: Sister Mary Madeleva Wolff, CSC: A Pictorial Biography* (Notre Dame, IN: Congregation of the Sisters of the Holy Cross, 1993).

11. Arntz Family History Committee, *A Chronological History of the Familie Arntz* (privately printed, 1989).

12. Plutarch, *Plutarch's Lives: Noble Greeks and Romans*, rev. ed., trans. John Dryden (London: Everyman's Library, 1969).

13. Judith Thurman, *Isak Dinesen: The Life of a Storyteller* (New York: St. Martin's Press, 1982).

14. Arnold Rampersad won the National Book Critics Circle award for his biography of Langston Hughes (1986). Rampersad and Jonathan Spence won MacArthur ("Genius") Prize Fellow awards in 1991 and 1988, respectively. Rampersad, Paul Mariani, and Phyllis Rose were National Book Awards finalists in 2007, 1983, and 1979, respectively.

15. T. S. Eliot, "Little Gidding," in *Four Quartets* (London: Faber and Faber, 1944), part 5, lines 239–42.

16. Sister M. Madeleva, CSC, *My First Seventy Years* (New York: Macmillan, 1959).

17. Madeleva, *My First Seventy Years*, xi.

18. Madeleva, *My First Seventy Years*, xii.

19. Emily Dickinson, "Tell all the truth but tell it slant," in *The Poems of Emily Dickinson: Reading Edition* (Cambridge, MA: The Belnap Press, 1998), 1263.

20. Mandell, *Madeleva*, 183.

21. Madeleva, *My First Seventy Years*, 125. See also Madeleva, letter to Mother Vincentia, CSC, dated October 21, 1933, Sister Madeleva Collection, Box 7, File 23, Saint Mary's College Archives, Notre Dame, IN.

22. Mandell, *Madeleva*, 100.

23. Madeleva, *My First Seventy Years*, 144.

24. See, for example, Mandell, *Madeleva*, 60, 95–96.

25. Sister M. Madeleva, CSC, *Knights Errant: And Other Poems* (New York: D. Appleton and Company, 1923). For more on Franciscan spirituality in this collection and Madeleva's other poetry, see Daniel P. Horan's chapter in this book.

26. Sister M. Madeleva, CSC, *A Child Asks for a Star* (Denville, NJ: Dimension Books, 1964).

27. M. L. Stevenson, personal interview, May 14, 1988.

28. Cornelius Hagerty, letter to Madeleva, dated April 19, 1929, Sister Madeleva Collection, Box 5, Folder 62, Saint Mary's College Archives, Notre Dame, IN.

29. Cornelius Hagerty, "Canoe Trips" (privately printed, 1965), 16.

30. Mandell, *Madeleva*, 99.

31. See Kate Shellnutt, "Report: Jean Vanier's L'Arche Hid 'Mystical-Sexual' Sect for Decades," *Christianity Today*, January 30, 2023, https://www.christianitytoday.com/2023/01/jean-vanier-l-arche-abuse-sect-report-thomas-philippe-catho/.

32. Gail Porter Mandell, *Madeleva: One Woman's Life* (Mahwah, NJ: Paulist Press, 1994).

33. Gail Porter Mandell, "Sister Madeleva Remembered: Why She Still Matters after Fifty Years, *American Catholic Studies* 125, no. 2 (2014): 89–96.

34. Most notably, Madeleva commissioned French muralist Jean Charlot's fifteen frescos symbolizing the fine arts, which decorate the main entrance to Moreau Center for the Arts. See Sally Geislar's chapter in this volume for more on Madeleva's transformation of the campus landscape.

35. Thomas C. Fox, "Sr. Madeleva Wolff forever changed the face of Catholic theology," *Global Sisters Report: A Project of National Catholic Reporter*, January 7, 2016, https://www.globalsistersreport.org/news/trends/sr-madeleva-wolff-forever-changed-face-catholic-theology-36166.

36. Tess Hayes, "Madeleva Wolff and the Relaxed Grasp: A Leader Then, a Leader Now," unpublished comprehensive essay, Saint Mary's College, 2024.

PART 1

MADELEVA'S LEGACY AS A WOMAN RELIGIOUS

2

Sister Madeleva's Spirituality of the "Relaxed Grasp"

A Legacy for Women Religious—Yesterday, Today, and Tomorrow

Margaret Eletta Guider, OSF

This chapter explores an unexamined aspect of the legacy of Sister M. Madeleva Wolff, namely, her particular contribution to the initial formation and ongoing transformation of women religious in the United States and abroad. The chapter begins with a reflection on the emergence and evolution of Sister Madeleva's own vocation and proceeds to examine the significance of her advocacy for the intellectual, theological, and human formation of women religious through the National Catholic Education Association, the School of Sacred Theology, and the Sisters Formation Conference—an advocacy that was and continues to be transformative for women religious not only in the United States but throughout the world. The chapter then goes on to pose a thought experiment regarding the unexplored consequences of the death of Sister Madeleva in 1964 for the renewal of religious life in the United States after Vatican II. Two questions emerge: Had she lived a bit longer, might Sister Madeleva's influence and wisdom have played a role in preventing or at least mitigating the polarization that occurred among U.S. women religious? Or was Sister Madeleva's legacy actually a contributing factor to what remains a question regarding the renewal and uncertain future of religious life in the United States? Fast-forwarding over the course of sixty years until the present time, the chapter proposes that the discovery or recovery of what may be described as Sister Madeleva's "spirituality of the relaxed grasp" offers U.S. women religious a glimpse into Sister Madeleva's final contribution and lasting legacy to our ongoing and ultimate formation, now and in the future.[1]

A Bit of Background

When I received the invitation to be part of this collection of essays exploring the local and lasting legacy of Sister Madeleva Wolff, CSC, I wondered, but hesitated to ask, whether it might have had something to do with a lecture I had given in April of 2023 at Boston College entitled "Roman Catholic Women Religious and the Transformation of Theological Education in the United States."[2] Coincidental or intentional, I do not know. In either case, a major feature of the presentation focused on Sister Madeleva's contribution to the lives of women religious in the United States and abroad. In short, the lecture was divided into two parts: "Before Sister Madeleva Wolff, CSC" and "After Sister Madeleva Wolff, CSC." The turning point was the significance of the School of Sacred Theology, a subject that is discussed at length in another chapter in this volume, "A School of Their Own," written by Professor Sandra Yocum. Truth be told, at the time of that Boston College lecture, I knew far more about Sister Madeleva, the college president and the innovative founder of the School of Sacred Theology, than I knew about Sister Madeleva, the woman religious. The invitation to be part of this project provided me with an opportunity to discover more about the importance of another dimension of her life and legacy, especially for those of us who have shared—and continue to share—with her the vocation to religious life. In all honesty, had I known nothing about Sister Madeleva but this one insight about the "relaxed grasp," she would have taught me what I consider to be the most important insight for making meaning of the years in religious life that I have known and those I have yet to live.

In late July of 2024, as I was walking the streets of Boston and pondering exactly how I would compose this essay, I came to the awareness that it was here in Boston, on July 25, 1964, that Sister Madeleva made her journey home to God. Given the sixtieth anniversary of her passing from this life to eternal life, I paused and wondered whether, somehow, I had stumbled unexpectedly into what the old Irish called a "thin place"—where boundaries between worlds cease to exist, where heaven and earth seem to touch.[3] Recalling a memorable aphorism from Morrie Schwartz, as recounted in the memoir written by Mitch Albom in his book *Tuesdays with Morrie*, "Death ends a life, not a relationship,"[4] I took a chance and engaged in a bit of an imaginative conversation with Sister Madeleva, beginning with the question: "Sister Madeleva, what five experiences of your life would you want women religious—across the lifespan and across continents—to remember? And what are five life lessons that are part the legacy you have entrusted to women religious through your spirituality of the *relaxed grasp*?" What follows are the fruits of what I would like to think of as an authentic transtemporal communication about what we as women religious are invited to value and carry on.

In the five reflections that follow, I present an answer to the first question, the context for making meaning of the answer, and an answer to the second question in the form of a life lesson.

Remembrance

> Always remember your vocation—your Galilee—the place where it all began—the place where you were first called and said yes.[5]

The Emergence of Mary Evaline Wolff's Vocation to Religious Life as a Sister of the Congregation of the Holy Cross

As an advocate of autobiography as theology, I began my pursuit of understanding Sister Madeleva's religious vocation by reflectively reading her memoir, *My First Seventy Years*.[6] I was profoundly challenged and inspired by her understanding of living one's religious life with a "relaxed grasp."[7]

Recounting the emergence of her vocation, she speaks of "how the grace of God has worked in the case of one girl out of hundreds."[8]

Growing up in the Midwest, in Cumberland, Wisconsin, to be precise, Mary Evaline was a nature mystic of sorts from an early age. Her encounters with the wonders of God's creation were constant and experientially relational. Her recollections—of family, school, childhood, catechesis, adolescence, friendships, mentors, and spiritual guides—laid a foundation for a journey that eventually would take the freshman at the University of Wisconsin to Saint Mary's College, thanks to an advertisement in *McClure's Magazine*, a popular periodical at the turn of the twentieth century known for investigative reporting.[9] The year was 1906.

Upon her arrival at Saint Mary's, though not enamored with the habit worn by the first Sister of the Holy Cross she encountered on campus, she did have an overwhelming sense of *belonging* as she entered Holy Cross Hall. She recalled her first sophomore English class. It was there that she first met the enchanting Sister Rita, the unforgettable muse who recognized the potential of the young poet who stood before her—all this and more. Sister Rita also was committed to encouraging Mary Evaline to stay on the path of self-discovery.

Independent in her thinking, Mary Evaline was not one to follow rules, especially those rules she judged as foolish. In her own estimation, she did not quite fit the profile of the usual Saint Mary's girl. However, two months after arriving on campus, something unanticipated occurred. She made her first retreat and was profoundly affected by the experience, of which she later remarked:

> To me it opened up spiritual worlds of which I think I must have had some intuition for which I know I had an immense and clamorous hunger. For the first time, the religious life was presented to my judgment and mind as well as my emotions. These told me that here was something that mattered, something worth doing and being. "Why had God made me?"...Clearly, religious life was what I most desired and for which I had most completely disqualified myself. God did not make sisters out of girls like me.[10]

Her sophomore year passed. Fall turned to winter, winter to spring, and spring to summer. Having concluded her initial year at Saint Mary's, Mary Evaline made her way back to her family in Wisconsin, acutely attuned to an unanswered question that was burning in her heart: "For what has God made me?"

Returning to Saint Mary's in September to begin her junior year, Mary Evaline found her way, once again, to a course taught by Sister Rita. As the year unfolded, she frequently found herself looking out of one of the north windows, observing the postulants and novices at recreation. Recounting this memory in her autobiography, Sister Madeleva goes on to speak of a walk by the riverbank with Sister Augustine. Having confided in Sister Augustine, to whom she had previously disclosed in an unguarded way the thought of becoming a Sister, Mary Evaline quickly and forthrightly stated that she was a most unlikely candidate. Nevertheless, the riverbank walk led to *the* conversation about religious life: "I listened breathlessly, reverently. 'I will do anything God wants me to do, if I can only find out what it is.' Sister responded simply, 'That is all one needs for a religious vocation.'"[11] The moment was apocalyptic.

At the conclusion of her junior year, before departing for the summer, Mary Evaline went to say good-bye to Sister Rita who entrusted her with an unexpected gift—a book. It was a copy of *The Story of Fifty Years*, the history about the Sisters of the Holy Cross that Sister Rita had written a few years earlier.[12] Before Mary Evaline's train ride to Madison ended, she was transformed. By the end of August, with the encouragement of Sister Augustine, she had written a letter to the Mistress of Novices requesting to enter the congregation, declaring what she described as "my absolute wish to become a Sister of the Holy Cross."[13] On September 14, 1908, the Feast of the Holy Cross, she was welcomed by Mother Barbara. Three months later, on December 10, 1908, she was received as a novice and given the name Sister Mary Madeleva—a trifecta of "the Mother of God, Magdalen, the friend of Christ, and Eve, the mother of humankind."[14] After twenty months in the novitiate, she professed her first vows in August of 1910 and was missioned to teach at the college and the academy. A few weeks before, on July 23, 1910, her beloved teacher and mentor, Sister Rita Heffernan, died of cancer at the age of fifty. In some way, this experience—relationally and theologically—created the conditions that led to Sister Madeleva's articulation and practice of what became a de facto spirituality of the "relaxed grasp."

Life Lesson

For women entering into the religious life,
quite likely there will be a woman religious who is
a powerful source of inspiration.
Be prepared from the outset, that this sister may not live long enough
to see one through to her first or final profession,
much less the years of accompaniment and companionship
that one may have hoped for and imagined.
Remember, death changes a relationship,
but the relationship does not end.

Remembrance

Trust your own spiritual experience, your intuition—be creative and courageous, dare to bring new interpretations to old understandings of all manner of things—understandings seemingly set in stone and immutable. Things can and do change.

The Evolution of Sister Madeleva's Religious Vocation and Its Application to Her Life as a Scholar, Teacher, Mentor, and Friend

In the summer of 1921, Sister Madeleva was missioned from Ogden, Utah, to Saint Agnes Convent in Los Angeles, California, to rest and to work as well. On the occasion of a visit to Berkeley, she obtained more information about the doctoral program at the University of California. Sowing seeds of hope, while suffering bouts of poor health and fatigue, she returned to Ogden for the 1921–1922 school year. In late April of 1922, she was informed that in the summer she would be returning to California to pursue graduate coursework in English at Berkeley. In the years that followed, she would multitask her way through doctoral studies, changes in local communities, writing her dissertation, and defending it on April 23, 1925, the first woman religious to earn a doctorate from the University of California at Berkeley.[15] Whatever biases, prejudices, and judgments those identified with the secular academy may have had about Roman Catholic women religious, every indication suggested that those in the secular milieu were somehow transfixed by Sister Madeleva's brilliance and moreover enchanted by that spark of divine light so difficult to deny.

In the endeavor to undertake a reading of Sister Madeleva's dissertation, *Pearl: A Study in Spiritual Dryness*,[16] it is fair to say that, over time, more than a few readers have been made aware of the limitations of their own scholarly backgrounds. Despite this fact, amid its pages, *every* reader shares a sense of amazement at the breadth and depth of Sister Madeleva's giftedness for philosophy, languages, literature, history, theology, and spirituality. Indeed, seen through the eyes of critical scholars as well as devoted admirers, she was unquestionably a Renaissance woman. However, in her own eyes, as a woman religious, she most certainly was no stranger—personally or vicariously—to the spiritual conditions that she brought to bear in the dissertation and addressed directly without gloss. In presenting *her* interpretation of *Pearl*, what she described as one of the most perfect of Middle English poems, she states:

> For the past half century careful and devoted scholars have been busy with the *Pearl*, yet research has pretty generally come out by the same door wherein it went....All the while material close at hand has been overlooked, and an obvious interpretation neglected. It is the interpretation of the *Pearl* as an exposition of spiritual dryness or interior desolation—one of the most familiar of spiritual conditions—with the subsequent questionings, hopes, and resignation which normally grow out of it. Such an interpretation I shall make.[17]

In the 209 pages that follow, Sister Madeleva does just that—concluding with the final words, "As a spiritual autobiography, the *Pearl* is perfectly true to type....I think that the *Pearl* is a miniature 'Paradiso' of the religious state, presenting a perfectly consistent exposition, revelation, and ecstatic climax of spiritual 'blues.'"[18]

Amid the realities of unsettling experiences and difficult times in community, Sister Madeleva's endurance, perseverance, and tenaciousness all contributed to the manner in which she artistically wove the threads of these adaptive challenges together with the threads of her many joys, accomplishments, recognitions, and graces received into a tapestry of life like no other.

Life Lesson

For sisters around the world currently exhausted; at times, unwell; facing multiple transitions; expectations for multitasking; complex and, at times, less than supportive community environments; resentful peers; and the scrutinies of superiors intent on "keeping others humble and in their place": *corragio*! Do not allow discouragement to undermine the simultaneous ability to piece together coursework in service of a degree that will enable one to use her gifts and fulfill the mission entrusted to her. The secret is to find mentors, make lifelong friends, and trust the process. God is faithful.

Remembrance

To lead—in all ways, whether great or small—one must practice discernment, wisdom, and versatility. Guided by inspiration, innovation, intuition, and indignation, enlarge your capacity to dream, to hope, to care, and to persevere.

Sister Madeleva's Advocacy for the Education and Formation of Women Religious in the United States and Beyond

In the early twentieth century, as vocations to religious life in the United States were on the rise, congregations entrusted with the education and faith formation of children and young women within their own institutions as well as diocesan parochial schools recognized that more than catechesis was needed in their academies and colleges, and more than catechesis and spiritual reading at meals was needed for the religious and theological formation of their own sisters.

Instead of framing the reality solely as a "problem" to be solved, Sister Madeleva dared to reimagine the reality as an adaptive challenge that required the creation of new conditions. She managed to make a way where there was no existing way. As president of Saint Mary's College in Notre Dame, Indiana, she exercised her influence in multiple ways: in partnership with others in the National Catholic Education Association; through the establishment of the School of Sacred Theology; as well as the consequential impact of her innovative ideas and actions on major superiors of women religious and the Sisters Formation Conference, as exemplified in her memorable address given at the National Catholic Education Association meeting in Philadelphia, April 21, 1949, entitled "The Education of Sister Lucy."[19] In her address, Sister Madeleva "painted an appealing portrait of 'Sister Lucy,' a young woman religious who received a full undergraduate education and was given adequate time and space to contemplate her vocation...only to state that Sister Lucy did not actually exist."[20] Sister Madeleva then went on to say,

> I need not tell you that Sister Lucy does not exist. But I know that we all should insist that she shall exist. We are here in part to bring her into existence. Sister Lucy is our 1949 model of the religious teacher of the future, her education and her training. She is the advanced payment of our debt to posterity.[21]

As for the School of Sacred Theology, suffice to say that it helped to provide, among others, countless women religious with a formal theological education. It represented a singular effort to meet what Bishop Edwin O'Hara described in a letter to Sister Madeleva as the overwhelming "demand for the advance of religious education on the part of teachers in our Catholic schools."[22] As Gail Porter Mandell observes in her book *Madeleva: A Biography*, Sister Madeleva's "primary concern in establishing the school had been a practical one: to ensure adequate preparation for those actually teaching theology in the Catholic school system, most of whom were nuns."[23]

In the years that followed, the School of Sacred Theology served—and, while no longer in existence, continues to this day to serve—as a model for other theological institutes, schools of theology and ministry, and university-based departments of theology and religious studies throughout the world. In 1955, it gave rise to Rome's *Regina Mundi*,[24] setting forth a worldwide movement[25] that would challenge—relationally and systemically—the gender barriers, cultural biases, and familial/congregational attitudes that so often were sustained and exacerbated by ecclesiastical, episcopal, and clerical prerogatives and prejudices, not to mention the internalized lack of confidence on the part of women religious themselves, who often devalued and diminished their own giftedness and underestimated their potential to match and exceed the achievements of their brothers in religion.

Life Lesson

If you give a Sister a fish, she will either find ways of making it feed many more than expected, or, if given to her alive, it is possible that she will build an aquarium for those who have never seen a fish. If you teach a Sister how to fish, in all likelihood, she will return to you one day to teach you alternative and better ways of fishing, perhaps become a fish scientist, manage a fishery that will feed the hungry, or write a dissertation on John 6:1–14 or John 21:1–14.

Remembrance

Life is short, even when it is comparatively long. Make amends, before it ends.

The Renewal of Religious Life in the United States and the Unexplored Significance of Sister Madeleva's Legacy for Women Religious

During the Second Vatican Council, structures for leadership and formation in communities of women religious became a subject of intense discussion and debate. In the years that followed, the reception and implementation of *Perfectae Caritas* and *Renovationis Causam* proved to be foundational. Among numerous quotable quotes, one that stands out as an eschatological echo of Sister Madeleva's voice and an acknowledgement of her legacy is that "the adaptation and renewal of religious communities depends very largely on the training of their members."[26]

As the "universal call to holiness" articulated in *Lumen Gentium* shed new light on the Church's long-standing tradition of hierarchical states of perfection, so too the advancement of collegiality, subsidiarity, and mutual accountability among bishops trickled down to religious congregations that required a rethinking and a reconfiguring of structures of power and authority. Congregations turned to leaders of the Sisters Formation Conference, the Religious Sisters Vocation Conference, and the Conference of Major Superiors of Women for guidance—many of whom directly or indirectly had come under the influence of Sister Madeleva's leadership and unrelenting advocacy for the intellectual, spiritual, professional, and human formation of women religious. Indeed, as an "influencer" par excellence, Sister Madeleva had planted seeds and the seeds took root. Yet like so many other prophets before her, she did not live long enough to see the fruits of her labors or to offer wise advice on the inevitable need for skillful pruning to guarantee future growth.

Mindful of the monumental changes and challenges that occurred in the lives of women religious subsequent to Sister Madeleva's death in 1964, a bit of speculative reflection on the unexplored consequences of her legacy on the renewal of religious life may offer some insight into the turbulence that followed. Had Sister Madeleva lived a bit longer, say six or seven more years, might her persistent influence and wisdom have prevented or at least mitigated the polarization that occurred among women religious in the United States? Specifically, the acrimonious divisions that occurred in 1971 within the Conference of Major Superiors of Women in the United States, an unreconciled split that continued for several decades between the Leadership Conference of Women Religious and what began as the *Consortium Perfectae Caritatis* and eventually became the Council of Major Superiors of Women Religious. Though "what if?" thought experiments are often unproductive, in this particular case perhaps an intentional recovery of Sister Madeleva's "spirituality of the relaxed grasp," while not sufficiently reflected upon in the past, arguably merits retrieval in the present and future.

With the passage of six decades, the number of U.S. women religious has declined from an estimated 180,000 in 1965 to 39,000 in 2021,[27] with an average age of eighty, and less than 1 percent under the age of thirty.[28] In light of the legacy of Sister Madeleva, how are women religious to interpret these "signs of the times"? Perhaps a glocal perspective is needed, one that takes account not only of the local reality of the United States but also the global reality of women religious in every land.[29] As many of the original Sister Lucys take their place among the "cloud of witnesses" (Heb 12:1), may their legacies of compassion, creativity, integrity, and innovation remain a source of inspiration for the Church and society...and hopefully, for a new generation of Sister Lucys willing to take a chance on living with a "relaxed grasp."

Life Lesson

There comes a time when the détente of "you go your way and I'll go mine" evolves into a graced encounter brought about by previously unimaginable experiences of vulnerability and interdependency.

Remembrance

Relax your grasp. Live into your legacy. Let God be God.

Sister Madeleva's Spirituality of the "Relaxed Grasp"

At the conclusion of Sister Madeleva's memoir, *My First Seventy Years*, she describes simply and succinctly the essence and evolution of her spirituality of the "relaxed grasp"—her very own collection of life lessons:

learning what it means "to live without props,"[30]
to experience holy indifference,
to loosen one's hold on all that we leave behind,
upon the death of loved ones "learning to let go in deference to Him,"[31]
in witnessing the poverty of others,
to ask oneself "What have my years taught me of the relaxed grasp?,"[32]
remembering "what I have had to let die
and must bury without regret."[33]

Throughout her religious life, and writing seven years before her death on July 25, 1964, Madeleva gave voice to a spirituality that I propose holds even greater significance for U.S. women religious today than it may have sixty years ago.

Among U.S. women religious, the language of legacy has become commonplace. But for too long, many have distanced themselves from the concept precisely because of the inevitable reality it discloses. Simply put, the days of our earthly lives are numbered—certainly individually, but also for some, collectively, as growing numbers of congregations anticipate coming to completion in the foreseeable future.

Given this inevitability, a number of questions arise, not only

"*Will* we be remembered?" but also "*How* will we be remembered?" "Is it important that we are remembered?" or "Is it sufficient that we made a difference, that we left the world a better place than we found it?" And "Even if the good that we have done—and continue to do—cannot be traced back to us by name, place, and date, is it sufficient that we did what was ours to do? That with God's grace, we became who we were meant to be?"

In the effort to offer a response to these questions, I propose that Sister Madeleva's "spirituality of the relaxed grasp" provides concise instructions on what may be described as the "*ultimate* religious formation" that, over the course of our lifespan, enables us to learn how to *live into* our legacy—and legacies.

Conclusion

During the question-and-answer session that occurred after my presentation at the conference for which this chapter was written, a member of the Sisters of the Holy Cross, Sister Mary Ellen Vaughan, fondly spoke of Sister Madeleva and offered to the assembly a firsthand reminiscence:

> I graduated from Saint Mary's College in 1961. It was Sister Madeleva's last year as President. She was a visible presence during my four years. Every Tuesday at 1 p.m., all students were required to attend a weekly convocation in O'Laughlin Auditorium, ordinarily led by the Dean of Students and usually covering a lot of *minutiae* of "Do's and Don'ts."
>
> Monthly, as her very busy travel schedule would allow, Sister Madeleva led the convocation. Those gatherings were inspiring, challenging, as Sister Madeleva invited us to become the women God was calling us to be.
>
> One of her topics that has stayed with me over these many years was what she called "the relaxed grasp." We were to learn to open our tightly clenched fists, grasping for control, and finger by finger open those fists to relax and receive all the gifts God wanted to give us.
>
> Years later, as I am now in my senior years, I find myself doing that simple spiritual practice to help me remember

that I am not in control and to keep my heart open to receive God's gracious gifts.

It seems appropriate to conclude with a testimony from one of Sister Madeleva's own sisters who kindly has provided every reader with the privilege of being one degree of separation from Sister Madeleva herself.

Life Lesson

What is remembered, lives.

—Native American Proverb

Notes

1. For a more detailed understanding of the significance of "the relaxed grasp" for Sister Madeleva, see Gail Porter Mandell, "The Relaxed Grasp," *Madeleva: A Biography* (Albany: State University of New York Press, 1997), 215–27.

2. A lecture given at the Clough School of Theology and Ministry on April 27, 1923, https://www.bc.edu/bc-web/schools/stm/sites/encore/main/2023/women-religious-theological-education.html.

3. See Kerri ní Dochartaigh, *Thin Places: A Natural History of Healing and Home* (Minneapolis: Milkweed Press, 2022).

4. Mitch Albom, *Tuesdays with Morrie: An Old Man, A Young Man, and Life's Greatest Lesson*, 25th anniversary ed. (New York: Crown, 1997), 192.

5. Pope Francis, "Homily for Easter Vigil, Holy Saturday," April 19, 2014, https://www.vatican.va/content/francesco/en/homilies/2014/documents/papa-francesco_20140419_omelia-veglia-pasquale.html#:~:text=Do%20not%20be%20afraid%2C%20do,not%20a%20kind%20of%20nostalgia.

6. Sister M. Madeleva, CSC, *My First Seventy Years* (New York: Macmillan, 1959).

7. Madeleva, *My First Seventy Years*, 169–72.

8. Madeleva, *My First Seventy Years*, xii.

9. See Harold S. Wilson, *McClure's Magazine and the Muckrakers* (Princeton, NJ: Princeton University Press, 2015).

10. Madeleva, *My First Seventy Years*, 28–29.

11. Madeleva, *My First Seventy Years*, 32.

12. Sister Mary Rita Heffernan, CSC, *A Story of Fifty Years*, from the Annals of the Congregation of the Sisters of the Holy Cross, 1855–1905 (Notre Dame, IN: Ave Maria Press, 1905).

13. Madeleva, *My First Seventy Years*, 33.

14. Madeleva, *My First Seventy Years*, 35.

15. Mandell, *Madeleva*, 85.

16. Sister M. Madeleva, *Pearl: A Study in Spiritual Dryness* (New York: D. Appleton and Company, 1925).

17. Madeleva, *Pearl*, 2–3.

18. Madeleva, *Pearl*, 209.

19. Sister M. Madeleva Wolff, *The Education of Sister Lucy: A Symposium on Teacher Education and Teacher Training* (Holy Cross, IN: Saint Mary's College, Notre Dame, 1949), 1–39.

20. See Mary Henold, Introduction to Document 1: Excerpt from Madeleva Wolff, CSC, "The Education of Our Young Religious Teachers," *National Catholic Education Association Bulletin*, 46 (August 1949): 254, included in *How Did Catholic Women Participate in the Rebirth of American Feminism?* (Binghamton: State University of New York at Binghamton, 2005). https://documents.alexanderstreet.com/d/1000674220.

21. See Mary Madeleva Wolff, "The Education of Our Young Religious Teachers," *National Catholic Education Association Bulletin* 46 (August 1949): 254.

22. "The Most Rev. E. O'Hara, Letter to Madeleva, 15 March 1948, College Archives," as quoted in Mandell, *Madeleva*, 188. See also Heather Grennan Gary, "How the Door Was Opened for Catholic Women Theologians," *U.S. Catholic*, December 2012, https://uscatholic.org/articles/201212/how-the-door-was-opened-for-catholic-women-theologians/.

23. Mandell, *Madeleva*, 188.

24. The Roman Institute of Sacred Studies Regina Mundi, aimed "at giving to religious, to members of societies without vows or of secular institutes, and in general to women and girls dedicated to the pursuit of perfection and apostolic work, a thorough training in sacred studies, so that they may be better prepared either for the work of government and the guidance of other religious, or for other apostolic work, especially as teachers or heads of women's colleges and institutions of higher studies…under the authority of the Sacred Congregation of Religious." See

L. S. Muir, "The Institute *Regina Mundi*," *The Furrow* 6, no. 8 (August 1955): 501–3, https://www.jstor.org/stable/27656739. In 1956, it became a Pontifical Institute. See *The Catholic Advocate* 5, no. 20 (May 19, 1956): 10.

25. See UISG, International Union of Superior Generals, "Regina Mundi in Diaspora," a scholarship program designed to guarantee access of women religious throughout the world to quality theological educations, https://oldsite.uisg.org/wp-content/uploads/2016/01/Regina-Mundi-ENG_2016-17.pdf.

26. See Sacred Congregation for Religious and Secular Institutes, *Renovationis Causam: Instruction on the Renewal of Religious Life*, January 6, 1969, introduction; see also Second Vatican Council, *Perfectae caritatis: Decree on the Up-to-Date Renewal of Religious Life*, October 28, 1965, §18, in *Documents of Vatican II*, ed. Austin P. Flannery (Grand Rapids, MI: Eerdmans, 1975), 635 and 621.

27. "FAQs," Center for Applied Research in the Apostolate, https://cara.georgetown.edu/faqs.

28. See Jessie Wardarski, "Takeaways from AP's reporting on Young Nuns," *Associated Press*, December 20, 2024, https://apnews.com/article/young-nuns-catholic-student-debt-aging-7af437d02f67ec85f8c2df63fcabb4d4.

29. *L'Osservatore Romano*, "New Church statistics reveal more Catholics, fewer vocations," *Vatican News*, April 4, 2024. In 2022, women religious "exceeded the number of priests across the world by almost 47%....Globally, they went from 608,958 professed women in 2021 to 599,228 in 2022, with a relative decline of 1.6%." While trends in Latin America bear some similarity to past trends in Europe, North America, and Oceania, the number of Sisters in Africa and Asia continues to grow, revealing modest increases.

30. Madeleva, *My First Seventy Years*, 169.

31. Madeleva, *My First Seventy Years*, 171.

32. Madeleva, *My First Seventy Years*, 172.

33. Madeleva, *My First Seventy Years*, 172.

3

A School of Their Own

Sandra Yocum

> Somewhere among all our magnificent Catholic young womanhood there must be another Catherine [of Siena], another Eustochium. Perhaps from our School of Sacred Theology she may emerge.
>
> Madeleva Wolff, CSC, *Courier* magazine, May 1945

As these words suggest, Sister Madeleva's romantic embrace of Catholic intellectual tradition combined with her convictions about women's intellectual ability informed her decision to take a calculated risk and establish Saint Mary's Graduate School of Sacred Theology in 1943. Under her presidency, Saint Mary's College became the first Roman Catholic educational institution in the world to offer women the opportunity to earn doctorates in theological studies. Sister Madeleva articulated these aspirations for women studying theology in the May 1945 issue of the Saint Mary's College *Courier*. With her usual dramatic flair, Madeleva surmised the contemporary context. "Christianity is at crucial war with the devil....Who is going to combat this condition? Who under God is going to preserve Christianity in our country?" Turning to the past, she described a fourth-century women's "study club" that helped Jerome translate the Bible into the Latin Vulgate. She recalled Catherine of Siena, who demanded that the pope return to Rome from Avignon, and Teresa of Avila, who reformed the contemplative Carmelite order. In her account of this women's history, "Two lay women gave us our Bible. One lay woman saved Rome for the Church. One cloistered nun reformed the spiritual life of her time."[1] She founded the School of Sacred Theology to prepare Catholic women to make comparable contributions to the Church in the fractious twentieth century.

The school's twenty-two years of existence (1944–1966) provided an important precedent. The precedent is not because it was the undisputed first to offer U.S. Catholic women avenues for graduate studies in theologically relevant topics. Catholic University of America (CUA) had offered women and laymen opportunities for advanced degrees in religion since 1931. Women could engage theological subject matter not only in CUA's graduate programs in religious education but also in philosophy, classics, English, history, and sociology. Yet, "theology" at this time referred to a very specific course of study, and CUA excluded women from that course of study in their Graduate School of Sacred Theology. In 1939, the College of Saint Bonaventure in New York began a summer master's program with a clearly recognizable theological curriculum in the Franciscan scholastic tradition. As will become clear later in this chapter, the Franciscan priest who founded that program had a very different vision of women's contributions to the study of the sacred science than did Sister Madeleva.

Two factors contribute to Saint Mary's program as precedent setting. First, Madeleva choose to replicate the curriculum of graduate studies in theology that served the ordained or soon-to-be ordained. Second, and just as important, she established a year-round graduate program with opportunities to complete a doctorate. Sister Madeleva did so to prepare a cadre of Catholic women intellectuals whose theological education prepared them to make critical contributions to the broader movements associated with Catholic Action in which laity (the nonordained) played a central role in a restoring the social order to Christ. As theology graduate programs proliferated in Catholic universities during the 1960s, the question as to whether women ought to be admitted into the study of theology had long ago been answered in the affirmative through Sister Madeleva's efforts.

Why a School of Sacred Theology?

Madeleva's long-standing romance with theology is clearly illustrated in her role as dean and de facto president of the Holy Cross Sisters' newly founded St. Mary's-of-the-Wasatch (1926). Gail Porter Mandell provides a delightful account of her efforts, noting that Madeleva drew her inspiration from Abbess Hilda's monastery school in Whitby. There, the abbess presided over the complete education of men as well as women.[2] In organizing the students' day, Madeleva "mandated that the 'first and best hour of the day' be devoted to the study of religion." On Saint Thomas Aquinas's feast day, Madeleva canceled classes to provide students with a unique opportunity to hear lectures on this first among Catholic intellectual lights.[3] Organizing such a day of study demonstrates Madeleva's ingenuity and ability to take advantage of a certain freedom in the less discipline-structured curriculum of higher education at that time.

Her commitment to fostering theological studies extended beyond the students. In 1932, Madeleva sponsored a summer program for her own congregation with a focus upon spiritual renewal. "Her tentative curriculum she divided into seven parts: prayer, the Liturgy, Scripture, dogma, philosophy, religious literature, and church music."[4] Over one hundred sisters participated in the program. So, Madeleva had some prior experience as she began to fashion not only a curriculum but also a vision for Saint Mary's Graduate School of Sacred Theology.

Sister Madeleva offered a brief account of the school's founding in her autobiography, *My First Seventy Years*. The account centers on a 1943 meeting of the National Catholic Educational Association (NCEA) at which attendees heard Saint Mary's president, Sister M. Madeleva, articulate her concerns about the current academic status of religion in Catholic colleges. Madeleva published an article, "Religion in College," in the 1943–1944 volume of *Journal of Religious Instruction* that provided a more in-depth account of her reasoning. She began by advocating the inclusion of student credit hours in religion courses on official transcripts.[5] Describing its omission served Madeleva's larger purpose to highlight the academic marginalization of the one subject that, in her estimation, must be central to any higher education identified as "Catholic." Madeleva then turned her focus to the necessity of establishing better educational opportunities in religion for laity and women religious. "Do you know any Catholic college or university open to women that offers a good course in Scripture, in church history, in dogma, in apologetics?"[6] After acknowledging summer theology-related courses offered at DePaul University, Creighton College, Marquette University, and Saint Louis University, she remained convinced that Frank Sheed's complaint about the lack of theology courses for laymen (and women) remained valid.

Establishing the School of Sacred Theology

What Madeleva had in mind was nothing less than a full-fledged graduate program in theology open to women. To that end, she had contacted several Catholic universities whose administrators claimed, according to Madeleva, that the war made it difficult to launch a new program. Madeleva found this response wanting, which she made abundantly clear in her 1943 address. To highlight Catholic higher education's failures, she quoted a November 1942 *Indiana University News-Letter* article featuring a "Student Religious Cabinet." Cabinet members promoted a degree that prepared students "to enter schools for advanced study in religion." The degree evidently advanced no particular religious commitments; an advisor provided the necessary academic structure. Madeleva, with her usual rhetorical aplomb, indicted Catholic educators. "This happens on a campus unhallowed by Sacraments, unsanctified by their presence of Christ in the Blessed Sacrament, uninspired by the indwelling of the Holy Spirit. What have we, with our supernatural resources, to show in comparison?"[7] She then called for "measures to provide the best possible training, to erect our courses in religion into departments, to make them the strongest and crowning departments in our colleges, to give wisdom its proper place in our curricula, to make our colleges literate in religion and Catholic in essence."[8]

Sister Madeleva's convictions translated into a bold action. As she recorded in her autobiography, "with that strange impulse outside [her] will," she volunteered Saint Mary's campus as the site for the graduate school. The women's college at the time did not even offer its five hundred undergraduates a religion major.[9] Madeleva's biographer Gail Porter

Mandell observed that Madeleva often employed rhetorical strategies familiar to women who sought to go beyond the norms of their day. "As a woman, Madeleva seems to have thought of herself as something of a David among Goliaths, invariably emphasizing her young age, small size, or lack of experience when comparing herself with men. Her weapons were an intelligence and a determination that few could match."[10] Her claim of "a strange impulse outside [her] will" as the impetus for founding the graduate school echoes the claims of Christian women of ages past who marshalled the Holy Spirit's support for their own strange impulses. Yet, clearly, her so-called "strange impulse" arose from a deep current of love for theologically informed intellectual life and her educational efforts to make that a reality in the curriculum that she oversaw.

Madeleva's wide-ranging national connections, combined with her "intelligence" and "determination," helped to expedite the NCEA's goal only a year after it had appeared unattainable. The declaration about founding a school was not quite as unanticipated as her autobiographical claim suggested. Early in the spring of 1943, Bishop O'Hara had begun urging Madeleva to found the school at Saint Mary's.[11] Madeleva had met Father Edwin V. O'Hara in Rome during her European travels. Discovering that they were both headed to the Holy Land, they decided to travel together.[12] This experience cemented their strong friendship.

Without a doubt, Edwin V. O'Hara proved an invaluable ally in the school's founding. His own ecclesial ministry in rural areas had made him keenly aware of the need to expand opportunities for Catholics to receive a theological education beyond the basics of the catechism. The prelate embraced Catholic Action and advocated training laity in apologetics following the Catholic evidence model. O'Hara, as chair of the National Catholic Welfare Conference's Committee on Confraternity of Christian Doctrine (CCD), supported an initiative among U.S. scholars to produce a new English translation of scripture.[13] O'Hara's confidence in Sister Madeleva's ability to succeed in founding a school of theology fits a pattern that his biographer described as one of his "modus operandi: a heavy investment in the competency and skills of strong-willed women."[14] According to school alumnae, he paid more than lip service, keeping his promise to employ any lay woman who graduated from the school in his diocese.

The year 1944 marked the official opening of the School of Sacred Theology, but Saint Mary's offered three courses in 1943. One of the three 1943 summer instructors, Father Michael Gruenthaner, SJ, became the school's first chancellor thanks to Madeleva's persistent "cajoling." The Jesuit was, at that time, a respected Catholic biblical scholar of the Old Testament and editor of the *Catholic Biblical Quarterly*. Certainly by today's standards, and even among some of his younger contemporaries, Gruenthaner's unyielding defense of a literal reading of the Adam and Eve story diminishes his scholarly legacy. His students, both Jesuits and Saint Mary's alumna, on the other hand, recall his teaching with great fondness. They recall his directing them to engage the actual text facilitated by his impressive knowledge of biblical Hebrew and his reportedly dramatic rendering of certain passages.

Madeleva's willingness to accept a scripture scholar as chancellor of the Graduate School of Sacred Theology stands out when one considers the dominance of neo-Thomism in 1944, the year of the program's official opening. To reduce the choice of Greuenthaner to his singular availability and willingness misses other possible reasons. Edwin O'Hara's desire to found a school coupled with his promotion of scripture study for Catholic laity suggests his influence in securing the Jesuit's services. Sister Madeleva also had a long-term interest in scripture, awakened through Mother Barbara in the novitiate. Until that time, she had never read the text nor possessed an English translation. "The poetry of the sacred text thrilled her. It became for her one of the most important influences on her own writing."[15] She opened her classes reading the prologue of John's Gospel especially to highlight the role of the Word.[16]

Designing a Curriculum

The earliest bulletin (1944) for the Graduate School of Sacred Theology certainly conveyed the driving force of a strong will. The bulletin boldly proclaimed the school's purpose: to honor their students' "right to participate according to their needs and abilities in the treasury of sacred doctrine handed down by the great doctors of the Church."[17] Sister Madeleva fully acknowledged the school's indebtedness to ongoing clerical support; the school's dedicated priest-professors made it possible for women to study formally and in depth their own theological traditions. At the same time, the bulletin's assertion of a "right" suggested that the school existed not as a favor granted through a clerical *noblesse oblige* but as a duty fulfilled by the school's founders, especially Sister Madeleva.

Her assessment of students' needs and abilities led her to seek the best people available to create a rigorous program of scholastic studies to militate against "teachers and apologists [who] are apt to be amateurish and inadequate." As the first bulletin noted, women teaching the faith require "the same type and degree of scientific preparation which the Catholic Church in her wisdom and age-long experience prescribes for her priests."[18] Madeleva looked to the educational institutions most respected in Roman Catholic circles for providing such sound theological training, that is, the seminaries shaped by the Pontifical Faculties of Theology. The phrase "scientific preparation" informed prospective students that the curriculum offered them training in scholastic theology, most notably in the work of Thomas Aquinas.

The initial program did modify the seminary curriculum to better serve its clientele, that is, primarily teachers rather than researchers, nonordained rather than soon-to-be-ordained. Since canon law excluded women from receiving pontifical degrees in theology, the first degree granted was an MA in religion. A student had to commit two full years and two summers. A PhD in religion followed in 1946, and the MA became a four-summer program and finally a five-summer obligation. The doctoral course work culminated in a one-and-half-hour oral exam. No dissertation was required. A paper of publishable quality was recommended, and candidates had to give at least one short talk to students, novitiates, or scholasticate.

The program's dedication to providing what was deemed throughout its existence the most up-to-date and rigorous of theological studies affirmed the significance of women participating in the wider church's mission. The bulletin implied that these women were among those whom "God has raised up" in this age to fulfill "the function of teaching, defending the faith against errors, correcting the wayward, leading men to the perfection of justice." The brochure actually identified these activities first as "the function of the Church's hierarchy, the apostolate, for which it is trained by the study of sacred doctrine."[19] Women, because they shared in the episcopal charism of teaching and defending the faith, needed similar training.

Which School Was First?

As already noted, other Catholic colleges had degree programs in theology open to women. In a 1950 article in *The Catholic School Journal*, Rev. Irenaeus Herscher, OFM, seeking to correct the claim of Saint Mary's being the first, pointed out that Saint Bonaventure's College and Seminary founded "a department of sacred theology for religious Brothers, Sisters, and lay teachers" in 1939. "The first Sisters to be graduated from the School of Sacred Theology received their master degrees in 1943, after completing five summer sessions. In other words, St. Bonaventure College already had graduates from its School in 1943, the year St. Mary's School of Sacred Theology was founded."[20] He reported an enrollment of one hundred sisters and offered to send brochures to anyone interested.

Father Thomas Plassmann, OFM, Saint Bonaventure's president from 1920 to 1946, founded the school. In a paper, "Religion for Nuns," preserved in Saint Bonaventure archives, he described a heated discussion at a NCEA meeting in Milwaukee on the topic "How to Teach Religion in Our Schools." In his words, "a few of the 'Sponsae Christi' crossed swords with one or two of the 'sacerdotes Dei.'" At a lull in the debate,

> a Sister, who for the moment took on the role of the "valiant woman" of Proverbs 31, rose to her feet, and with courage in her voice and fervor in her heart, thus addressed the Rev. gentlemen of the cloth: "Why all this secretiveness about your theology? Is there anything in it that we Sisters should not know, or are we judged incapable of grasping it? For years and scores of years we are doomed to ask the same simple catechetical questions over and over again. If we do want to know more about these beautiful truths, we are handed a somewhat more detailed explanation of the Catechism—but a book of theology, never. We should like to know more, if for no other reason than our own satisfaction and spiritual comfort. We love our work, but it is tough to be told all the time that for a fuller explanation we shall have to wait until we enjoy the Beatific Vision in the realms above."[21]

The anonymous sister's incisive comments motivated Plassmann to found a summer master's degree to serve "Sisters and Teachers of Religion."

Plassmann reassured those concerned that Sisters ought not engage the complexities of speculative theology. "There is nothing to hide [in theology], and, if able masters lead them on through some of the deeper speculations, there is no danger of going astray." Plassmann then speculated that "Sisters possess perhaps more of the charisma of faith, of the 'Credo ut intelligam,' than is given to us [priests]." The Franciscan's aspirations for the women studying theology at Saint Bonaventure were more circumscribed than those of his Holy Cross counterpart, Sister Madeleva.

> Of course, we theologians do not want the Sisters to learn more than we know ourselves. That would be disastrous, though for a neophyte in the sanctuary or pulpit it might serve as a powerful stimulant....The purpose is not, to train Theologians or professors of Theology or writers of theological treatises, but teachers of Religion in order that they may acquire a fair understanding of Religion as a science, which is Theology.[22]

Father Plassmann and Sister Madeleva inhabited the same Catholic lifeworld in which the faithful, particularly laity, are to be formed for engagement in and with that secular lifeworld to overtake it through an integration of rational inquiry and devotion. Sister Madeleva, however, had far greater aspirations for the alumnae of St. Mary's Graduate School of Sacred Theology that simply gaining "a fair understanding of Religion as a science."

The "valiant woman" proved to be a recurring theme in narrative accounts of women's quests for theological education. In *The Catholic School Journal* (1950), Mary Fitzgerald reflects upon the many new opportunities for women to study theology during the summer, all of which, she asserts, "can trace their lineage to the first founded and most formally organized of such schools, St. Mary's School of Sacred Theology of Notre Dame, Ind." She then gave an account of Madeleva's initiative that suggests far more resistance than any found in Madeleva's own public reflections.

> When Sister Madeleva, president of St. Mary's College, bravely asserted that she would found a graduate school in which women might study theology, a shocked and dismayed

> silence was the response—but a new era in Catholic education began. Those who now complacently contemplate what Sister Madeleva's decision has brought about have no comprehension of what travail she endured. When she began her search for professors, pious eyebrows were raised, and learned foreheads drawn. Shall it be whispered that those who should have hurried to her [support], hesitated, doubting both the rock of her inspiration and the rod of her will. But alone and valiantly, she persisted in her efforts. From the most discouraging beginning and inconceivable opposition in the summer of 1943, St. Mary's School of Sacred Theology has grown surely and securely.[23]

Fitzgerald then observed that the school's success inspired others to found similar programs. Herscher's account of Saint Bonaventure's summer school was probably a direct response to Fitzgerald's claim about Saint Mary's.

Defending and Expanding Women's Theological Education

Four years after Saint Mary's offered its first theology graduate courses, Sister Madeleva once again came to the defense of "Theology for Women in America." This 1947 public lecture began with one of her favorite rhetorical strategies: a reminder that "to teach any of the secular subjects assigned her," the state required a Sister to have a bachelor's degree for elementary and a master's, at least eventually, for secondary and college teaching. By describing the state's high expectations for those teaching secular subject matter, she highlighted Catholic negligence in preparing those teaching sacred subject matter. The lack of preparation, according to Madeleva, explains why most religion courses "have been the least interesting, the most poorly taught, consequently the least popular in the curriculum."[24] Madeleva offered a remedy: the study of theology. Anticipating those who insisted that priests ought to teach theology courses, she simply noted that demand far exceeds supply. Women, especially Sisters, whether trained or not, are teaching religion. Madeleva insisted that a Catholic teacher of religion "should have had at least a minor in religion in undergraduate school and some additional graduate work." True to her presentation's title, the education she had in mind is open to all Catholic women. "There is no intrinsic reason why the lay teacher cannot and should not prepare to teach religion." After establishing the necessity of graduate education in theology for women, Madeleva then proceeded with some carefully chosen language to justify the founding of Saint Mary's Graduate School of Sacred Theology. "There was no graduate school in the United States where any woman could qualify for a Doctor's or a Master's degree in religion with theology and scripture [*sic*] as the content subjects."[25] She was correct, since Catholic University's content was not theological per se and Saint Bonaventure's only offered a master's degree in the summer.

Madeleva then reminded her audience that Saint Mary's program was "an experiment, the result of a study made by the Problems Committee of the Midwest Regional Unit of the Catholic Educational Association." In providing a basic program outline, she communicated a rigorous course of studies. The doctorate required "two years of Theology: fundamental, dogmatic, moral, spiritual; Church history, the Encyclicals with three summer sessions of Sacred Scriptures; Greek, Hebrew, archaeology, hagiography, Canon Law are included as requirements or electives." No dissertation is required. "An adequate piece of research is required and a public defense of some significant theological truth. The course concludes with a public examination on some significant theological truth." Madeleva emphasized the "graduate level" quality of the courses taught by a notable faculty, "some of the best scholars in scripture and theology in America." To further emphasize the program's academic quality, she mentioned that students currently enrolled included graduates of "Harvard, Johns Hopkins, the Catholic University of America."[26] An indication of Madeleva's commitment to graduate level studies was, as the previous description suggests, the apparent emphasis on acquiring reading proficiency in foreign languages. Alumnae noted that students unfamiliar with Latin were at a distinct disadvantage in meeting the professors' expectations in the study of Aquinas. Biblical Hebrew and Greek were initially required but Hebrew proved too difficult to absorb in a semester and soon became optional. Reading ability in French and German were strongly recommended.

Madeleva extolled the benefits of Saint Mary's educating women in theology. From its modest beginnings in 1943 to 1947, the presence of the graduate school already had an enormous impact on the undergraduate curriculum. "Two sisters prepared in the graduate school, assisted by two priests, are fulltime [*sic*] teachers." Effective teaching of these women and their clerical assistants had increased religion majors and minors. Academic benefits appeared to be only a minor subplot in the larger story of women's deliberate engagement in theological studies. Madeleva described "a palpable growth in charity among students and teachers, a great joy of spirit, a supernatural point of view, an elevation in the entire level of thinking and living." She claimed these effects to have exceeded Saint Mary's boundaries. "Everywhere students are encouraged to enter seriously and joyously into the great supernatural laboratories of theology, queen of the sciences, and the study of the revealed word of God." And in case anyone had any lingering doubts about women teaching theology to other women, Madeleva proclaimed, "Courses in scripture and theology are being taught in the right way by the right teachers, to the right students in many places throughout America."[27]

Madeleva then turned her attention to the undergraduate, incorporating her into this expansive narrative featuring women studying theology. She asked, "What can a girl do with such a college or graduate preparation for life?" Her first response, which St. Thomas would surely have approved, even if utterly surprised that the response came from a woman, was simply—"be." In contrast to secular education, which begins and ends in this world, theological education begins in the "supernatural" and ends in "immortality." Not to leave this world completely aside, Madeleva assured her listeners that undergraduates who enter into the supernatural realms through theology can prepare them for the more familiar professions, especially those in "social services" and that even more familiar "vocation of wife and mother." Madeleva then placed Saint Mary's graduate students at the center of her grand narrative about twentieth-century enthusiasm for theological studies.

> For half a century, mad with science, our teachers and our students have been starving for an opportunity to study the greatest of sciences. Twenty-five years ago Frank Sheed remarked that there was no place in America where a layman could study theology. Today at Saint Mary's College, sisters and laywomen not only study theology and Latin, they are familiar with the Scriptures in the Hebrew and the Greek. They qualify for degrees of Master and Doctor of Philosophy in religion.[28]

Madeleva then deftly moved from this particular place and time to the eternal. "Once Saint Augustine wrote beautifully, 'God Himself is the country of the soul.' Today the women of America, religious and lay, college teachers and their students are entering into the rich theological and scriptural heritage of this their native land."[29] Others had used "pioneer" to describe Madeleva's endeavor. But the founder herself described women studying theology as natives returning to their homeland, that is, God.

Notes

1. Madeleva Wolff, CSC, *Courier* 19, May 1945.
2. Gail Porter Mandell, *Madeleva: A Biography* (Albany: State of New York University Press, 1997), 91.
3. Mandell, *Madeleva*, 93.
4. Mandell, *Madeleva*, 109.
5. Sandra Yocum Mize, *Joining the Revolution in Theology: The College Theology Society* (Lanham, MD: Rowan and Littlefield, 2007), 19.
6. Sister M. Madeleva Wolff, CSC, "Religion in College," *Journal of Religious Instruction* 13 (1943–1944): 726.
7. Madeleva, "Religion in College," 729.
8. Madeleva, "Religion in College," 730.
9. Sister M. Madeleva, CSC, *My First Seventy Years* (New York: Macmillan, 1959), 115.
10. Mandell, *Madeleva*, 177.
11. Mandell, *Madeleva*, 185.
12. Mandell, *Madeleva*, 132.
13. Timothy Michael Dolan, *"Some Seed Fell on Good Ground": The Life of Edwin V. O'Hara* (Washington, DC: The Catholic University of America Press, 1992), 126–55.
14. Dolan, *"Some Seed Fell on Good Ground,"* 152.
15. Mandell, *Madeleva*, 53.
16. Mandell, *Madeleva*, 57.
17. Saint Mary's College 1944 Bulletin in "Bulletins: Graduate School of Theology" File, Saint Mary's College Archives.
18. Saint Mary's College 1944–1945 and 1946–1947 Bulletins, in "Bulletins: Graduate School of Theology" File, Saint Mary's College Archives.

19. Saint Mary's College 1948–1949 Bulletin, 14, in "Bulletins: Graduate School of Theology" File, Saint Mary's College Archives.

20. Irenaeus Herscher, OFM, *The Catholic School Journal* 50 (1950): 22A.

21. All of the quotes in this discussion of Father Plassmann's account are taken from his paper entitled "Theology for Nuns," in Plassmann Collection, Box 1, St. Bonaventure University Archive.

22. Plassman, "Theology for Nuns," in Plassmann Collection, Box 1, St. Bonaventure University Archive.

23. Mary Fitzgerald, "Theology and Women," *The Catholic School Journal* 50 (May 1950): 32A.

24. Madeleva, "Theology for Women in America," September 13, 1947, Saint Mary's College Archives.

25. Madeleva, "Theology for Women in America," 2–3.

26. Madeleva, "Theology for Women in America," 3–4.

27. Madeleva, "Theology for Women in America," 4.

28. Madeleva, "Theology for Women in America," 5.

29. Madeleva, "Theology for Women in America," 5.

4

Set Up to Burn Out

Lessons from Sr. Madeleva Wolff, CSC's Experiences of and Responses to "Burnout"

Jessica Coblentz

U.S. women religious are often lauded as workplace pioneers who created and stepped into professional roles previously unavailable to women.[1] And because of their courageous faith, perseverance, and the lasting results of their ministries, it is easy to romanticize their labor. In reality, these women were often handed interminable workloads without adequate preparation, while sexism and clericalism regularly left them underappreciated. Today's growing attention to worker "burnout," especially among women and those who occupy "caring professions," invites renewed reflection on all this: Were women religious set up to burn out?

In dialogue with literature that theorizes burnout, this chapter looks to Sr. Madeleva Wolff, CSC, as a case study on experiences of and constructive responses to worker burnout. After showing that Madeleva's personal writings evince features of what we today call "burnout," I argue that her life challenges us to grapple with the pitfalls of contemporary labor conditions and the shadow side of worker ideals, especially those grounded in faith.

What Is Burnout?

So, first, what is burnout? With growing attention to worker burnout across the last few decades, especially during the COVID-19 pandemic, there is an expanding body of academic and popular literature on the subject.[2] As a result, writes Jonathan Malesic, it can seem that "everyone is burned out, but no one knows what that means."[3] Fortunately for us, Malesic recently published *The End of Burnout*, a book that charts the social and scientific history of burnout and advances an incisive analysis of its problems and potential remedies.

Malesic clarifies that while today's notion of burnout didn't emerge until the 1960s, it has several related antecedents, including acedia, melancholia, and neurasthenia—all exhaustion disorders of some kind.[4] A few features distinguish contemporary burnout from these and other conditions, however. For one, burnout is defined by a constellation of three symptoms—exhaustion, cynicism, and despair—which manifest concurrently but to varying degrees depending on the person.

Next, these symptoms are occasioned by a distinctive coupling of social causes that also differentiate burnout. Burnout results from a confluence of the working conditions under which a person labors, on the one hand, and from the cultural and spiritual ideals that a person brings to that work, on the other.[5] These dual social causes help to explain why the concept of burnout has proliferated since the 1970s, when labor conditions broadly diminished, "contribut[ing] to shortfalls regarding the fairness, autonomy, community, and values people experience at work."[6]

Meanwhile, the ideals that one brings to the job affect how a worker experiences these conditions. The ideals that lead to burnout make "a promise: engage with your work, and you will earn more than a salary. You will earn social dignity, moral character, and spiritual purpose," explains Malesic.[7] In language particularly apt for a chapter on this topic, he suggests that the worker ideals cultivated by our communities often inspire our perseverance to become "work saints"—so, not just workers, but noble workers.

Yet working conditions and these ideals rarely align, a reality that makes burnout a fundamentally ironic experience. Malesic draws on the late literary critic Lauren Berlant, who coined the term "cruel optimism" to describe ironic experiences like this.[8] "Cruel optimism is 'when the object that draws your attachment actively impedes the aim that brought you to it initially.'" Malesic illustrates this irony with his own experience of academic burnout, recalling, "I was pursing worthy goals in my career—learning, teaching others, contributing to a community of fellow scholars—but the pursuit itself exhausted me, made me cynical, and threw me into despair. And in doing so, it undermined my ability to attain those very goals."[9]

We see here how the worker ideals that draw someone into the workplace are undermined by the very conditions of that workplace. In this situation, the aspiring work saint becomes a "work martyr"—a worker who submits to her own destructions in the name of lofty labor ideals. (According to Malesic, the work martyr is today's "typical worker.")[10]

Was Sister Madeleva Set Up to Burn Out?

Madeleva was often regarded as a "woman ahead of her time," but Malesic's history of burnout indicates that it would be an anachronism to literally diagnose her with this condition.[11] However, the dual social causes that engender today's burnout—those working conditions and worker ideals—certainly shaped Madeleva's career and seemed to contribute to symptoms we today associate with burnout.

Working Conditions

First, regarding her working conditions, Madeleva had little say over her occupational role at any given time; she went where and did what her superiors directed, even when they did so against her explicit request. This lack of autonomy, which Malesic associates with a diminished work environment, was a common condition of religious life.[12] Still, when combined with the absence of adequate worker preparation and the astonishingly long hours that Madeleva worked throughout her career, we see a portrait of extraordinarily difficult working conditions.

Madeleva's very first teaching assignment is a striking example of the inadequate professional preparation she received, and it was, by her own account, indicative of larger trends among women religious of her day, who were underprepared to serve as educators at nearly every level.[13] Less than a month into Madeleva's postulancy with Sisters of the Holy Cross, which began at the start of what would have been her senior year at Saint Mary's College, the superior of her community asked her to teach an English class at Saint Mary's Academy, the sisters' local high school. In her autobiography, Madeleva recounts her reaction to this request: "I was sure that I could scarcely wash dishes or sweep a floor well enough to be allowed to do either in the convent. I had never thought of being a teacher of any kind." Nevertheless, she began teaching English "the next morning, in a room before students, with books that [she] had never seen."[14]

Madeleva eventually completed her bachelor's and master's degrees, though she did so while her responsibilities multiplied. She maintained "a heavy and mature teaching schedule" at the college while carrying "additional and exacting loads of writing, sponsoring student publications, and class organizations." Again, this was apparently typical, for in her recollection of all this, she tells us, "The young sister is a magnet for jobs of many kinds."[15]

These examples from Madeleva's early career evince a lack of autonomy, a lack of professional preparation, and the sheer amount of work she was doing. Indeed, Madeleva claimed "to work twenty-five hours out of twenty-four," which, combined with other chronic mental and physical health issues, often put her on bedrest or even in the hospital for days at a time.[16] Members of the congregation, family, and friends regularly pointed out that this exhaustion was a result of her stress and overwork—something she herself conceded.[17]

Madeleva's time in the Western United States provides additional examples. In 1919, Madeleva was sent to the mission territory of Ogden, Utah, to lead Sacred Heart Academy, where she "pushed herself past exhaustion" so much so that in 1921, her superior sent her to California "to rest" for the summer. Madeleva "did not rest" there, according to her biographer, Gail Porter Mandell, and soon after went onto doctoral studies at Berkeley before returning to Ogden to serve as founding dean of the college that the congregation established there.[18] With her success as a college dean came ever more frequent illness, during which her local superior "refused to bend any of the convent rules, no matter how ill Madeleva might be."[19] This, again, shows how a lack of autonomy contributed to her challenging circumstances.

As her teaching and administrative career succeeded and took their toll, Madeleva's career as a published poet prospered. Yet this labor, too, was constrained by her extraordinary work conditions. Madeleva saw poetry as "a distillation requiring undistracted time in large quantities" but asserted, "This no sister that I know of has ever had."[20] Thus, for her, "Insomnia came as a solution. A sonnet and a short lyric good enough for immediate publication were not infrequently the fruit of one sleepless night." She adds, "Exhaustion was inevitable."[21] She also resigned to another solution—her sickbed—writing, "Having never had time within an always heavy and demanding schedule to do any writing, I have done what I have done chiefly when ill, often in hospitals."[22] Recall that the physical exhaustion she mentions here is one of the symptoms of burnout, and her resignation to it suggests another of burnout's symptoms—despair.

Worker Ideals

Per Malesic, it is the ideals that one brings to difficult working conditions like these that engender burnout. For her part, Madeleva was nothing if not a woman of noble ideals and lofty aspirations—a fact evident from the very beginning of her time at Saint Mary's. The Sister famously recounts that what led her to transfer there from the University of Wisconsin after her freshmen year of college was a search for something "more" for her life.[23] That longing for meaning and purpose animated her education, her religious life, and her decades of ministry as a scholar, teacher, and administrator.

Malesic explains that for many noble workers, their labor is not simply an obligation but a means to dignity and value. One recurring theme in Madeleva's reflections is an awareness that her success was an opportunity to demonstrate the dignity of her communities. For instance, in defiance of anti-Catholicism, Madeleva approached poetry as an opportunity to demonstrate the capacity and equal value of the Catholic mind, vowing, "As a Catholic and a sister I would write well enough for acceptance by the secular press, or I would not write at all."[24]

Among the first women to earn a PhD from Berkeley, Madeleva saw her doctoral studies as another opportunity to prove the intellectual worth of herself and most notably, womankind. Mandell recounts that there, as with the other esteemed institutions of higher education that Madeleva would occupy, she "prided herself on holding her own as one of few females in a predominantly male environment." She "thought of herself as something of a David among Goliaths, invariably emphasizing her young age, small size, or lack of experience when comparing herself with men."[25] Madeleva had reasons to be proud: Her professors lauded her coursework, her first collection of poetry went to press during her doctoral studies, and she won a book contract for her dissertation before its completion. And yet, of her Berkeley years, she also recalls "the spasms of panic, the chronic 'if I fail' state of mind which all but overwhelmed my waking hours."[26]

Madeleva believed that her work as an educator and administrator also served a unique higher purpose, for "A Catholic education is…an investment in eternity."[27] Of Catholic women's education in particular, she observed, "Girls achieve a type of womanhood when educated with girls which differs from the results of coeducation." She adds, however, "Perfection is not achieved without costs. The women's colleges in the United States are monuments to the enterprise, the sacrifice, and the fortitude of women."[28]

A memorable chapter from Madeleva's autobiography called "Wanting Things Badly Enough" is evidence of how her drive to provide Catholic women with a unique and exceptional education shaped her labor. The chapter is a litany of Madeleva's grand hopes for Saint Mary's during her presidency—student and faculty residence halls, a new infirmary, home economics and foreign language laboratories, a student recreation center—in response to which she poses the question, "Do we want these badly enough?" The implication is that if she and the college deem something worthwhile enough, then they will work tirelessly until it is realized. "These things must come," Madeleva asserts. "We want them badly enough."[29]

Summing up the overall effects of Madeleva's ideals on her work life, Mandell conveys how the spiritual underpinnings of her work drove Madeleva to persevere despite the challenges of her circumstances:

> Madeleva's confidence that nothing can be amiss in a life dedicated to serving God…shaped her philosophy and transformed any and every circumstance, however unpleasant in itself, into an opportunity for spiritual growth. Ironically, it also impelled her to work hard, certain that her every effort was supremely meaningful because it served a higher purpose than her own. Her faith in the providence of God reassured her that all would be well in the end.[30]

The Irony of Burnout

In Madeleva's life, we also witness the sad irony of burnout culture—that is, how work conditions and worker ideals give rise to "work martyrs." Mandell highlights how Madeleva's drive to live a life of service to God is precisely what exhausted her, often to the point of inhibiting her ability to serve God:

> Knowing and loving [God], she sought to serve, but service itself seemed to separate her from the One for whom she declared herself willing to sacrifice everything—except love itself. Madeleva coped with her contradictions by collapsing....She then consented to spend anywhere from a few days to several weeks in a hospital or rest home—an annual occurrence in midlife. Seldom allowing herself to do nothing even there, she used the time to read, meditate, and write an occasional poem or two....Her hospital stays became in a sense retreats for the body and the mind, which whether Madeleva consciously recognized it or not, were as necessary for her as the spiritual retreats scheduled regularly for all sisters.[31]

In view of Malesic's sketch of burnout, it is not romantic but concerning that Madeleva came to see her exhaustion—much of which was contingent on her constant overwork—as a holy "retreat" because it was her only access to the spiritual practices that most connected her to the God she longed to serve.[32]

This is especially concerning because the poetry writing that she deferred to these "retreats" was, according to Mandell, "an activity she found essential to her development as a religious person."[33] It "had from the first been Madeleva's way to God, intimately connected with her life of prayer."[34] Again, it is easy to romanticize the poet as a "work saint" whose drive to write kept her awake at all hours, writing even when her exhaustion put her in the hospital. "That's how much the work meant to her!" we might be inclined to say. The reality is that with so little time to write or revise amid the work demands of serving God, she perceived no choice but to relegate her most important spiritual practice to "after midnight or as she lay in her sickbed."[35]

Lessons for Today

The combination of Madeleva's work conditions, her faith-informed work ideals, and the ways they often combined to hold her back lead me to conclude that Madeleva was indeed set up to burn out. The makings of burnout were all there: The exhaustion and despair of burnout were also present, though I don't detect a great deal of cynicism in her. In general, it is not a stretch to say that she experienced some approximation of what we today call "burnout."

More interesting than a retrospective diagnosis for Madeleva, though, is what her experience and response to it can teach us about navigating burnout today. These lessons stand out for their enduring relevance, I argue, despite the few, quite harsh words Madeleva dedicated to mental health in her own writings. In one essay from her 1961 collection on higher education, Madeleva attributes growing public concern for mental health to communist propaganda and "quackeries." "The sanity of our nation is under question, under attack," she bemoans.[36] Although she adds the caveat that she is "not talking about careful and expert care of our health in all its aspects, physical, mental, moral, spiritual," her larger message suggests that Madeleva probably would have resisted the label of "burnout" had it existed in her time, if not for the reason of personal pride then for the sake of the nation.[37] Madeleva's example nevertheless affords several lessons for addressing workers' psychological well-being in our own time, when such flippant treatments of mental health are no longer acceptable.

A first lesson comes from Madeleva's response to her own experience. One might think that these struggles would compel a woman of her professional rank to improve the conditions of those under her direct supervision. Unfortunately, Madeleva admits that she was difficult to work with at times.[38] It would be a mistake to think that the conduct of one boss is what burnout culture hangs on, however. Malesic warns that most individual or interpersonal solutions cannot remedy the broadscale, social causes of burnout; this is what so many of today's calls for individual "self-care" get wrong.[39] Structural change is crucial for improving work conditions, and in this regard, Madeleva accomplished a great deal. Madeleva's experience of difficult work conditions familiarized her with the challenges of teaching with little to no professional preparation, and it prompted her to make religious teacher training programs a significant part of her life's work.

For example, she was instrumental in establishing comprehensive, full-time graduate theological education for women religious. After unsuccessfully petitioning several priest-serving graduate theology programs to admit women religious as students, Madeleva established the equally rigorous and traditional graduate School of Sacred Theology at Saint Mary's in 1943. Though this groundbreaking program would prepare Catholic women of various vocations to serve as professional theologians and lay ministers as well as teachers, Mandell emphasizes that "Madeleva's primary concern in establishing the School of Sacred Theology had been a practical one: to ensure adequate preparation for those actually teaching theology in the Catholic school system, most of whom were nuns."[40] That is, she determined to better the circumstances of young sisters who were sent to teach in parochial schools just as she had been.

The Sister Formation Movement was Madeleva's second structural contribution. As a member of the National Catholic Education Association (NCEA), Madeleva was for years "the loudest voice among those asking for a special section" on the preparation of nuns for teaching careers.[41] Eventually appointed to lead this committee, she chaired the special NCEA session dedicated to the preparation of sister-teachers that served as a launchpad for the First National Congress of the Religious of the United States in 1952 and the official establishment of the Sister Formation program in 1954—both of which were shaped by Madeleva's persistent leadership.[42]

When it comes to burnout today, Malesic warns of "bad advice about burnout [that] assumes—as we all often do—that institutions and systems of culture are immutable, almost God-given."[43] These two examples of institutional innovation show that, though Madeleva resigned herself to perpetual exhaustion due to the perceived immutability of her own work conditions, she never resigned to the impossibility of changing the systems and structures of professional preparation for other women religious, especially those embarking on careers in education. In this way, Madeleva exemplifies the commitment to structural change that is necessary for addressing the social causes of burnout in our own time. Rather than lauding individual practices of self-care or shifting jobs in search of a slightly better boss—helpful as those may be—we should learn from Madeleva that lasting, broadscale change to our working conditions will require the ambitious belief that professional and institutional structures can change as well as the determination to change them.

A second lesson from Madeleva concerns the ideals that we bring to our work. Madeleva's work had spiritual purpose, which inspired her self-sacrifice to the point of persistent exhaustion and little time for the poetry and prayer that most connected her with the source of that spiritual purpose. Though such mission-driven work exists in the nonreligious workplace, Madeleva's life puts into focus how religious contexts, where labor is explicitly and collectively sacralized, can reinscribe these ideals with particular force.

Just a few months apart in 2019, articles in two major American Catholic periodicals addressed burnout among Catholic ministers, and in them we hear echoes of the spiritual ideals that compelled Madeleva to sacrifice so much.[44] One former Catholic high school principal told *America* magazine that while the job was overwhelming at times, he initially thought this was "just the cost of the cross."[45] Another Catholic, Amy, observed how Catholic nonprofit employees tie "vocation to job, [making] it so that people give so much to their job"; this leaves people "set up for burnout."[46] In these anecdotes we see that, still today, when one's job is part and parcel with God's work, workers may find it challenging to close shop for the day no matter how trying their work conditions may be.

Like these secular lay ministers, those in religious life today may likewise remain "set up for burnout" because of the ideals that animate their work. According to Sandra Schneiders,

> Religious women work harder and longer for less pay than anyone in the Church with comparable qualifications. They are more often than not too responsible for their own good, remaining in ministerial positions that are patently abusive because of their commitment to God's people. Without any coercive pressure from superiors these Religious not only make their annual retreat (sometimes at the price of vacation) but also attend summer courses, prayer workshops, days of reflection, personal development seminars, and lectures....Religious are conscientious participants, often at the price of already scarce free time, in congregational tasks.[47]

Whereas prior to the reforms of the Second Vatican Council when the work of religious might have been more dependent upon enforced authority and communal obligation, Schneiders suggests that personal conviction—such as "commitment to God's people"—frequently inspires today's religious, especially women religious, to remain busy, self-sacrificing laborers, often under challenging working conditions. Reflection on the pitfalls of Madeleva's spiritual ideals should prompt us to bring a critical lens to the personal convictions that motivate ministry today. While sisters' ideals can bring a fulfilling sense of purpose and meaning to their vocational life, we know that these ideals can also compel religious who are working even "harder and longer" to burn out just like their secular lay counterparts.

Critical inquiry into the role of the spiritual ideals of today's women religious is all the more urgent in view of the fact that Schneiders observes a collective "soul fatigue" amid their busy ministerial lives. Schneiders draws on the work of Carmelite theologian Constance FitzGerald to develop her own account of this collective malaise.[48] Bringing Malesic's account of burnout into conversation with the contemporary realities of "soul fatigue" amid ministerial overwork may contribute additional insights for understanding religious life today. And while Schneiders's observations here pertain specifically to women religious, I suspect that men's communities share many of these experiences and would likewise benefit from engagement with Malesic's insights and critical reflection on Madeleva's example and the ideals that animate their work.

While these examples indicate that the dangers of faith-informed work ideals endure in our own time, Malesic believes that aspects of contemporary religious life also have the potential to relativize or reframe these ideals—not only among religious women and men but for all people. Malesic urges Americans to ground their dignity and value in something other than work, and he points to one religious community, the Benedictines, as inhabitants of a work counterculture that prioritizes one's identity in God above all. Because the liturgy dictates the Benedictine workday—no matter how productive or unproductive their working hours—this community embodies the foundational theological conviction that their value is independent from work. Their dignity is a gift from the God to whom they pray, first and foremost.

That Malesic points to this contemplative community as a model of alternative, sustainable work ideals is striking because Madeleva often spoke of her own longing for a more contemplative religious life, especially when she seemed most burnt out.[49] Malesic's proposal, paired with Madeleva's organic yearning for contemplation, signals both the problem of how spiritually driven work can get in the way of the spiritual life and a potential spiritual path beyond burnout. The solution to burnout is not a mass migration into contemplative religious life but rather an embrace of the lessons we can learn from privileging of God and self overwork. A life that prioritizes one's grounding in God regardless of work might serve as a helpful preventative and alternative to a life driven by spiritual work that hardly has time for God.

A third lesson concerns the memorialization of Madeleva and other women religious. Everyday hagiographies of Madeleva often emphasize her accomplishments while omitting her struggles as a worker.[50] In addition to being historically incomplete, these omissions can reinscribe troubling messages about women's work today. A romantic view of Madeleva's work parallels contemporary myths of a woman's ability to "have it all," which overlook the physical, emotional, and spiritual tolls of women's work, past and present.[51] In secular life, contemporary American women are frequently told that, despite the continued injustice of their labor conditions inside and outside the home, they can maintain a successful career and family life if they work hard enough—if they "want it badly enough," as Madeleva might put it. Meanwhile, Schneiders's portrait of contemporary religious life is not so different, with many sisters stretching to meet the demands of their congregations and the broader church and world. While there is good reason to venerate Madeleva and many other women religious of the past as pioneering models of women in the workplace, glamorizing their labor runs the risk of perpetuating today's detrimental myths of women's labor and normalizing the conditions and ideals that have often made their work so difficult.

Only by passing on the honest, messy realities of Madeleva and other work martyrs will we truly honor what she and so many other women religious endured to accomplish all that they did. And perhaps more pressing still, it's only in telling the messier story of their labor that we will be able to learn from the good and bad that they model for today's workers—religious and secular, women and men, old and young alike.

Notes

1. An earlier version of this essay was published as "Set Up to Burn Out: Lessons from Sr. Madeleva Wolff, CSC's Experience of and

Responses to 'Burnout,'" *Review for Religious* 2, no. 2 (2023): 151–62, 10.1353/rfr.2022.0023. I am grateful to *Review for Religious* for permission to reprint the essay here.

2. See, for example, Jennifer Moss, *The Burnout Epidemic: The Rise of Chronic Stress and How We Can Fix It* (Boston: Harvard Business Review Press, 2021); Emily Nagoski and Amelia Nagoski, *Burnout: The Secret to Unlocking the Stress Cycle* (New York: Random House, 2020); Anne Helen Petersen, *Can't Even: How Millennials Became the Burnout Generation* (Boston: Mariner Books, 2021).

3. Jonathan Malesic, *The End of Burnout: Why Work Drains Us and How to Build Better Lives* (Oakland: University of California Press, 2022), 19.

4. Malesic, *The End of Burnout*, 13.

5. Malesic, *The End of Burnout*, 55.

6. Malesic, *The End of Burnout*, 14.

7. Malesic, *The End of Burnout*, 14.

8. Lauren Berlant, *Cruel Optimism* (Durham, NC: Duke University Press, 2011).

9. Malesic, *The End of Burnout*, 21.

10. Malesic, *The End of Burnout*, 138.

11. Gail Porter Mandell, *Madeleva: One Woman's Life* (Mahwah, NJ: Paulist Press, 1994).

12. See Malesic, *The End of Burnout*, 98–100.

13. Sister M. Madeleva Wolff, CSC, *My First Seventy Years* (New York: Macmillan, 1962), 110–11.

14. Madeleva, *My First Seventy Years*, 36.

15. Madeleva, *My First Seventy Years*, 44–45.

16. Madeleva, *My First Seventy Years*, 49.

17. Gail Porter Mandell, *Madeleva: A Biography* (Albany: State University of New York Press, 1997), 112.

18. Mandell, *Madeleva*, 71.

19. Mandell, *Madeleva*, 111.

20. Madeleva, *My First Seventy Years*, 147.

21. Madeleva, *My First Seventy Years*, 46.

22. Madeleva, *My First Seventy Years*, 147–48.

23. Marjorie Hall Walsh, "Sister Madeleva: Lyric Poet" (master's thesis, Creighton University, 1962), 1.

24. Madeleva, *My First Seventy Years*, 45.

25. Mandell, *Madeleva*, 177.

26. Madeleva, *My First Seventy Years*, 54.

27. Madeleva, *My First Seventy Years*, 136.

28. Madeleva, *My First Seventy Years*, 129.

29. Madeleva, *My First Seventy Years*, 108.

30. Mandell, *Madeleva*, 220.

31. Mandell, *Madeleva*, 221.

32. See Mandell, *Madeleva*, 72 and 112.

33. Mandell, *Madeleva*, 53.

34. Mandell, *Madeleva*, 221.

35. Mandell, *Madeleva*, 72.

36. Sister M. Madeleva, CSC, *Conversations with Cassandra: Who Believes in Education?* (New York: Macmillan, 1961), 15.

37. Madeleva, *Conversations with Cassandra*, 16.

38. Mandell, *Madeleva*, 105.

39. Malesic, *The End of Burnout*, 154.

40. Mandell, *Madeleva*, 188.

41. Mandell, *Madeleva*, 189.

42. Mandell, *Madeleva*, 188–90; See also Madeleva, *My First Seventy Years*, 113. Further evidence of the lasting effects of Madeleva's structural innovations, the Sister Formation Movement gave birth in 1976 to what is today the Religious Formation Conference (RFC). RFC continues to serve women's and also men's congregations throughout the United States and the world. See *Religious Formation Conference*, https://www.relforcon.org/.

43. Malesic, *The End of Burnout*, 12.

44. Kaya Oakes, "When Professional Catholics Burnout," *America* (June 28, 2019), https://www.americamagazine.org/faith/2019/06/28/when-professional-catholics-burn-out; Teresa Coda, "As Lay Ministries Flourish, Ministers Struggle with Burnout," *US Catholic* (October 15, 2019), https://uscatholic.org/articles/201910/as-lay-ministries-flourish-overworked-ministers-struggle-with-burnout/.

45. Oakes, "When Professional Catholics Burnout."

46. Oakes, "When Professional Catholics Burnout."

47. Sandra Schneiders, IHM, *Finding the Treasure: Locating Catholic Religious Life in a New Ecclesial and Cultural Context* (Mahwah, NJ: Paulist Press, 2000), 157.

48. Schneiders, *Finding the Treasure*, 159–209.

49. See Mandell, *Madeleva*, 88.

50. See, for example, Thomas C. Fox, "Sr. Madeleva Wolff Forever Changes the Face of Catholic Theology," *National Catholic Reporter* (January 7, 2016), https://www.globalsistersreport.org/news/trends/sr-madeleva-wolff-forever-changed-face-catholic-theology-36166.

51. For commentary on the enduring prevalence of this myth, see Anne-Marie Slaughter, "Why Women Still Can't Have It All," *The Atlantic* (July/August 2012), https://www.theatlantic.com/magazine/archive/2012/07/why-women-still-cant-have-it-all/309020/.

5

Sr. Madeleva Wolff's Spirituality of Vision

Margaret M. Gower

This chapter considers the language of vision in the theology and spirituality of Sr. M. Madeleva Wolff, CSC (1887–1964). I argue that, in "vision," Madeleva finds a notion capacious enough to support her as she spans diverse theological and spiritual influences and authorities as well as diverse vocational interests and activities. First, I situate Madeleva's notion of vision in theological and spiritual context, offering special attention to her sacramental worldview, notion of beauty, and notions of poetry and poetics. From there, I suggest that, in the Beatific Vision, Madeleva finds a theological ideal, spiritual practice, and ultimate end that is prioritized in three currents within Christianity in which she stands: monasticism, mysticism, and Thomism. In all, I review Madeleva's sources and consider her constructive contribution to a theology and spirituality of vision, especially as it connects to Christian life and Christian education.

Madeleva describes seeing in creation as a spiritual practice that trains us for the Beatific Vision. The natural, creation, cannot be separated from the supernatural, God. Madeleva affirms the traditional notion of the transcendentals, the idea that there are eternal attributes of being that have their source in God, that God *is* perfectly, that exist to some degree in all of creation (including in human beings, made in God's image and likeness) in ways that echo God and point to God, that attract us, and that draw us to God. In the ancient philosophical tradition, the medieval Scholastic tradition, and Madeleva's own neo-Scholastic context, there was not one set list but overlapping understandings of the most basic properties of being. For Madeleva, they are truth, goodness, and beauty. So, when we notice beauty in the world, we are offering our attention to God, as in prayer. And, for Madeleva, the right response to seeing beauty is making beauty. For her, that is poetry above all. But she explains that

> there can be quite properly a poetics of every art: the seeing, the making, the singing of music, of the graphic arts, of fiction, of the sciences surely. There is a poetics of education, the creative process of making, through the vision of truth, of charity, the emotional intensities of goodness and beauty, out of a responsive girl a responsible woman.[1]

In poetics, especially the poetics of education, Madeleva sees "traffic between mortality and immortality, between space and the infinities."[2] The ultimate end of the poetics of education is immortality, infinity, and the Beatific Vision. Madeleva sees "vision" prioritized in monasticism, mysticism, and Thomism alike.

Sacramentality, Beauty, and Poetry

In a special way, Madeleva affirms the sacramentality of creation, the presence of God in the world. Madeleva seems to feel deeply that every place in creation, every place in the world that God made and God loves, is a possible site of encounter with God. More than accessible to us, God is waiting for us. For Madeleva, part of what it means to be Christian is to "see" God in creation, so that we can encounter God in creation. She sees the natural world and liturgical spaces alike as training grounds for this kind of seeing that leads to knowing God. She describes nature as cathedral and churches as gardens.[3] God dwells in these places, not *more* than in other places, but *more visibly*, at least for the one in training to see. In her 1959 autobiography *My First Seventy Years*, Madeleva writes,

> All knowledge then reflects God's omniscience. The lowliest matter displays the wonder of His creative art. Only when we

> know matter as God's creation do we truly know it, can we love and use it intelligently. Only when we know the world as God's world and the place of His love can we be happily at home in it, can we be literally and holily secular.[4]

For Madeleva, our relationship with creation will not be right, and we will not be comfortable as creatures in creation, until we see and know each place as God's place—as a place where God dwells and loves. She describes the correspondence between human seeing and knowing and God's ultimate seeing and knowing. When we see spiritually, which is a kind of knowing, we can see the material stuff of the world as that which God has made and sees as good. This is as true for "humble" (from the Latin word, *humus*, for ground, earth) matter as for majestic matter.[5] When we learn to see and know the world in this way, then we will be happy and at home in God's love and in our life on earth. Then we will know that we, too, are stuff of "the world" ("literally and holily secular," as Madeleva puts it) and part of the matter created by God. Madeleva, the wordsmith, turns the conventional meaning of *secular* on its head. She is not referring to the world, or time and space, *as opposed to* the Church, or the eternal and celestial, but to the world *as* a spiritual place. The supernatural is accessible to us in the natural world. We are part of the matter made by God. And we will be happy and holy when we accept our status as creaturely, spiritual *because* we are "secular."

Madeleva's notion of the sacramentality of creation is the theological and spiritual context for her notion of beauty. For Madeleva, beauty is "God's visibility," and beauty requires care.[6] Madeleva writes "that of the trinity—goodness, truth and beauty, each an equation for God—beauty is the most palpable, the most irresistible. I have called it God's visibility."[7] God *is* in the humble and the majestic alike. But, in beauty, the presence of God *is more visible* to us. Beauty helps us to see, to know, God. As Madeleva's biographer Gail Porter Mandell has argued,

> Madeleva had long regarded beauty as a tangible manifestation of the divine, the most accessible to humans of all God's attributes. Her devotion to beauty corresponded with her belief that the transcendent may be experienced through the senses as well as the soul; that the love of God involves the entire person, including the body....Madeleva believed that beauty draws souls to God more effectively than preach-

> ing or proselytizing. Not that a beautiful aspect or object in itself is God, but it can act sacramentally to reveal the reality of God's presence both to the maker and to the partaker of beauty.[8]

For Madeleva, then, beauty is a way of knowing God. Madeleva differentiates this notion of beauty from constraining notions of beauty for women. In contrast to a kind of beauty characterized by primping and prodding or painting, Madeleva wants to inspire the kind of beauty that is expressed in the common project of making her students "educated women for God's sake."[9] Bearing the influence of the Thomist and neo-Thomist ideas predominant at the time, her idea is that each one is in the image of God, and their work together is to perfect *that* resemblance. The very force of beauty, however, means that it is susceptible to misuse. The idea of beauty can be distorted and used to hurt persons, especially women. As Madeleva sees it, the very power of beauty explains "the ever-prevailing diabolism by which the devil takes such prompt and seductive possession of physical and human beauty....The grossness with which celluloid [i.e., the movies, "Hollywood"] has exploited the beauty of our young womanhood sickens me."[10] Indeed, in her weekly convocations as president of Saint Mary's College, Madeleva spoke often about beauty, criticizing representations of women in popular culture, and encouraging, instead, the "beauty of being," conferred by Christian education.[11]

So, beauty requires safeguarding. Madeleva wants to participate in that care. She writes that "we wanted to build a home for beauty."[12] Taking up the language of the transcendentals for the persons of the Trinity, Madeleva revises and reprioritizes the motto of Eric Gill (1882–1940). She explains that

> years ago, Eric Gill wrote, "Take care of goodness and truth, and beauty will take care of herself." I had not found this so. Perhaps because our care of goodness and truth had been mistaken or inadequate. At any rate, I had watched beauty go begging for a home and a family....I am inclined to rearrange Eric Gill's neat statement to read: "Take care of beauty, and goodness and truth will take care of themselves."[13]

Madeleva's sense that beauty needs to be cared for and protected from those who would use it for harm seems almost eerie in light of what scholars now know—and which Madeleva had no way of knowing—about Gill's sexual abuse of those in his care.[14] Madeleva knows that it is wrong to let beauty fend for itself. Beauty requires care. And part of what it means to be Christian is to be a caregiver for beauty in the world.

Madeleva develops her notion of beauty in the commencement address, entitled "Go, Sell What You Have" that she offered at Cardinal Stritch College in Wisconsin on June 2, 1963.[15] She describes the world's blindness and education's special sight, "the vision of truth," that engenders holiness.[16] Madeleva frames her words to the graduates as "a plea."[17] She says: "I should like to ask you to give back, to safeguard, if necessary, to bring back beauty to God."[18] She recalls for them that "we define and think of God as infinite Truth, Goodness, Beauty. We adore Him as infinite Truth, as infinite Goodness."[19] She asks them: "How many of us have fallen on our knees for even five minutes in adoration of the infinite Beauty that is God?"[20] And she charges them: "Give this beauty that is truth, that is goodness, to the poor, to a purblind [i.e., blind or almost blind] world. Through you it may come to identify truth and goodness with beauty, and so with God."[21] In the end, Madeleva asks the graduates to accept from her the appeal of the nineteenth-century English Jesuit priest and poet to "give beauty back...to God, beauty's self and beauty's giver."[22] The line that Madeleva includes here is from "The Leaden Echo and the Golden Echo," intended to be part of a drama on St. Winifred, which Hopkins began in 1879 but never completed. The two companion poems were designed as a choral song for two groups of girls to mark and celebrate the difference between mortal and spiritual beauty. Hopkins's work shifts from considering beauty in the world—"Despair, despair, despair, despair"—to a kind of representation of the resurrection of the body—"Spare!"[23] For Madeleva, the point seems to be that, at the end, God will save all beauty, including our bodies. But, until then, it is for us to see and safeguard beauty and, in so doing, see, know, and love God.

For Madeleva, herself a poet and an interpreter of poetry, poetry has a special status as the language of beauty. She writes,

> a great world and a great work are open to us as students and teachers, the worlds and work of contemplation and creative thought, of insight, of the divinization of the spiritual in the world of our five senses. The translation of our discoveries into the language of beauty should follow. We should see visions. We should dream dreams. We should write poems.

> All of us can be seers. Most of us can be makers. Some of us can be singers.[24]

Participants in the project of Christian education are, in a special way, in training for "insight," for seeing, in the spiritual sense. Many are compelled by beauty seen to beauty make. As Madeleva explains, "the person who does this, who exercises this art [of making], is the poet, the maker. But first [they] must see the possibilities within persons, places, things for such making, such creation. First, [they] must be a seer. [They] must have vision, insight. This in certain magnitudes, constitutes inspiration."[25] In her view, "a true seer" cannot stop with seeing. A true seer "must become a maker."[26] Some set out insights of all kinds in the language of beauty, which is, of course, also the language of truth and goodness. For Madeleva, this is poetry.[27] Echoing the Thomist and neo-Thomists terms predominant at the time, Madeleva lifts up poetry as a kind of key ingredient in the activity of art. Poetry helps us to see and to know, and it helps us to express what we see and know. So Madeleva writes: "What grace is to the moral life poetry is to art, supernaturalizing and transfiguring the simplest, the common things. It ministers spiritual nourishment to our emotional needs."[28]

The title of her address at Cardinal Stritch College captures this idea: "Go, Sell What You Have." At the heart of the talk is the Gospel lesson: "'Go, sell what you have and give to the poor.'"[29] After she charges the graduates "to go and sell what you have," she both asks and answers:

> What have you? A college education, a trained mind, a disciplined will, the intellectual virtues of wisdom, knowledge, art, the enveloping moral virtue of prudence, the gifts of the Holy Spirit. You have the greatest commodity in human being, the product of the biggest and best business in the world. You have a liberal education.[30]

And she goes on: "Because you are supernatural graduates, I want you to be supernatural in utilizing your education, to know and to love as God does. You are [God's] daughters. I want you to give your supernatural gifts to the poor."[31]

> What are they? Faith, courage, love, goodness, truth, beauty. These you must give to the poor. Who are the poor? Everyone.

> There is no person in all the world, nor ever has been, who has not need for at least one of these gifts. God...begs for our love.
>
> Why are we all so poor? Because we constantly waste our inheritance, the good things in our Father's house, and feed on the husks of swine....Pierre Teilhard de Chardin tells us that "God waits for us in things"—but how obtuse we have become to these possible encounters![32]

God is here, waiting. But most of us cannot focus to see. So Madeleva appeals to the graduates to share the fruits of their Christian education, above all, truth, goodness, and beauty, with the world.

Madeleva cites the French Jesuit priest, scientist, and theologian Pierre Teilhard de Chardin (1881–1955) as a source for her conclusion. The line that she quotes is from his *The Divine Milieu*, where he uses the language of "seeing" to explain his project and his argument. He writes that he puts forward "no more than a practical attitude—or, more exactly perhaps, a way of teaching how to see."[33] Teilhard explains:

> I shall not attempt to embark on metaphysics or apologetics. Instead, I shall turn back, with those who care to follow me, to the Agora. There, in each other's company, we shall listen to St. Paul telling the Areopagites of "God, who made man that he might seek him—God whom we try to apprehend by the groping of our lives—that self-same God is as pervasive and perceptible as the atmosphere in which we are bathed. He encompasses us on all sides, like the world itself. What prevents you, then, from enfolding him in your arms? Only one thing: your inability to see him."[34]

He concludes, "God truly waits for us in things, unless indeed [God] advances to meet us."[35] Madeleva offered her address at Cardinal Stritch College the year after Teilhard had been tagged for concern by the Vatican. Teilhard's work was not published until after his death in 1955 "because of disciplinary measures from the Congregation for the Doctrine of the Faith (formerly the Holy Office) during his life. The popularity of his books *Human Phenomenon* and *The Divine Milieu* led to the *monitum*, or warning, in 1962 for "ambiguities and indeed even serious errors.""[36] *The Divine Milieu* was published in English in 1957, although Teilhard composed it around thirty years earlier. So Madeleva seems expansive in her sense of whom to read and use, even citing Teilhard by name in a public talk the year after he received the *monitum*.

In sum, Madeleva's sacramental worldview, her notion of beauty, and her notions of poetry and poetics animate her spirituality of vision. There is something of God in creation. We can see God in creation. We can see God in beauty. Even more than truth and goodness, beauty is our surefire way to know God. We feel it and we find it (so, God) irresistible. And, sometimes, we are compelled to act on it. For Madeleva, poetry is the language of beauty. It helps us to know God and to love God.

The Vision of God

Madeleva was formed by and committed to monasticism, mysticism, and Thomism. In "vision," she finds a common theological ideal, spiritual practice, and ultimate end that is prioritized in each of these currents within Christianity.[37]

First, Madeleva uses language of vision in the context of the Beatific Vision.[38] For Madeleva, the ultimate end of poetics and, especially, the poetics of education, is the Beatific Vision, which she tends to list with immortality and infinity. With roots in scripture, the notion of the Beatific Vision is an attempt to name the immediate (that is, unmediated) knowledge of God that is experienced in heaven.[39] It is called *vision* in order to distinguish it from the knowledge of God which is available to the human mind in the present life. It is called *beatific* because, in this knowledge, the human person finds perfect happiness. Madeleva anticipates "heaven the Beatific Vision," where human persons will see God face-to-face.[40] For "heaven is a place of complete happiness."[41]

Monasticism has tended to place special priority on the Beatific Vision. John Cassian (ca. 360–430), the most influential writer on early monasticism, recommends a spirituality that includes a "hermeneutical method that places a primacy on striving to realize the beatific vision so desired by his desert forebears."[42] For Cassian, purity of heart is the way, and the Beatific Vision is the end. As the historian Katie Bugyis demonstrates in her chapter in this volume, Madeleva has a sense of herself as a Sister of the Holy Cross, a vowed woman religious, participating in a common project with other Christian religious. Madeleva sees her religious life in the monastic life.

Mysticism has also tended to place special priority on the Beatific Vision. Madeleva was interested in mysticism since at least her days as a doctoral student at the University of California at Berkeley, where she studied English medieval poetry with special attention to mystical poetry. When Madeleva received her obedience to serve as president of Saint Mary's College, the college magazine announced that "in addition to her executive duties, she will head the department of English and offer courses in mysticism, creative writing, and contemporary poetry."[43] Indeed, during her first two years as president, Madeleva taught two courses in the English Department, "one in writing, one in literary criticism," according to her autobiography.[44] And at the Catholic University of America (CUA) in the summer session from June 28 to August 8, 1935, she taught graduate students in "English S. 353: Mysticism in English Literature" and "English S. 355: The Poetry of Chaucer other than the Canterbury Tales." According to the CUA course catalog, "Mysticism in English Literature" was "a study of eminent mystical writers and writing from 'The Dream of the Rood' to 'The Hound of Heaven,'" using C. F. E. Spurgeon's *Mysticism in English Literature* (1913).[45]

The author of the one required text listed in Madeleva's CUA course description is the English professor Caroline Frances Eleanor Spurgeon (1869–1942). Madeleva's use of Spurgeon's text points to Madeleva's own place in this important generation of women, including Evelyn Underhill (1875–1941) and Simone Weil (1909–1943), writing about mysticism, sometimes as they studied it and sometimes as they experienced it. As the scholar of mysticism Bernard McGinn has described, the twentieth century is like the thirteenth century as a period of new development for women writing about God as scholars of mysticism and/or as mystics themselves.[46] Madeleva and the trailblazing programs that she founded, the School of Sacred Theology at Saint Mary's College (f. 1943) and the undergraduate major in theology at Saint Mary's College (f. 1946–1947), are part of this high-point moment in the history of women writing God-talk, especially mystical God-talk. In her essay entitled "Dame Julian of Norwich" (first published in 1955), Madeleva admires Julian's *shewings*, or showings, and emphasizes Julian's visions from God to her spiritual eyes. She describes how "with profound penetration and unerring orthodoxy she looks into the face of Mary, upon the crucified Christ, beyond the anthropomorphic, to the Beatific Vision of the Trinity. She takes us with her all the way."[47]

Thomism has also tended to place special priority on the Beatific Vision. Even in her essay on Julian, Madeleva refers to "the present revival of Thomistic philosophy."[48] In the light of the neo-Scholasticism that predominated in Catholic academic contexts after the promulgation by Pope Leo XIII of *Aeterni Patris* (1879) and the proclamation of Thomas Aquinas as patron of all Catholic universities (1880), the curriculum of the School of Sacred Theology at Saint Mary's College was predominantly neo-Thomist.[49] And, as Mandell has described, Madeleva attended each class meeting. So, in the coursework that she herself had secured—expanding opportunities for authoritative credentialing in God-talk for laypersons, including women—Madeleva found the language of vision, as an end and also as an experience. In Thomas and the neo-Thomists, Madeleva encountered the notion of the *summum bonum*, the highest good, the ultimate end toward which all human action is directed. Learning from ancient philosophers, above all Aristotle, and theologians, especially Augustine and Boethius, Thomas proposes that the ultimate end for all human persons is God, the uncreated good, who alone can perfectly satisfy, and that this experience (that is, attainment or enjoyment) of God makes humans happy.[50] In the end, for Thomas, "final and perfect happiness can consist in nothing else than the vision of the Divine Essence."[51]

Madeleva incorporates this capacious notion of vision as a common theological ideal, spiritual practice, and ultimate end of Christian life into her notion of education. She makes the case for Christian education in general and Christian education for women in particular in the language of vision. Ultimately, education is for the Beatific Vision; it prepares us for union with God at the end. Madeleva explains that "Saint Mary's came into existence one hundred years ago to teach youth that they are children of God, that they are immortal, and to prepare them through all the avenues of mind and soul for the perfection of that immortality."[52] Addressing students, she writes, "Your immortality has been predetermined in large part by the degree of your personal intimacy with wisdom, by the intensity of your love of truth and your persevering fidelity to it."[53] Secondarily, education offers perspective; it enables us to bear suffering in life. Madeleva thinks that part of the purpose of Christian education (the secondary part because it is a temporal good, not the ultimate good) is to make students secure for life on earth.

This is not about status or wealth. She locates true security in God alone. "You can be secure only when you can stand everything that can happen to you."[54] Two of the examples she offers of this perspective that enables suffering to be seen rightly are stories of alums who are mothers who bear grave loss, the death or imminent death of a child.[55] Madeleva had been giving careful thought to this particular experience of suffering since her time at Berkeley, where she wrote her doctoral dissertation on the medieval poem "Pearl," an account of the experience of the loss of a child.

Madeleva's ideas also follow in the tradition of Boethius's *The Consolation of Philosophy* (523). Boethius (ca. 480–584) composed the text from prison while he awaited execution. From the sixth century forward, it was an influential text in Christian theology and philosophy. Indeed, Chaucer (ca. 1340s–1400), on whom Madeleva worked with special interest as a scholar and teacher, had translated it into English. And Madeleva points to Queen Elizabeth I, who, she writes, "made the first version into modern English of Boethius' *Consolations of Philosophy*."[56] Sr. Maria Assunta Werner, CSC (1916–1995) has described both Madeleva's interest in Boethius and her eminent professor's response to her interest during her time at Oxford (1933–1934).

During the Trinity term Sister attended lectures by C. S. Lewis on medieval poetry. Because of illness, he missed three of the nineteen lectures advertised for the course. At his suggestion to the students, Sister wrote to ask him to lecture on Boethius; Lewis responded with three lectures, not one, on *The Consolation of Philosophy*.[57]

Conclusion

In all, this chapter has traced the language of vision in Madeleva's theology and spirituality, situating it within her sacramental worldview, notion of beauty, and notions of poetry and poetics and within her currents of special influence and authority, monasticism, mysticism, and Thomism. What comes through in her use of language of vision is, in fact, a spiritual practice of seeing and making, divinizing, "supernaturalizing and transfiguring."[58] In training for the Beatific Vision, the Christian person practices seeing beauty in the world. Some feel compelled by beauty seen to beauty make. Receiving a Christian education, students do this when they make their lives into expressions of the beauty that is also truth and goodness. Even today, the vestiges of Madeleva's theology and spirituality of vision are seen in the idea, set out in the mission statement of Saint Mary's College, that intellectual vigor, aesthetic appreciation, religious sensibility, and social responsibility expand together—that they are, not discrete, but dependent goods.[59]

Notes

1. Sister M. Madeleva, CSC, *Conversations with Cassandra: Who Believes in Education?* (New York: Macmillan, 1961), 40.

2. Madeleva, *Conversations with Cassandra*, 41–42.

3. Gail Porter Mandell, *Madeleva: A Biography* (Albany: State University of New York Press, 1997), 232.

4. Sister M. Madeleva, CSC, *My First Seventy Years* (New York: Macmillan, 1959), 137.

5. Thanks to Eric Bugyis for this etymological insight.

6. Madeleva, *My First Seventy Years*, 104.

7. Madeleva, *My First Seventy Years*, 104.

8. Mandell, *Madeleva*, 230.

9. Madeleva, *Conversations with Cassandra*, 41.

10. Madeleva, *My First Seventy Years*, 104.

11. As Mandell has demonstrated, "Female beauty was a frequent theme in the president's addresses to the student body of Saint Mary's. She attacked the image of beauty promulgated by the media of her day. In her opinion, this image pressured women to look 'not like themselves, but like pitiful parodies of the motion picture deities of the moment.' She redefined the notion of 'true beauty' as 'beauty of being—apart from hairdos and cosmetics,' and stressed that only Christian education conferred it." Mandell, *Madeleva*, 180. Mandell is quoting from Madeleva's "Why Do We Educate Our Daughters?" in *Conversations with Cassandra* (1961). The passage reads in full: "Standardizations in all areas and on every level tend to dominate their learning, their living. They look at and listen to the same vapidities, the worst as well as the best that celluloid has to offer. They are pressured to look, not like themselves, but like pitiful parodies of the motion picture deities of the moment. One need not elaborate. Against standardization from lipstick to leotards, the college girl today must fight the difficult fight of keeping her independence,

of being simply and completely herself." Madeleva, *Conversations with Cassandra*, 18–19.

12. Madeleva, *My First Seventy Years*, 104.

13. Madeleva, *My First Seventy Years*, 104–5.

14. Gill was an English sculptor, designer of typefaces (including Gill Sans and Perpetua, which are standard in Word), and a convert to Catholicism. Since his death and after Madeleva's time, scholars have learned about Gill's incestuous and abusive sexual relationships. See Eric Gill, *Beauty Looks After Herself: Essays* (New York: Sheed & Ward, 1933).

15. Madeleva offered her remarks during the college's years as a Catholic women's college, after its period training the Sisters of St. Francis of Assisi and before opening to men.

16. Madeleva, *Conversations with Cassandra*, 40.

17. Sister M. Madeleva, CSC, *Horizons: Reflections on a Liberal Education* (Notre Dame, IN: Sisters of the Holy Cross, 1981), 10.

18. Madeleva, *Horizons*, 10.

19. Madeleva, *Horizons*, 10–11.

20. Madeleva, *Horizons*, 11.

21. Madeleva, *Horizons*, 11.

22. Madeleva, *Horizons*, 11.

23. Gerard Manley Hopkins, "The Leaden Echo and the Golden Echo (Maidens' song from St. Winefred's Well)," in *Poems Of Gerard Manley Hopkins: Now First Published*, ed. Robert Bridges (Humphrey Milford, 1918), 55–57.

24. Madeleva, *Conversations with Cassandra*, 46.

25. Madeleva, *Conversations with Cassandra*, 39.

26. Madeleva, *Conversations with Cassandra*, 39.

27. Mandell has described how "Madeleva's experience as a poet and as a nun had shaped her ideas on beauty. As a young religious, she had seen what she referred to as the 'overwhelming beauty' of God through prayer, and her need to express that vision resulted in poetry. As a graduate student at Berkeley, she defined the religious poet who writes from such experience as 'the soul satisfied by union' who sings, and wrote that this type of poet, which she called 'mystical,' realizes that 'Earth, life, the soul, the Church, [them]self are wedded to God in a very ecstasy of love. All creation is a multiple mirror, dedicated to the reflection of these unions.'" Mandell, *Madeleva*, 230. Mandell is quoting Madeleva's analysis of Francis Thompson's poetry in an essay enti-

tled "Religious Poetry" that she published in *Chaucer's Nuns and Other Essays* (1925).

28. Madeleva, *Conversations with Cassandra*, 46.

29. Madeleva, *Horizons*, 9. See Mark 10:21, Matt 19:21, and Luke 18:22.

30. Madeleva, *Horizons*, 9.

31. Madeleva, *Horizons*, 10.

32. Madeleva, *Horizons*, 10.

33. Pierre Teilhard de Chardin, *The Divine Milieu: An Essay on the Interior Life* (New York: Harper Torchbooks, 1960), 46. See also Pierre Teilhard de Chardin, *The Divine Milieu: Pierre Teilhard de Chardin*, trans. Siôn Cowell (Liverpool, UK: Liverpool University Press, 2012), 3.

34. Teilhard de Chardin, *The Divine Milieu*, 46. See also Teilhard de Chardin, *The Divine Milieu*, trans. Siôn Cowell, 2.

35. Teilhard de Chardin, *The Divine Milieu*, 47. See also Teilhard de Chardin, *The Divine Milieu*, trans. Siôn Cowell, 4. Madeleva names and quotes Teilhard again at the end of her address. "You are the holy women of this world and your day. As Pierre Teilhard de Chardin says, 'In each soul, God loves and partly saves the whole world which that soul sums up in an incommunicable and particular way.'" Madeleva, *Horizons*, 16.

36. Heidi Schlumpf, "Time to Rehabilitate Teilhard de Chardin?," *National Catholic Reporter*, January 27, 2018, https://www.ncronline.org/news/time-rehabilitate-teilhard-de-chardin.

37. Mandell has suggested that "as she grew older, Madeleva continued to associate poetry in a particular way with the vision of God and to describe the devotion to poetry as a form of worship." Mandell, *Madeleva*, 231.

38. It is beyond the compass of this study, but I am interested in pursuing the question of Madeleva's use of the work of Kenneth Escott Kirk (1866–1954) on the Beatific Vision. Kirk's *The Vision of God: The Christian Doctrine of the Summum Bonum* is a classic in moral theology. Kirk presented his ideas as the Bampton Lectures at the University of Oxford in 1928, published them in 1931, and expanded and reissued the book in 1934. So Kirk's work coincides with Madeleva's year at Oxford (1933–1934). Indeed, while Madeleva was at Oxford, Kirk was the Bishop of Oxford in the Church of England (a position he held from 1937 to 1954) as well as the Regius Professor of Moral and Pastoral Theology at Oxford (a position he held from 1933 to 1938). From a

genealogical perspective, I'm interested to consider Kirk's influence on Madeleva. And, from an ecumenical perspective, I'm interested to learn whether Kirk, positioned as he was within the Church of England and the Oxford Movement, was one of the theological thinkers that Madeleva was reading, talking with, and learning from almost thirty years before the Second Vatican Council.

39. See, for example, "'Come,' my heart says, 'seek his face!' Your face, Lord, do I seek" (Ps 27:8), "Blessed are the pure in heart, for they will see God" (Matt 5:8), and "For now we see in a mirror, dimly, but then we will see face to face. Now I know only in part; then I will know fully, even as I have been fully known" (1 Cor 13:12). All biblical quotations are from the NRSV translation.

40. Madeleva, *Conversations with Cassandra*, 58.

41. Madeleva, *Conversations with Cassandra*, 46–47.

42. Christopher J. Kelly, "Cassian's Hermeneutics: Purity of Heart and the Vision of God," in *Patristic Theories of Biblical Interpretation: The Latin Fathers*, ed. Tarmo Toom (Cambridge, UK: Cambridge University Press, 2016), 109.

43. Sister Maria Assunta Werner, CSC, *Madeleva: Sister Mary Madeleva Wolff, C.S.C., A Pictorial Biography* (Notre Dame, IN: Saint Mary's College, 1994), 75.

44. Madeleva, *My First Seventy Years*, 94.

45. *The Catholic University of America Announcements for the Years 1935–1936 and 1936–1937*, vol. 15 (Washington, DC: The Catholic University of America, 1935), 36, and C. F. E. Spurgeon, *Mysticism in English Literature* (Cambridge: Cambridge University Press, 1913).

46. Bernard McGinn, "'The Violent Are Taking It by Storm' (Mt. 11:12): Reflections on a Century of Women's Contributions to the Study of Mystical Spirituality," *Spiritus: A Journal of Christian Spirituality* 13, no. 1 (2013): 17–35.

47. Madeleva, *Conversations with Cassandra*, 132–33.

48. Madeleva, *Conversations with Cassandra*, 130.

49. Mandell has described how the school offered "courses on the Old and New Testaments, fundamental, dogmatic, moral, ascetical, and mystical theology, church history, papal encyclicals, biblical archaeology, hagiography, and canon law for religious." Mandell, *Madeleva*, 186.

50. Thomas Aquinas, *The "Summa Theologica" of St. Thomas Aquinas*, trans. Fathers of the English Dominican Province (London: R. & T. Washbourne, 1920), https://www.newadvent.org/summa/2003.htm.

51. Thomas Aquinas, *The "Summa Theologica."*

52. Sister M. Madeleva, CSC, "Education for Immortality," in *A College Goes to School: Centennial Lectures* (Notre Dame, IN: Saint Mary's College, 1945), 164. Madeleva developed this idea in her 1944 lecture "Education for Immortality," which was her contribution to the special lecture series that the college hosted during the academic year in commemoration of the century since its founding. The next year, the lectures were published together as *A College Goes to School* (1945).

53. Madeleva, "Education for Immortality," 166.

54. Madeleva, *Horizons*, 16. See also Madeleva, *Conversations with Cassandra*, 19: "We must educate our daughters to the fact that we are secure only when we can stand everything that can happen to us."

55. Madeleva, *Conversations with Cassandra*, 42–43.

56. Madeleva points to Elizabeth to support her argument for women's education. "Educated women, it appears, have always been with us. Our problem is not to find them; our problem is to match them." Madeleva, *Horizons*, 23.

57. Maria Assunta, *Madeleva*, 66. See also Madeleva, *My First Seventy Years*, 75–76. Mandell and others have described Madeleva's friendship with the British writer C. S. Lewis (1898–1963).

58. Madeleva, *Conversations with Cassandra*, 46.

59. Saint Mary's College, "Saint Mary's College Mission Statement," 2025, https://www.saintmarys.edu/about/leadership/college-mission.

PART 2

MADELEVA'S LEGACY AS A POET AND SCHOLAR

6

"A Modern Madam Eglantine"

Sister Madeleva and Chaucer's Nuns

Katie Ann-Marie Bugyis

On April 22, 1959, Sister M. Madeleva (1887–1964) wrote to C. S. Lewis (1898–1963), chair of Medieval and Renaissance English at Magdalene College at the University of Cambridge, to inform him that she was traveling to Europe that summer and wished to visit him. Madeleva had made Lewis's acquaintance when she was pursuing further graduate studies at the University of Oxford in the 1933–1934 academic year. In the Trinity term, Madeleva had taken his course "The Prolegomena to the Study of Medieval Poetry"—"the best course [she had] ever had anywhere," she had remarked in a letter to her General Superior, Mother M. Vincentia (1867–1949)—and she had remained in correspondence with him ever since.[1] In her 1959 letter, Madeleva asked Lewis: "May I call on you. As an American I could not be reconciled to a day in Cambridge with the omission of such an amenity. Please, however, do not let me intrude on leisure or privacy that you may need much more than a call from a modern Madam Eglantine."[2] Lewis responded five days later, insisting, "But of course you must call!"[3] And he directed her to come to Oxford instead, where he planned to vacation. During her travels, Madeleva did spend a day in Oxford, but she left no record of a meeting with Lewis.[4]

Among the many details of Madeleva's life to be gleaned from her letter to Lewis, it is significant that she identified with Madam Eglantine, one of the pilgrims that the late fourteenth-century English poet Geoffrey Chaucer created for his *Canterbury Tales.* In his opening portrait of Madam Eglantine, the narrator Chaucer observed that she was the prioress of the community of Benedictine nuns at the priory of St. Leonard, Stratford-at-Bow, located on the eastern outskirts of London, and that she was accompanied by "another nonne," who served as "hir chapeleyne," and by "prestes thre."[5] Chaucer described at length Madam Eglantine's appearance and comportment, including how she smiled, sang the Divine Office, spoke French, dined at table, cared for animals, and wore the signs of her religious profession, from the "ful semyly...wympul pynched" on her head to the "smal coral...peire of bedes" about her arm, on which hung a gold brooch bearing the inscription "Amor vincit omnia [Love conquers all]."[6] Madeleva herself owned and prominently displayed in her office at Saint Mary's College bellows that had been carved with the same inscription (see figure 1). In her autobiography, *My First Seventy Years*, published in the same year she hoped to see Lewis again, Madeleva explained that the inscription on the bellows was "a nice supplement to the motto on the medal of Madame Eglantine, in Chaucer."[7]

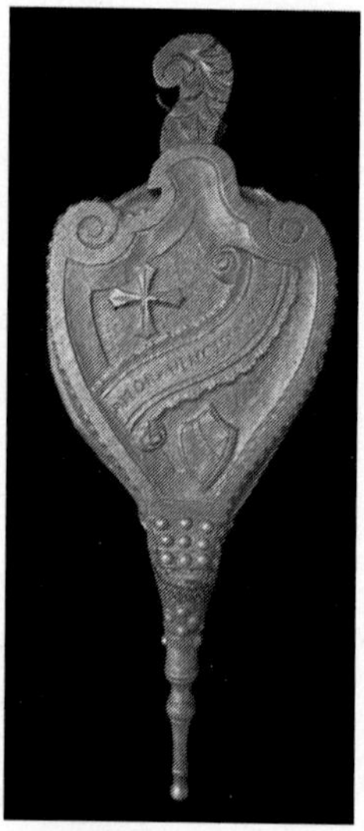

Fig. 1: Sr. M. Madeleva Wolff's Bellows (Saint Mary's College Archives).

Madeleva's identification with Madam Eglantine may surprise and even trouble those familiar with more modern studies of Chaucer's Prioress, which often read her character as vain, worldly, and disobedient to the Rule and customs ostensibly governing her life as a Benedictine nun, and also interpret the tale she tells to the band of pilgrims about a "litel clergeon" as violently anti-Semitic.[8] But when Madeleva began her formal study of Chaucer's *Canterbury Tales* in a graduate seminar in 1922, the prevailing criticism of the Prioress was focused almost exclusively on her portrait in the General Prologue—"the amiable foibles" of her character and "the delightfully imperfect submergence of the woman in the nun," as Madeleva's teacher at the time, John Livingston Lowes (1867–1945), a visiting professor from Harvard University, had noted in an earlier article.[9] Far less attention was given to the Prioress's tale.

It was not until after the Second World War, when the atrocities committed against the Jews under Hitler were made public knowledge, that scholars began to raise ethical concerns about the anti-Semitism of the tale, its teller, and its author.[10]

For Lowes's seminar, Madeleva wrote a paper entitled "Chaucer's Nuns." She later published it in two collections of her essays—first in *Chaucer's Nuns and Other Essays* in 1925 and then, without revision, in *A Lost Language and Other Essays on Chaucer* in 1951.[11] In her essay, Madeleva reflected the prewar trend in Chaucerian scholarship of attending primarily to the Prioress's characterization in the General Prologue, but she departed radically from the latest criticism, including Lowes's, by attempting to free the Prioress from "a secular point of view" that failed to recognize and appreciate the religious significance of her appearance and comportment.[12] Without apology, Madeleva interpreted the Prioress as a Catholic and a nun. She firmly believed that her experiences of consecrated life as a Sister of the Holy Cross gave her unique insight into the Prioress's character. Observations of the Prioress made by someone from any other state of life, even by Chaucer himself, were liable to distortion because they could never understand her as fully as another nun could. Over five hundred years separated Madeleva from the Prioress, and though Madeleva acknowledged certain differences in the rules, customs, and practices of their religious observances, she also insisted on a universality and timelessness to essential features of every nun's observance in the Western Christian tradition, most especially the "subtle change" her whole self underwent because of "the mystical but most real relation between [her] soul and God" and "the rules and customs and religious practices of the particular community in which the individual [sought] to perfect that mystical relation."[13] A woman who committed her life to undergoing this "subtle change" was a nun, according to Madeleva, no matter when she lived or what community she entered. It was this shared definition that encouraged Madeleva to identify her fellow Sisters of the Holy Cross and herself with the Prioress. In doing so, Madeleva defended the sincerity of all their religious vocations.

Madeleva, the Medievalist

By her own account, Madeleva's attraction to medieval studies began in earnest when she was a first-year student at the University of

Wisconsin at Madison. In the fall of 1905, she enrolled in a yearlong general survey of medieval history taught by Dana Carleton Munro (1866–1933) and George Clarke Sellery (1872–1962).[14] Madeleva judged their course to be "a thoroughly satisfying experience in education" for her.[15] She admitted, "Certainly, I have had more scintillating, more spectacular professors, but none have ever taught me more."[16] For her, the Middle Ages meant "art, architecture, evolving cultures, the Benedictine schools, the Crusades, the guilds"—all topics covered in the course.[17] She declared: "The great loves of my life are in so much of all this."[18] The course expanded her understanding of the world and its past: "I, a freshman from a microscopic town in the northern woods [of Wisconsin], was assigned for a term paper, 'A Commentary on the Rule of Saint Benedict.' At last I had come to a teacher who addressed himself to my mind."[19] Madeleva's close reading of the Rule of Saint Benedict as an undergraduate shaped how she later understood her vocation as a Sister of the Holy Cross. In her account of her novitiate in her autobiography, she remarked: "Studying our Rule took me straight back to the Rule of Saint Benedict on which I had written a term paper."[20] Later still, in her essay "Chaucer's Nuns," Madeleva acknowledged that she lived "under a modified form" of the Rule of Saint Benedict.[21] This acknowledgment was vital to her argument: "the Nuns themselves, to be interpreted at all, must be interpreted in relation to their Rule, their customs, and the community prayer by which their entire lives were regulated."[22] And Madeleva was better prepared to "regard…them simply in the light of the Prioress's Rule" than other scholars of Chaucer's *Canterbury Tales* because she had committed her life to following a similar Rule.[23]

According to Madeleva's transcript, the next medieval course she took was Old English, sometime between 1916 and 1918, for a special Master's program in English offered in the summers by the University of Notre Dame to Sisters of the Holy Cross on Saint Mary's campus.[24] But it was the graduate seminar on Chaucer with John Livingston Lowes at the University of California, Berkeley, in the summer of 1922, that proved decisive for Madeleva's intellectual formation and scholarly career. That spring, while she was principal of Sacred Heart Academy in Ogden, Utah, she had been informed by her local superior, Sister M. Celsus (1855–1927), that she was to go to Berkeley for a summer session of graduate work in English.[25] "By choice," she registered for Lowes's course because she was a "medievalist by every attraction," as she later confessed in her autobiography.[26] In Lowes, she found a "rare teacher and rare friend."[27] For her final paper, she decided to study "Chaucer's Nuns from inside the convent," a topic that "seemed ideal and opportune" to her.[28] When Lowes returned the paper, he pronounced it "ready for publication."[29]

Two years later, Madeleva sent "Chaucer's Nuns" in a collection with four other essays she had completed in graduate coursework to D. Appleton and Company for consideration for publication. On June 17, 1924, Rutger Bleecker Jewett (1867–1935), vice president and editor of the publishing house, wrote to Madeleva to inform her that he found the essays to "show deep scholarship and an amazing grasp of both life and literature," but he worried that "the general book buying public will not be keen for such a volume," and wondered whether there would be "a demand for such a book in Catholic institutions."[30] He affirmed again that "these essays are of a high literary quality and of genuine worth," and would "publish them with pride and great pleasure," if he could "see any chance of breaking even financially."[31] He insisted that he needed to "see a market sufficient to justify the cost of publication" before embarking on the enterprise.[32] A month later, Jewett followed up with Madeleva to say that he had decided "to take the risk" to publish her collection of essays, if she was "willing to forego royalties on the first edition of a thousand copies."[33] He concluded that "the quality of these essays is so high" that he could not "reject the manuscript."[34] Two days before, Jewett had a publishing agreement for *Chaucer's Nuns* drawn up between D. Appleton and Company and the Sisters of the Holy Cross and sent to Madeleva's General Superior, Mother M. Aquina (1852–1927), for her signature on behalf of the community.[35] The collection was to be published under Madeleva's religious name. On July 23, Madeleva sent a letter to Mother Aquina from Holy Rosary Academy in Woodland, California, where she had been living and teaching while pursuing her doctorate at Berkeley. Madeleva assured Mother Aquina that all of the essays in *Chaucer's Nuns* had been

> written as class assignments at summer schools and so have been no infringement on the time that belongs to my teaching or other duties. The book will have a real value to scholars and will be, I think, fairly representative of the work of the Sisters of the Holy Cross; more substantial than a less serious but more popular work....This present manuscript

> will be more valuable to us as teachers, I think, though it may not bring in big receipts at once.[36]

Mother Aquina consented to the publication of *Chaucer's Nuns* and signed the agreement with D. Appleton and Company.

Madeleva's determination to publish *Chaucer's Nuns* with a secular press was in keeping with her practice of submitting her poetry "first to secular rather than to Catholic magazines."[37] In her autobiography, she explained:

> I had heard so much about Catholics being unable to receive recognition because they were Catholics. I resolved not to permit mediocrity in my writing to be attributed to my religion. As a Catholic and a sister I would write well enough for acceptance by the secular press, or I would not write at all.[38]

Beyond publishing with a secular press, Madeleva was determined to analyze works of English literature authored by Catholics as a Catholic and a vowed religious and to prove that previous criticism on this literature failed to grasp their essential meaning. In a letter to Mother Aquina written while she was working on her dissertation on the theme of "spiritual dryness" in the fourteenth-century Middle English poem *Pearl*, Madeleva rejoiced:

> I am so enthusiastic about [my thesis] for it all works out just as I had thought, and all the professors here as well as the most eminent critic on the subject, who visited here some weeks ago, agree that I am right and all of them are wrong. It is good to have beat them at their own game with the simple weapons of Catholic lore, the Imitation of Christ, the Rule of St. Benedict, and the like. Professor Lehman is anxious to have it published, in part at least, in one of the learned journals. This will mean recognized scholarship for Holy Cross among the English scholars of the world.[39]

Madeleva did publish her dissertation—*Pearl: A Study in Spiritual Dryness*—with D. Appleton and Company in 1925, the same year as *Chaucer's Nuns*.[40]

Seven years later, Madeleva wrote an article entitled "Scholarship for Catholic Women" that, in part, addressed the need for scholarship by Catholics. She observed that current research in history, science, literature, and languages was

> being done chiefly by non-Catholic scholars, and their equipment is, in many cases, pitifully meager because of the heritage of which their Protestantism has deprived them. They cannot look at the ninth-century cope or monstrance, they cannot read an eleventh-century martyrology or thirteenth-century Mass Book with anything approaching understanding. They go to endless pains trying to explain expressions that, to a Catholic, are obvious.[41]

She especially lamented that Catholics had

> surrendered Dan Chaucer, "the morning star of English song," unconditionally to our friends, the enemy. Chaucer is studied with tolerance, I might say, in our colleges; Catholic criticism of Chaucer almost does not exist. We have been squeamish about some of the Canterbury Tales, perhaps, while reading with complacency more shocking things in the daily papers, more innocuous things in our daily fiction. And so we have missed, mayhap, the reverence, the Catholicity, the faith and simple condition of Chaucer in the conclusion of the *Parson's Tale*, not to speak of the *Prioress's* and the *Second Nun's Tales*.... Why do we not get into the heart of our Catholic literature?[42]

Around the time this article was published, Madeleva hoped to make a study of "the implicit Catholicism of Chaucer."[43] By then, *Chaucer's Nuns* was out of print, and she did not think it likely that it would be printed again.[44] She planned to use the titular essay of her earlier collection as one of the chapters.[45] But she was long delayed in completing the proposed volume. In 1934, her superiors chose her to serve as the third president of Saint Mary's College, and "the impact of administration," as she later explained to C. S. Lewis, was "desolating as far as adventures in mere thinking are concerned."[46] It was not until 1951, seventeen years into her presidency, that Madeleva published *A Lost Language and Other Essays on Chaucer* with Sheed and Ward. She reprinted "Chaucer's Nuns" as the second essay in the collection. In all the essays, but most especially in the first, "A Lost Language," she endeavored to recover "fairly convincing evidences of a persistent warp of sincere piety and devotion through all the gay woofs of life and convention that pattern [Chaucer's] work."[47] In a letter to Madeleva on April 18, 1951, C. S. Lewis thanked her both for having a copy of *Lost Language* sent to him and for writing it: "There has been nothing like it before and it emphasises a side of Chaucer too often neglected."[48] Four years later, Madeleva had this pious and devout Chaucer visually represented in one of the fifteen frescoes created by the artist Jean Charlot (1898–1979) to ornament the façade of Moreau Hall, the new fine arts building under construction at Saint Mary's College (see figure 2). Madeleva worked closely with Charlot to design the frescoes.[49] Like many earlier portraits of the poet, the Chaucer in Charlot's fresco holds rosary beads in his hand, but unlike any of those portraits, this Chaucer points upward to God.[50]

Fig. 2: Jean Charlot's Fresco of Geoffrey Chaucer for Moreau Hall at Saint Mary's College, courtesy of the Jean Charlot Collection, University of Hawai'i at Mānoa Library.

Madeleva and Chaucer's Nuns

In her essay "Chaucer's Nuns," Madeleva also took care to represent the Catholic Chaucer. She made several inferences about his familiarity with vowed religious life. In trying to determine the religious custom that dictated why the Prioress "was cleped madame Eglentyne," Madeleva considered the possibility that it was "self-chosen" and that "the chooser was Chaucer."[51] Even so, she thought: "his choice was a canny one, I admit, with the canniness of a journalist."[52] Similarly, Madeleva's defense of the motto *Amor vincit omnia*, inscribed on the brooch hanging from the Prioress's rosary beads, depends in large part on her conviction that "Chaucer himself had seen it so many times in some convent parlor, possibly in Norfolk where a ring bearing the same inscription has been unearthed and where there was a large Benedictine convent in Chaucer's time."[53] Concerning the Divine Office, or hours of prayer sung every day in religious communities, Madeleva asserted:

> Chaucer must have been familiar with the Divine Office, so familiar that he knew how it should be said....he must have been at some convent for only there could he have heard the "service divyne entuned."...One might go further and infer that through business or ties of kinship he must have been well acquainted with some community; a stranger or a casual visitor does not ordinarily hear the religious chanting the Office, or if he does, he is not able to interpret it as Chaucer does.[54]

To her suggestion that Chaucer may have been personally connected to a religious community, Madeleva added a footnote, citing Thomas Lounsbury's *Studies in Chaucer*, which listed records for two Elizabeths with the surname Chaucer who were Benedictine nuns at different convents in the late fourteenth century.[55] Like many scholars before and after her, Madeleva was tempted to wonder whether Chaucer had a daughter or another female relative who was a Benedictine nun. In studying the tales told by the Prioress and the Second Nun, Madeleva thought that it was

> abundantly evident to any reader, to the religious most of all, that Chaucer knew personally, even intimately, Sisters; not

> only that, he had talked with many of them, I should say; had listened to their stories....Whether he got the text of the little clergeon from Gautier, or Cæsarius, or the Paris Beggar Boy, or the unknown X is a point on which research may ponder futilely; but that he knew the story from the lips of some old Nun before he knew any of these would not surprise me in the least....I like to think of Chaucer, the child, a "little clergeon" himself perhaps, or later "his felaw" listening again and again to the stories of the childish singer of the *Alma Redemptoris*, of the "corones two," and of the martyrdom of St. Cecilia from the lips of some dear old Sister, an aunt or a grandaunt, perhaps—who knows?[56]

More than familiarity with conventual life, Chaucer had great admiration for the Prioress and the Second Nun as vowed religious, on Madeleva's reading. She criticized scholars who suggested that "Chaucer had in mind an ambiguous meaning for the motto, 'Amor vincit omnia' or an eye to its cheaper journalistic value."[57] Such suggestions, to her mind, were "unworthy and inconsistent with [Chaucer's] attitude of pronounced respect toward the Prioress."[58] Likewise, those scholars who declared that the two nuns' motivations for undertaking the pilgrimage to Canterbury were anything but spiritual clearly misjudged Chaucer's assessment of them. Madeleva insisted:

> nowhere does Chaucer give us any reason to think that his Nuns were of a tramp or derelict order; the reverence and courtesy of which he specifically says they were worthy is proof enough that he was depicting the typical "ninety-nine who need not penance" Sister rather than the well advertised one who does.[59]

Madeleva was also of the opinion that the Prioress was not a young nun, as many scholars had thought, but a "cheerful dignified, kindly woman of fifty years, perhaps."[60] Chaucer's choice of subject, Madeleva claimed, was not only in keeping with the Rule of Saint Benedict's strictures on electing superiors, but also further proof of the "greater perfection" of his artistry.[61] She explained:

> He has given us some one much harder to paint with his brush of words than a young Nun in whom the young woman is as

> yet imperfectly submerged. That task might have tempted his immaturity. But here is his picture of a woman a decade or more beyond middle age (my opinion) sweetened and spiritually transformed by the rules and religious practices of her choice, who can be in the world without being of it, gracious without affectation, and friendly without boldness.[62]

Here, Madeleva countered the reading of her former professor John Livingston Lowes, who asserted that the details of Chaucer's description of the Prioress "suggest still youthful flesh and blood behind the well-pinched wimple…not only in his account of the amiable foibles of the Prioress, but in his own choice of words and phrases, Chaucer suggests the delightfully imperfect submergence of the woman in the nun."[63]

For all his astute and respectful observations of vowed religious life, however, Chaucer still misunderstood certain features of it, in Madeleva's estimation. Near the beginning of her essay, she emphasized: "He was representing the visible effects of a spiritual life of which he had no experimental or vicarious knowledge. That fact should be italicized in considering critically his accomplished task."[64] By "spiritual life," Madeleva was referring to the "mystical but most real relation between the soul and God" that effected the transformation of self experienced by vowed religious. In an unpublished treatise entitled "The Nun and Her Relation to Christ's Mystical Body," possibly written just after she had made her final vows in 1914, Madeleva affirmed for her fellow Sisters of the Holy Cross that

> sanctity can be achieved in many ways but if I can grow into understanding of my mystical relationship with Christ, and into complete cooperation, I shall know and experience the heavenly paradoxes of my life in God. I shall be one of the holiest, happiest members of His Mystical Body.[65]

Madeleva believed that Chaucer could never have fully known and experienced this mystical relation as a married layman. He was not espoused to Christ as the Prioress, the Second Nun, or Madeleva had been at their consecrations. His deficiency in knowledge and experience of the spiritual life, according to Madeleva, led him to misinterpret the Prioress's solicitous care at table to keep her habit clean as "apparent over-daintiness."[66] Madeleva thought, too, that "even Chaucer might not have been able to account exactly for" the spirit of mortification that directed the Prioress to reach "ful semely after hir mete."[67] And "the chief significance" of the Prioress's "ful semyly…wympul pynched"—an evident sign to Madeleva of a habit worn "modestly and becomingly as the uniform of [a nun's] high vocation"—"may have deceived even Chaucer."[68] Madeleva was also not sure whether the poet was "consciously or unconsciously, making [the Second Nun] live according to her rule and supplying her with legitimate and ordered occupation against the evil of idleness."[69] And in representing "the natural overflow of [the Little Office of the Virgin's] most beautiful and fitting parts into [the] more worldly speech [of the two nuns]," "Chaucer may not have known just how deep the this undercurrent was."[70] If that was the case, Madeleva declared, "the more glory to him for representing what he observed but did not understand."[71]

Madeleva thought that contemporary scholars of the Prioress and the Second Nun, especially those without experience of or even familiarity with the vowed religious life, were at greater risk of misunderstanding what Chaucer had observed and tried to represent in the two pilgrims. Not only did such scholars see the nuns "through the less luminous distance of five hundred years" since Chaucer had created them, but they also occupied "a secular point of view" that limited or distorted their vision of the objects of their analysis.[72] Madeleva explained: "Criticism seems to have followed methods of microscopic analysis of them out of their habitual environment."[73] Scholars taking this analytical approach to the Prioress and the Second Nun did not assess their appearance or comportment according to the Rule of Saint Benedict or the customs that directed the communities of Benedictine nuns in Chaucer's day. They judged the two pilgrims instead according to their own, often mistaken assumptions of how nuns were expected to appear and behave in the late fourteenth century. They accused the Prioress in particular of being insufficiently nunlike. In her discussion of the nun's dress and conduct at table, for example, Madeleva cited R. K. Root's summation of the Prioress's character as "distinctly likeable, but also a little ridiculous" in her "many affectations" and "pains" to imitate a courtly manner.[74] "So much trivial comment," Madeleva thought, "ha[d] been expended" upon the Prioress's table manners, and she engaged with it "rather resentfully" in her essay. "None of them," Madeleva pointed out, "ever wore a religious habit, nor had the least idea of what real distress a Sister feels at getting a spot on her habit, especially at table."[75] They could not, therefore, understand why the

Prioress took such great care when she was eating. More fundamentally, they struggled to recognize that "Chaucer in depicting the Nuns was not dealing merely with women wearing a particular and conspicuous costume, symbolic of religion, but women whose whole selves had undergone a subtle change."[76] Only someone who had experienced this change could see the Prioress and the Second Nun for who they really were.

To correct previous scholars' "microscopic analysis" of the Prioress and the Second Nun, Madeleva sought to provide a "telescopic synthesis of them in their environment."[77] She viewed the nuns' characters more "in the light of their rules, customs, and community prayers than by the measure of a social life that they had voluntarily abandoned," because she believed that such a view could make "a fruitful and nearer-to-truth study of Chaucer's Nuns."[78] It could also yield "a more human, if not a different, understanding of them" than previous criticism had shown.[79] For example, to interpret the Prioress's "smylyng…ful symple and coy," Madeleva "would go sooner to the *Rule of St. Benedict*, with which Chaucer was easily familiar, than to the pastorelle of the fourteenth century where Professor Lowes hunts the phrase with such characteristic thoroughness."[80] Citing chapter 53 of the Rule on hospitality, Madeleva argued that the Prioress's smiling was "the minimum of hospitality that she must have felt for strangers at home or abroad."[81] Similarly, Madeleva invoked chapter 55 of the Rule on the provision of clothing and shoes to explain the Prioress's concern to keep her habit clean while at table: "She was wearing not only a clean, but a new habit, which she would be expected to give up on her return to her convent."[82]

No less essential to Madeleva's "telescopic synthesis" were her appeals to the personal experiences of contemporary vowed religious women, including her own, as sources for verifying and legitimizing the appearance and comportment of the Prioress and the Second Nun. Madeleva confirmed her observation of the Prioress's spirit of mortification at table not only by referencing a passage from chapter 39 of the Rule on the proper amount of food, but also by asserting that "the verriest novice knows that mortification is the mainspring of religious life and bodily mortification is practiced in some measure by all religious at table."[83] Likewise, in her defense of the Prioress's feeding leftover scraps to her "smale hondes," she contended:

> this custom is as old as St. Francis and his brother Wolff, I suspect. Personally, I see every day of my life a Sister with

> as "tendre a herte" as the Prioress—an old Sister, by the way—gathering choice bits of meat and creamy milk for our excellent mouser, Fluff, and scattering "wastel breed" to the little warblers and finches around our door. I should say that this good Sister's heart goes out to the canine world to such degree that more than one "hounde" greets her with barks of joy. One would have to live in a convent to appreciate fully what Chaucer has really done in these sixty lines of the *Prologue.*[84]

Madeleva cited the Prioress's keeping of pets and her care for other animals as further proofs of her older age: "A Sister of fifty or sixty can have a bird or a dog or a cat with propriety; a Sister of thirty would scarcely think of such a thing."[85] And only a more mature nun would have been "so charitable and so pitous" as to weep over "a mous / kaught in a trappe" as the Prioress did.[86] Madeleva insisted: "Human nature in respect to mice has not changed since those times. No young Nuns that I have ever met, and they are many, would have been moved to tears at such a sight; most of them would certainly have screamed or have wanted to."[87] Madeleva also defended the inscription *"Amor vincit omnia"* on the Prioress's brooch by noting that

> this is one of the commonest of epigrams among religious, and I know that one could find it worked in cross stitch, or painted in all the varying forms of realistic and conventional art and framed as a motto in dozens of our convents in our very unmystical and unmedieval United States to-day.[88]

No less ubiquitous in Madeleva's time were the tales told by the Prioress and the Second Nun:

> They are just the stories that Sisters are telling to the smaller and even the grown children in Catholic boarding schools the world over to-day; they are the stories that the children clamor for again and again and never tire of hearing. It was there that I heard them before I knew of Geoffrey Chaucer; and the Nuns' tales took me back, not to manuscripts, nor sermons, nor even to the lives of the saints, but to the stories told by Sisters in our recreations at boarding school.[89]

Madeleva maintained that the "suggestions" she offered about the likely origins of the Prioress's and the Second Nun's tales arose "from homely experience rather than from scholarly research," but she still hoped that they might "lead to new clues and methods of approach" in future studies of the nuns.[90]

The Reception of *Chaucer's Nuns*

Several readers of Madeleva's essay have praised her for incorporating her personal experiences as a vowed religious in her analysis of the Prioress and the Second Nun. In his foreword to *Chaucer's Nuns*, Benjamin Lehman (1889–1977), Madeleva's dissertation chairman at Berkeley, wrote:

> At length...comes a student who is a scholar (and is therefore not out to edify), who has insight (and is, therefore, not boring), who is a nun and aware of the singular continuity of tradition in religious communities....She brings these leverages of her intellectual and spiritual and physical state to bear upon those sisters who long ago moved with others on to Canterbury...the result is an essay which no library, no lover of Chaucer, no student of the religious life in communities can do without.[91]

Relatedly, albeit less effusively, Herbert S. Gorman (1893–1954), in his review of *Chaucer's Nuns* for the *New York Times* in 1925, remarked:

> She contributes something important to our knowledge of that delectable Prioress yclept Eglantine....The writer being a nun herself, a member of one of those unchanging orders that have come down through the centuries living under eternal rules, understands Chaucer's nuns, senses their secret minds and the reasons for their attitudes toward the great world.[92]

And in his reassessment of the Prioress and the Second Nun in an article published in *The Chaucer Review* in 1996, Henry Ansgar Kelly advised: "We should be prepared to take more seriously the favorable judgment about Chaucer's nuns arrived at by Sister Mary Madeleva, who was not only a working medievalist...but also a working nun, whose insights into living the common religious life should carry real weight."[93]

Other readers of Madeleva's essay have taken issue with her treatment of the Prioress and the Second Nun as real historical figures that could be distinguished from Chaucer. On June 1, 1925, John Livingston Lowes wrote to Madeleva to say that he was "still more impressed by its value" upon reading her essay again in its published form and thought that she had "made a contribution of utmost value," but he had certain concerns:

> You know infinitely more about Chaucer's nuns as nuns than I possibly can—that is to say, your knowledge is intimate from within. Chaucer, on the other hand, couldn't, I think, know them in quite that way; and at that sole point he and I stand on common ground. In a word, I can't help thinking that whereas I have undoubtedly not laid sufficient emphasis on the Prioress as she herself was, you, perhaps, have not quite sufficiently taken into account the fact that Geoffrey Chaucer (Heaven save the mark!) was not himself a nun.[94]

Florence H. Ridley, in her 1965 monograph *The Prioress and the Critics*, voiced her concern more forcefully:

> It is not as Sister Madeleva seems to think, that the poet in drawing his portrait copied a nun from life, faithfully, but without understanding what he saw; making, as it were, a photographic representation of a real person....Chaucer created the Prioress, and so he understands her better even than another nun could do.[95]

Anthony Bale, in an article for the inaugural issue of *New Chaucer Studies: Pedagogy and Profession* in 2020, extended Ridley's criticism, objecting not only to the historical reality Madeleva had granted the Prioress and the Second Nun but also to her identification with them: "Madeleva thus saw the Prioress as a direct ancestor, an accurate portrait of herself, one that she was especially well-placed to understand: critical ambiguities about the Nun were 'misinterpretations' both by the critics and by Chaucer himself."[96]

In Madeleva's defense of the Prioress, Bale was especially troubled by her discussion of the nun's tale: it "was not rooted in rehabilitating the violence and stereotypes of 'The Prioress's Tale', but rather that the tale represents an authentically and conventionally Catholic practice which persisted into Madeleva's own early twentieth-century convent."[97] Madeleva's admission that stories like the one told by the Prioress were still being told by sisters in Catholic boarding schools and convents and that she had first heard them from sisters at their recreations seemed to be emblematic of the anti-Jewish culture of the Roman Catholic Church at the time. Bale observed: "Madeleva's critical practice and her perceptions of Chaucer's Prioress relied on the elision of the agency and identity of the Jews from 'The Prioress's Tale'—indeed Madeleva never once wrote the word 'Jew' or 'Jews' in her 1925 essay, 'Chaucer's Nuns', on the Prioress."[98] Emmy Stark Zitter, in an article published in *The Chaucer Review* in 1991, even more emphatically denounced how Madeleva "so blithely states [that] such fraudulent stories about Jews" were still being told by Catholic sisters in her day.[99] With pointed irony, Elisabeth M. Orsten, in an article published in *Florilegium* in 1992, remarked: "In her defence of the Prioress, Sister Madeleva seems to be as sentimental as the good lady herself. Perhaps for that very reason she captures better than any more academic critic the spirit in which Madame Eglentyne tells her tale."[100] In their review of scholarly criticism of the Prioress in their 2017 monograph *The Critics and the Prioress*, Heather Blurton and Hannah Johnson acknowledged that Madeleva "feels compelled to rally to the Prioress's defense, but she does so on the grounds of her mores and deportment as a nun, and displays no special concern about the tale's content."[101] They emphasized that, in focusing on the Prioress's portrait, Madeleva "certainly reflects the broadly shared sense among early twentieth-century scholars that the anti-Semitism of the story was simply *there*, requiring little in the way of explanation or analysis."[102] In a footnote, Blurton and Johnson briefly reflected on the politics that may have informed such a stance toward the text: "In a universe of thought prior to the Holocaust, and preceding Vatican II, assumptions about Jewish-Christian relations were obviously much different than they were to be later."[103] The constraints of space prevented Blurton and Johnson from elaborating on this point, but it is worth further consideration in Madeleva's case.

Madeleva and Anti-Semitism

It is impossible to know fully another's mindset and its determining influences, especially at such a historical remove, but I think it is unlikely that Madeleva's "elision of the agency and identity of the Jews from 'The Prioress's Tale'" was motivated by malicious or even conscious anti-Semitism for at least two reasons: her friendship with Benjamin Lehman and her involvement in the National Conference of Christians and Jews. From the summer of 1922 to the winter of 1925, when she was researching, writing, and trying to publish *Chaucer's Nuns*, she was learning from Benjamin Lehman, the English professor at Berkeley who served as a mentor throughout her doctoral studies and as the chairman of her dissertation committee. After she had completed his seminar on nineteenth-century literature in the summer of 1922, he wrote to her superior, Mother Aquina, urging her to allow Madeleva to pursue a doctorate in English at Berkeley.[104] Lehman also advised Madeleva to publish *Chaucer's Nuns* and *Pearl: A Study in Spiritual Dryness* and wrote a foreword to the former work.[105] Lehman was a nonpracticing Jew, but he openly shared his struggles with faith and religion in his meetings and correspondence with Madeleva.[106] In a letter he wrote to her on March 30, 1924, he admitted: "All my ways, these weeks and months, have taught me how great and how beautiful is your Catholic and monastic simplification. Unhappily I only see, and feel dramatically. If once it became lyric, of me and my being—but it will not, I know too well."[107] And in a letter she wrote to him sometime before the publication of her poem "The Swimmer," possibly in 1925, Madeleva remembered: "This afternoon and once before you spoke to me of Faith in terms of a spring-board; had you ever thought of it under the figure of swimming?"[108] Lehman and Madeleva maintained a close friendship for the rest of their lives.

On April 16, 1951, he wrote to her to celebrate the arrival of his copy of *A Lost Language*: "How *C's Nuns* stand firm and happy-making, after these years. And how the others make us raise the 'feel' of that incomparable man as Catholic in a Catholic world. Many thanks to you for writing them, and for again thinking of me when the press had done its work."[109] And on April 23, 1964, in what would be her last letter to Lehman before her death three months later, Madeleva recalled that it was on that day, in 1925, that she had defended her dissertation:

> I never can quite understand, nor account for, your great kindness to me, growing out of the providential mistake I made in blundering into your seminar on *Nineteenth Century Ideas.* How deeply and truly we have experienced the lived life since then and how vicariously we have shared the areas in which our common, and often basic, interest lie. Life is a magnificent experience looking back, even more than looking forward.[110]

She went on to announce that she was scheduled to give a commencement address to the Evangelical Lutheran canonesses at Valparaiso University the following month, and that she had spoken to a group of Presbyterians in Indiana and to a group of Episcopalians in Michigan in the past two months. She remarked: "We have had the most stimulating conversations and relationships in all these cases. The barriers of separation are becoming less and less effective as barriers."[111]

Beginning in 1930, Madeleva became formally involved in interreligious dialogue. In that year, she joined the National Conference of Christians and Jews (NCCJ), which had been founded in 1928 as part of the Federal Council of Churches' Commission on International Justice and Goodwill

> to promote justice, amity, understanding and cooperation among Protestants, Catholics and Jews, and to analyze, moderate and finally eliminate intergroup prejudices which disfigure and distort religious, business, social and political relations, with a view to the establishment of a social order in which the religious ideals of brotherhood and justice shall become the standards of human relationships.[112]

The NCCJ became an independent organization in 1932.[113] In its founding document, the "Ten Commandments of Good Will," the NCCJ recognized: "Perhaps no page of history, called Christian, bears more blots and stains upon it than that which records the relations of Christians and Jews during almost two thousand years."[114] In her study of the NCCJ, Victoria Barnett also noted that it "rejected the proselytization of Jews and stressed the need to address anti-Judaism in interpretations of Christian texts."[115] Madeleva remained an active member of the NCCJ until her death in 1964. She consistently listed it among her professional activities in resumes and questionnaires. In 1958, she received a Brotherhood Award from the South Bend–Mishawaka Roundtable of the NCCJ "in grateful tribute to Sister Madeleva's dedicated work in the intellectual, spiritual, and cultural development of women of all faiths."[116] On October 13, 1961, Lewis Webster Jones (1899–1975), then president of the NCCJ, wrote to Madeleva to invite her to be a charter member of the newly formed National Honor Corps of the NCCJ.[117] She was already serving the NCCJ as a member of its board of trustees, so Jones also invited her to attend a reception with President John F. Kennedy (1917–1963) at the White House later that November. Madeleva traveled to Washington, DC, and attended the reception with Sister M. Mildred Dolores (1908–1991), then president of Dunbarton College of the Holy Cross. In a letter to Jones on October 9, 1963, to express her regret for not being able to attend the upcoming meeting of the board that November, Madeleva reminisced about her thirty-three years of service in the organization: "Since my first active participation in the National Conference of Christians and Jews dates back to 1930, I think that I may possibly be the oldest living member of the Conference. My seniority, at any rate, is a matter of great joy to me."[118]

Given the atrocities of the Holocaust as well as Madeleva's longstanding engagement with Jewish-Christian dialogue, it is lamentable that she did not revise her essay "Chaucer's Nuns" for republication in 1951 to address the anti-Semitism in the Prioress's tale. Meeting the many demands of her office as the president of Saint Mary's College for seventeen years probably kept her from staying up-to-date with the latest developments in scholarship on Chaucer's poetry. It is notable that, of the seven essays she collected in *A Lost Language*, only "Chaucer's Nuns" referenced secondary sources, and they all predate 1925, the year in which the essay was originally published. Madeleva intended the volume to attract readers "who would like to know our first and greatest narrative poet in his inimitable humanity without Middle English and the idiom of research."[119] She clearly missed the call made by other scholars after the Second World War to critique the anti-Semitism of Chaucer, the Prioress, and her tale. Would that she hadn't because her criticism would have carried significant moral weight as a Catholic sister.

Meeting the demands of her presidential office for so many years probably strengthened Madeleva's identification with the Prioress. By 1951, she could appreciate more fully how difficult it was for a nun in a position of leadership to balance the active and the contemplative lives, to "be in the world without being of it."[120] Madeleva's friend James A. Eldridge (1920–1978) captured this tension well in his tribute to mark the tenth anniversary of her death: "Her life was a paradox. In 1908 she sought the anonymity of the convent, but in 1957, when she celebrated her seventieth birthday, she was a nationally famous educator, poet, college president, lecturer and hostess."[121] Gail Mandell also observed in her 1997 biography of Madeleva: "Like Chaucer's prioress, for whose piety she argued vehemently while at Berkeley, Madeleva's ambiguities defy definitive interpretation. Behavior that some might consider worldly, she justified as part of her religious and professional mission."[122] Madeleva was a "a modern Madam Eglantine," as she told C. S. Lewis in 1959, and she had her critics, too.[123] She could not help but remain resolute in her support of the Prioress: to defend the sincerity of her religious vocation was to defend her own and those of her fellow sisters in active ministry. They were all the same to Madeleva and deserving of respect.

I am grateful to Eric Walerko, Archivist of Saint Mary's College Archives, and to Sr. Timothea Kingston, Archivist of the Congregation of the Sisters of the Holy Cross Archives, for their guidance in studying the materials in their care. I also appreciate the feedback I received on this essay from Jessica Coblentz, Susan Mancino, Molly Gower, and Eric Bugyis.

Notes

1. Madeleva, letter to Mother Vincentia, May 8, 1934, Congregation of the Sisters of the Holy Cross Archives. In a letter Madeleva wrote to Mother Vincentia the following month, she affirmed: "[C. S. Lewis] has been most courteous to us Sisters and is one of the most honest-minded teachers I have ever had"; Madeleva, letter to Mother Vincentia, June 9, 1934, Congregation Archives. Similarly, in a letter to W. H. Lewis (1895–1973) written five months after his brother's death, Madeleva declared C. S. Lewis "was among the very greatest teachers that I had or would have"; Madeleva, letter to Lewis, April 21, 1964, Saint Mary's College Archives.

2. Madeleva, letter to Lewis, April 22, 1959, College Archives.

3. Lewis, letter to Madeleva, April 27, 1959, College Archives.

4. Madeleva, letter to Sister M. Loreto, July 5, 1959, Congregation Archives. See, too, Gail Porter Mandell, *Madeleva: A Biography* (Albany: State University of New York Press, 1997), 238.

5. Geoffrey Chaucer, *Canterbury Tales*, in *The Riverside Chaucer*, ed. Larry D. Benson, 3rd ed. (Boston: Houghton-Mifflin, 1987), I.163–64.

6. Chaucer, *Canterbury Tales*, I.151, 158–59, 162.

7. Madeleva, *My First Seventy Years* (New York: Macmillan, 1959), 151.

8. Chaucer, *Canterbury Tales*, VII.503. Such criticism of Chaucer's Prioress is too extensive to cite in full here. For a recent study with a comprehensive bibliography, see Heather Blurton and Hannah Johnson, *The Critics and the Prioress: Antisemitism, Criticism, and Chaucer's Prioress's Tale* (Ann Arbor: University of Michigan Press, 2017).

9. John Livingston Lowes, "Simple and Coy: A Note on Fourteenth-Century Poetic Diction," *Anglia* 33 (1910): 440–51, 442.

10. On these developments, see Blurton and Johnson, *The Critics and the Prioress*, chap. 1.

11. Madeleva, *Chaucer's Nuns and Other Essays* (New York: D. Appleton and Company, 1925), 3–42; Madeleva, *A Lost Language and Other Essays on Chaucer* (New York: Sheed and Ward, 1951), 27–60.

12. Madeleva, *Chaucer's Nuns*, 17.

13. Madeleva, *Chaucer's Nuns*, 4.

14. Madeleva, *My First Seventy Years*, 21. See, too, The University of Wisconsin Catalogue 1905–1906 (Madison, 1906), 115.

15. Madeleva, *My First Seventy Years*, 21.

16. Madeleva, *My First Seventy Years*, 21–22.

17. Madeleva, *My First Seventy Years*, 21.

18. Madeleva, *My First Seventy Years*, 21.

19. Madeleva, *My First Seventy Years*, 22.

20. Madeleva, *My First Seventy Years*, 36.

21. Madeleva, *Chaucer's Nuns*, 20.

22. Madeleva, *Chaucer's Nuns*, 5.

23. Madeleva, *Chaucer's Nuns*, 20.

24. Transcript of Sister M. Madeleva (Wolff), Congregation Archives. See, too, Mandell, *Madeleva*, 62.

25. Madeleva, *My First Seventy Years*, 50.

26. Madeleva, *My First Seventy Years*, 51.

27. Madeleva, *My First Seventy Years*, 51.

28. Madeleva, *My First Seventy Years*, 51–52.

29. Madeleva, *My First Seventy Years*, 51. See, too, Lowes, letter to Madeleva, February 3, 1923; and Lowes, letter to Benjamin Lehman, October 4, 1924, College Archives.

30. Jewett, letter to Madeleva, June 17, 1924, Congregation Archives.

31. Jewett, letter to Madeleva, June 17, 1924.

32. Jewett, letter to Madeleva, June 17, 1924. Madeleva's response to Jewett, if she wrote one, was not archived.

33. Jewett, letter to Madeleva, July 18, 1924, Congregation Archives.

34. Jewett, letter to Madeleva, July 18, 1924.

35. Publication agreement between D. Appleton and Company and the Sisters of the Holy Cross, July 16, 1924, Congregation Archives.

36. Madeleva, letter to Mother Aquina, July 23, 1924, Congregation Archives.

37. Madeleva, *My First Seventy Years*, 45.

38. Madeleva, *My First Seventy Years*, 45.

39. Madeleva, letter to Mother Aquina, undated, Congregation Archives.

40. Madeleva, *Pearl: A Study in Spiritual Dryness* (New York: D. Appleton and Company, 1925).

41. Madeleva, "Scholarship for Catholic Women," *The Catholic Educational Review* 30 (1932): 21–32, 25.

42. Madeleva, "Scholarship for Catholic Women," 28–29.

43. Madeleva, letter to Mother Vincentia, Fall 1933, Congregation Archives.

44. Madeleva, letter to Mother Vincentia, November 5, 1933, Congregation Archives.

45. Madeleva, letter to Mother Vincentia, November 5, 1933.

46. Madeleva, letter to Lewis, May 1, 1951, College Archives.

47. Madeleva, "A Lost Language," 26. Madeleva first published this essay as "Chaucer's Lost Language," *Thought* 10 (1936): 555–65.

48. Lewis, letter to Madeleva, April 18, 1951, College Archives.

49. See, for example, Madeleva, letter to Charlot, July 28, 1955, Jean Charlot Collection, University of Hawai'i at Mānoa Library. See, too, Mandell, *Madeleva*, 235.

50. In his *Regiment of Princes*, Thomas Hoccleve (ca. 1369–1426) insisted of Chaucer: "Althogh his lyf be qweynt, the resemblance / Of

him hath in me so fressh lyflynesse, / That to putte other men in remembrance / Of his persone, I have heere his liknesse / Do make to this ende, in soothfastnesse— / That they than han of him lost thoght and mynde, / By this peynture may ageyn him fynde"; *Regiment of Princes*, ed. Charles R. Blyth, TEAMS Middle English Texts (Kalamazoo, MI: Medieval Institute Publications, 1999), 4992–98. A portrait of Chaucer accompanies this passage in the copy of Hoccleve's *Regiment* in London, British Library, Harley MS 4866, fol. 88r, which was created between 1411 and 1412. This is one of the earliest surviving portraits of Chaucer, and it features the poet holding rosary beads in his left hand and pointing to the word *liknesse* in the parallel text with his right hand. Madeleva was familiar with this portrait; she discussed it in her essay "A Lost Language": "The Hoccleve portrait by which the world best knows him a thoughtful, quiet man with snowy hair and beard and, like his Prioress, about his arm a pair of beads he bears. Critics say it is his rosary"; "A Lost Language," 16–17. She probably had this portrait in mind when she commissioned Charlot to create a fresco of Chaucer for Moreau Hall.

51. Madeleva, *Chaucer's Nuns*, 10.

52. Madeleva, *Chaucer's Nuns*, 10.

53. Madeleva, *Chaucer's Nuns*, 19.

54. Madeleva, *Chaucer's Nuns*, 12.

55. Thomas R. Lounsbury, *Studies in Chaucer: His Life and Writings*, 3 vols. (New York: Harper & Brothers, 1892), I.100.

56. Madeleva, *Chaucer's Nuns*, 35–36.

57. Madeleva, *Chaucer's Nuns*, 18.

58. Madeleva, *Chaucer's Nuns*, 18.

59. Madeleva, *Chaucer's Nuns*, 27–28.

60. Madeleva, *Chaucer's Nuns*, 23.

61. Madeleva, *Chaucer's Nuns*, 21.

62. Madeleva, *Chaucer's Nuns*, 21–22.

63. Lowes, "Simple and Coy," 441–42.

64. Madeleva, *Chaucer's Nuns*, 5.

65. Madeleva, "The Nun and Her Relation to Christ's Mystical Body," 13–14, Congregation Archives.

66. Madeleva, *Chaucer's Nuns*, 14.

67. Madeleva, *Chaucer's Nuns*, 15; Chaucer, *Canterbury Tales*, I.136.

68. Madeleva, *Chaucer's Nuns*, 17; Chaucer, *Canterbury Tales*, I.151.

69. Madeleva, *Chaucer's Nuns*, 33.

70. Madeleva, *Chaucer's Nuns*, 35.

71. Madeleva, *Chaucer's Nuns*, 35.

72. Madeleva, *Chaucer's Nuns*, 3, 17.

73. Madeleva, *Chaucer's Nuns*, 3.

74. Madeleva, *Chaucer's Nuns*, 14; R. K. Root, *The Poetry of Chaucer: A Guide to Its Study and Appreciation* (Boston: Houghton, Mifflin, and Company, 1906, repr. 1922), 190.

75. Madeleva, *Chaucer's Nuns*, 14.

76. Madeleva, *Chaucer's Nuns*, 5.

77. Madeleva, *Chaucer's Nuns*, 5.

78. Madeleva, *Chaucer's Nuns*, 28.

79. Madeleva, *Chaucer's Nuns*, 28. Madeleva was playing here with Lowes's claim that Chaucer's description "leaves the Prioress charmingly human, without a suggestion of the sensuous"; "Simple and Coy," 442.

80. Madeleva, *Chaucer's Nuns*, 7; Chaucer, *Canterbury Tales*, I.119. Madeleva cited Lowes's article "Simple and Coy."

81. Madeleva, *Chaucer's Nuns*, 8.

82. Madeleva, *Chaucer's Nuns*, 13–14.

83. Madeleva, *Chaucer's Nuns*, 15.

84. Madeleva, *Chaucer's Nuns*, 15–16; Chaucer, *Canterbury Tales*, I.146, 150, 147.

85. Madeleva, *Chaucer's Nuns*, 24–25.

86. Chaucer, *Canterbury Tales*, I.143, 144–45.

87. Madeleva, *Chaucer's Nuns*, 25.

88. Madeleva, *Chaucer's Nuns*, 19.

89. Madeleva, *Chaucer's Nuns*, 37–38.

90. Madeleva, *Chaucer's Nuns*, 35, 37.

91. Madeleva, *Chaucer's Nuns*, x–xi.

92. Herbert S. Gorman, "Writers Come to Judgment in Books of Criticism," *New York Times*, March 15, 1925.

93. Henry Ansgar Kelly, "A Neo-Revisionist Look at Chaucer's Nuns," *The Chaucer Review* 31 (1996): 115–32, 126; reprinted in Henry Ansgar Kelly, *Law and Religion in Chaucer's England* (Burlington: Ashgate, 2010), X.

94. Lowes, letter to Madeleva, June 1, 1925, College Archives.

95. Florence H. Ridley, *The Prioress and the Critics* (Berkeley: The University of California Press, 1965), 21.

96. Anthony Bale, "Reflections on Chaucer, Pedagogy, and the Profession of Medieval Studies," *New Chaucer Studies: Pedagogy and Profession* 1 (2020): 6–17, 8.

97. Anthony Bale, "Reflections on Chaucer," 6–17, 8.

98. Anthony Bale, "Reflections on Chaucer," 9.

99. Emmy Stark Zitter, "Anti-Semitism in Chaucer's *Prioress's Tale*," *The Chaucer Review* 25 (1991): 277–84, 282.

100. Elisabeth M. Orsten, "Madame Eglentyne in Her Day and in Ours: Anti-Semitism in *The Prioress's Tale* and a Modern Parallel," *Florilegium* 11 (1992): 82–100, 87.

101. Blurton and Johnson, *The Critics and the Prioress*, 19.

102. Blurton and Johnson, *The Critics and the Prioress*, 19.

103. Blurton and Johnson, *The Critics and the Prioress*, 19–20n16.

104. Lehman, letter to Mother Aquina, August 19, 1922, Congregation Archives.

105. Madeleva, *Chaucer's Nuns*, x–xi. See, too, Madeleva, letter to Mother Aquina, undated, Congregation Archives.

106. Mandell, *Madeleva*, 82–86.

107. Lehman, letter to Madeleva, March 30, 1924, College Archives.

108. Madeleva, letter to Lehman, April 3, (1925?), Lehman Papers, Bancroft Library, University of California, Berkeley.

109. Lehman, letter to Madeleva, April 16, 1951, College Archives.

110. Madeleva, letter to Lehman, April 23, 1964, College Archives.

111. Madeleva, letter to Lehman, April 23, 1964.

112. This quotation was taken from the NCCJ's 1928 bylaws; Victoria Barnett, "'Fault Lines': An Analysis of the National Conference of Christians and Jews, 1933–1948" (PhD diss., George Mason University, 2012), 42.

113. For the history of the NCCJ, see Victoria Barnett, "Fault Lines"; Barnett, "Ecumenical Protestant Responses to the Rise of Nazism, Fascism, and Antisemitism during the 1920s and 1930s," in *Religion, Ethnonationalism, and Antisemitism in the Era of the Two World Wars*, ed. Kevin P. Spicer and Rebecca Carter-Chand, 356–377 (Montreal: McGill-Queen's University Press, 2022), 360, 367.

114. Barnett, "Ecumenical Protestant Responses," 367. See, too, Barnett, "Fault Lines," 85.

115. Barnett, "Ecumenical Protestant Responses," 367.

116. The citation on the award was quoted by Jennifer Helman, "Saint Mary's Grande Dame," *The Old Courthouse News*, Winter 1977.

117. Jones, letter to Madeleva, October 13, 1961, College Archives.

118. Madeleva, letter to Jones, October 9, 1963, College Archives.

119. Madeleva, *A Lost Language*, i.

120. Madeleva, *Chaucer's Nuns*, 21–22.

121. James A. Eldridge, "A Heavenly Tramp," *Chillicothe Gazette*, July 27, 1974.

122. Mandell, *Madeleva*, 107.

123. Madeleva, letter to Lewis, April 22, 1959, College Archives. For example, Madeleva received significant pushback from alumnae, parents, current students, and even members of her own community when she decided to integrate Saint Mary's College and to admit the first Black student in 1941. See Madeleva, *My First Seventy Years*, 98–99.

7

THE *SUMMUM BONUM*

Sister Madeleva's Irish Sojourn, 1934

Thomas O'Grady

In the fall of 1933 and the winter and spring of 1934, the academic year before she assumed the presidency of Saint Mary's College, Sister Madeleva enjoyed a memorable period of postgraduate study at Oxford University in England. Working with legendary professors and littérateurs, she apparently moved comfortably within, between, and among the scholarly, literary, and social circles of that esteemed institution… and beyond.

As she documents in her memoir *My First Seventy Years*, her foothold in Oxford gave Sister Madeleva ready access to many sites of literary and ecclesiastical interest in England: Canterbury, Stratford, the Cotswolds, Sussex, York, Whitby, Haworth, Chester. From another foothold in Hyères on the French Riviera, she and Sister Verda Clare ventured even farther afield, visiting Genoa, Rome (where they had an audience with Pope Pius XI), and Naples; they even got as far as Alexandria and Cairo in Egypt and Jerusalem, Gethsemane, and Nazareth in the Holy Land. Additional travels took Sister Madeleva to Assisi, Siena, Florence, and Milan as well as to Freiburg in Germany and Paris and Chartres in France. She also made her way to Le Mans, the home base, in the middle of the nineteenth century, of Father Basil Moreau and the founding sisters of the CSC order. But as she attests outright in describing her departure from Oxford and England in July of 1934, the *summum bonum*[1]—the ultimate good—of her nine months abroad lay across the Irish Sea where she had arranged an afternoon visit with Nobel Laureate poet William Butler Yeats at his suburban Dublin home and also a ten-day visit with her "devoted friend,"[2] celebrated Irish man of letters and storyteller Seumas MacManus, in rural County Donegal in the northwest corner of Ireland.

Beginning in the 1890s, MacManus crisscrossed America repeatedly for more than three decades, entertaining and charming audiences by playing the part of a hearthside *shanachy*—a traditional Irish "teller of tales" and "singer of songs."[3] Apparently Sister Madeleva first met him in Utah in the 1920s while he was on one of his many speaking tours in the United States and she held positions first at the Academy of the Sacred Heart in Ogden, where she was a teacher and then principal, and then at College of Saint Mary's-of-the-Wasatch, where she was president, in Salt Lake City. (In *My First Seventy Years*, she mentions that MacManus "spent more than one fortnight" at Wasatch, "bringing us the authentic and all-but-lost epic art of the shanachie."[4]) He had reached out to her at Oxford, asking Catholic chaplain Father Ronald Knox to forward to her a letter addressed to "Sister Mary Madeleva of the Rocky Mountains"; the letter caught up with her in Hyères.[5] The three pages she devotes to the hospitality afforded her by MacManus is conspicuously filled with riches that reflect Sister Madeleva's powers of observation and her deep appreciation of Irish culture; that appreciation is evident as well in her description of her visit to a place of pilgrimage in County Donegal and also of her final two days in rainy Galway City that would eventually inspire a very memorable poem. Yet even the mere three sentences she gives to her time with Yeats reveals, with some scholarly unpacking, the richness of that experience as well.

"An Acre of Grass"

From the chapter in her memoir describing her Irish adventure, one can infer that her meeting with Yeats was facilitated by MacManus, though by the evidence of an exchange of letters between Sister Madeleva and University of Notre Dame president Father Charles O'Donnell, himself a poet of some repute, her visit was probably encouraged by O'Donnell, through whom Yeats had sent her an autographed copy of his iconic poem "The Lake Isle of Innisfree." Responding to O'Donnell,

Madeleva wrote in a letter dated January 15, 1933, that she was "tremulous with happiness":

> There have been so many hard, almost unbelievable things to face these past years that the advent of pure joy is almost terrifying...."The Lake Isle of Innisfree" will be only less precious to me than the manuscript copies of some of your own poems which I keep carefully.[6]

Her Irish sojourn thus commenced in Dublin on a Sunday in July "spent with the Yeatses at Rothfarnham [*sic*], with 'Willie,' his kindly wife, his robust daughter."[7] In 1918, shortly after his marriage to Georgie Hyde-Lees, Yeats had begun restoring a decaying sixteenth-century Anglo-Norman stone tower house in east County Galway that he had bought in 1917. Naming it Thoor Ballylee, he wrote lines dedicating it to his wife:

> **To be carved on a Stone at Thoor Ballylee**
>
> I, the poet William Yeats,
> With old mill boards and sea-green slates,
> And smithy work from the Gort forge,
> Restored this tower for my wife George;
> And may these characters remain
> When all is ruin once again.[8]

While the tower remained for Yeats a vital symbol of poetic aspiration—his volume titled *The Tower* (1928) includes some of his most enduring poems—he and his family lived there only sporadically, mostly in the summers: its dampness and the remoteness of its location proved untenable for the self-described "sixty-year-old smiling public man," and by 1929 the site began again to slip into disrepair.[9]

In 1932, Yeats signed a thirteen-year lease on Riversdale House, a comfortable home on an acre or so of land in the south Dublin suburb of Rathfarnham, a residence well suited for his personal and domestic circumstances at the time. As he explained in a letter to a friend, this lease "will see me out of life": "At any rate the home will be there while the children are being educated and making friends."[10] In a poem titled "An Acre of Grass," written two years after Sister Madeleva's visit and three years before his death in France in 1939, he describes his waning time spent at Riversdale:

> Picture and book remain,
> An acre of green grass
> For air and exercise,
> Now strength of body goes;
> Midnight, an old house
> Where nothing stirs but a mouse.[11]

In that same letter to his friend in 1932, Yeats expressed particular pleasure with how the grounds of the house gave him "a big old fruit garden all to myself" and with how "the study opens into it and it is shut off from the flower garden and the croquet and tennis lawns and from the bowling-green."[12]

From Sister Madeleva's very brief account in *My First Seventy Years*, Yeats evidently shared those special spaces with her after picking her up by car[13] at the convent in Dublin where she was staying: "Tea and cakes, a walk in the garden prefaced our real visit in his library where the great-hearted, white-haired Irish poet, without his greater birthright of faith, talked with me."[14] Thus did the soon-to-be President of Saint Mary's College, herself a widely published poet, step foot into the intimate world of the preeminent poet of her time; and thus does she figure, implicitly, in a second poem of Yeats's—"What Then?"—set explicitly at Riversdale:

> All his happier dreams came true—
> A small old house, wife, daughter, son,
> Grounds where plum and cabbage grew,
> Poets and Wits about him drew.[15]

Did Sister Madeleva interact much with "kindly" Mrs. Yeats and daughter Anne (who would go on to become a designer of theater sets and costumes and, though lesser than her grandfather and her uncle before her—John B. Yeats and Jack B. Yeats—a painter of some renown)? That is difficult to determine, but her describing fifteen-year-old Anne as "robust" seems to reflect her awareness that she had been a sickly child. (From her account in *My First Seventy Years*, Sister Madeleva appears not to have met son Michael at all.)

Probably, Yeats's wife and daughter withdrew when the two poets sat down together in that study/library to discuss literary matters. If their conversation touched on Yeats's two reading tour stops at the University of Notre Dame, in 1904 and 1933, the first including classroom visits at Saint Mary's, Sister Madeleva makes no such mention. (Interestingly, notwithstanding her issue with his deficient "birthright of faith"—which in her private journal led her to describe him as "an Irishman manque [*sic* manqué]: a man without a spiritual home"[16]—the Church of Ireland–raised Yeats, who became invested deeply in Theosophy and other esoteric forms of mysticism, felt very comfortable at Notre Dame, writing to one friend in the wake of his 1904 visit: "The Fathers were a delight, big merry Irish priests who told me fairy stories & listened to mine & drank punch with me on Friday night."[17]) Nor does she mention whether Yeats brought up her poem "Penelope," which Father O'Donnell had apparently shared with him during his 1933 visit to campus. (In a letter to Sister Madeleva dated January 12, 1933, Father O'Donnell recounts that after Yeats read the poem carefully twice, he remarked that it had what "most recent American poetry lacked, namely, 'passion.'"[18]) Drawing on Madeleva's journal, biographer Gail Mandell adds details omitted from the account of her visit in *My First Seventy Years*: Yeats "talked of Lady Gregory [his collaborator in launching the Irish Literary Revival in the 1890s], gave his opinion of A. E. [Irish poet and mystic George Russell], whose verse he was then reading, and spoke of Gandhi."[19] Mostly, though, their interaction seems to have been centered on Yeats reading to her from his own poems—perhaps from his most recent volume, *The Winding Stair and Other Poems* (1933), perhaps a poem like "In Memory of Eva Gore-Booth and Con Markiewicz":

> The light of evening, Lissadell,
> Great windows open to the south,
> Two girls in silk kimonos, both
> Beautiful, one a gazelle.[20]

Or perhaps "Coole Park and Ballylee, 1931":

> Under my window-ledge the waters race,
> Otters below and moor-hens on the top,
> Run for a mile undimmed in Heaven's face
> Then darkening through 'dark' Raftery's 'cellar' drop,

Run underground, rise in a rocky place
In Coole demesne, and there to finish up
Spread to a lake and drop into a hole.
What's water but the generated soul?[21]

Intriguingly, Yeats also recited for Sister Madeleva poems drawn "from those of that kindred Gaelic muse, Ella Young."[22] Now a mostly overlooked figure even in the realm of Irish letters, Young was an active and charismatic presence in both political and literary circles in Dublin in the first two decades of the twentieth century; a militant nationalist and a Theosophist, a children's storyteller and a poet, she made her way to the United States in the 1920s and from 1925 to 1932 held the position of lecturer in Irish Myth and Lore at the University of California, Berkeley. Much of her writing drew on the cultural motifs of the Irish Literary Revival of the late nineteenth and early twentieth centuries, a literary movement that Yeats himself branded "the Celtic Twilight." An educated guess would have Yeats reading to Sister Madeleva from Young's 1920 volume, *The Rose of Heaven*: not only does its title resonate with Yeats's own early volume *The Rose* (1893)—which includes, among other rose-centered poems, one titled "The Rose of the World"—but also the book was illustrated by Young's close friend Maud Gonne, the decades-long object of Yeats's obsessive affection and desire. "Was there another Troy for her to burn?" Yeats asked in a poem, casting her in the epical role of Helen.[23] In fact, scholars tend to agree that the image of the rose at the center of Yeats's imagination symbolized not only spiritual and eternal beauty, and not only an idealized projection of Ireland, but also Maud Gonne herself. Cut out of early Yeatsian cloth, the opening stanzas of the title poem of Young's volume typify the misty crepuscular affect of many of her poems:

The Rose of Heaven

I had for heritage a sword
And a rich cloak of cramoisie;
I gave them both away to you
With the good hound that followed me.

You took the cloak between your hands
And broidered on the silken hem

Strange beasts and flowers and golden stars:
It was great joy to look at them.

You graved a rune upon the sword;
You kissed the hound between the eyes;
You said, "Take back your gifts again,
Keep tryst with me in Paradise."[24]

Whether or not she fully realized it in the moment, in her few hours in the heady company of Yeats, Sister Madeleva began her very rich fortnight of travels in Ireland by breathing rarefied air indeed.

St. Patrick's Purgatory and Beyond

Following her afternoon in Rathfarnham, Sister Madeleva left Dublin and made her way northerly, no doubt by train, first to Dundalk in County Louth, then on to Enniskillen in County Fermanagh, and finally to the village of Pettigo, which straddles the border of County Donegal. From there either a hired automobile or, possibly, a horse-drawn trap shuttled her to the shore of Lough Derg in the southeast corner of Donegal from which she was ferried by "two stout oarsmen" to Station Island, the location of St. Patrick's Purgatory, the site of an arduous religious pilgrimage dating at least to the twelfth century.[25] (Legend has it that Christ revealed a cave on the island—the entrance to purgatory—to St. Patrick in the fifth century.) Perhaps she was inspired to visit by a poem written by her friend Father O'Donnell, who had died in June:

Lough Derg, Lough Derg, how chant the waves along
  Thy solemn shores, and in the flowing air
Drift murmurs of an unforgotten song
  And of remembered prayer.[26]

Ordinarily, the site was open only to those committed to the full three-day pilgrimage, which included fasting, minimal sleeping, and incessant praying. In an account of the pilgrimage published ten years after Sister Madeleva's visit, Irish writer Alice Curtayne sets the timeless scene:

> [The pilgrim] will embark on a mountain-locked lake that is just as secluded to-day as when Saint Patrick was attracted to its solitude. The physical features of the landscape have remained practically unaltered through the centuries. Its lonely aspect is the same as in the fifth century; the eye may still rest on all that Patrick saw: in the west, Croagh-Breac (the Speckled Stack); in the east, Kinnagoe; behind the one the same solemn sunsets, above the other appear the same fresh dawns.[27]

Curtayne also details the grueling experience of the pilgrimage itself:

> It is a three-day pilgrimage and a minimum period of residence on the island is prescribed: from three o'clock on the afternoon of the first day to half-past eleven on the morning of the third day. The pilgrim is obliged to fast on each of the three days. When he arrives on the island, his first duty is to remove his shoes. He must go barefoot until he is about to leave the island again. Thus he finds himself at once in the grip of a rigid discipline, extremely uncomfortable. He will probably not like it. He is not meant to like it.[28]

Presumably Sister Madeleva had special access through the intercession of Seumas MacManus and, after being welcomed by the Canon, enjoyed a mostly touristic visit to the site, joining the pilgrims in prayer and also "stopping at the beds of Saint Patrick and Saint Brigid and the great Basilica, the central places of devotion."[29] Returning to the mainland, she was met by MacManus, who drove her by car fifteen miles deeper into Donegal, to the village of Mountcharles, where she was welcomed by his cousin, a Mrs. Tierney, with whom she lodged.

Interestingly, her account of her time spent in Mountcharles and vicinity—which includes encounters with several local "characters"—is filtered through her reading of *The Way It Was With Them* (1928), a novel by another Donegal writer, Peadar O'Donnell, probably recommended to her either by MacManus or else by Father O'Donnell, whose parents were natives of Donegal. Originally titled *Islanders*, the narrative is set on the tiny island of Inniscara located off the coast of a somewhat larger island, Arranmore, which sits off the coast of Donegal around forty miles from Mountcharles. Centered on Mary Doogan, a widowed mother of nine children, and her eldest son, twenty-two-year-old Charles, the novel dramatizes the nobility of spirit prevailing within a family and a community despite the unrelenting poverty of purse determined by subsistence living off dauntingly stony soil and a fickle sea. Replete with romantic intrigues, heartache and heartbreak, acts of heroism and feats of endurance—and even a subplot thread involving a nationalist rebel on the run—the narrative is infused with local color that clearly enchanted Sister Madeleva and by life-affirming themes carried by engaging twists and turns of plot. As Northern Irish essayist Robert Lynd observes in his introduction to the American edition of the novel, "we positively rejoice in the heroism of human beings who can force a living from the rocks and live in charity with one another among the uncharitable stones," adding, "Mr. O'Donnell has mingled laughter and tears, the poetry and the prose of life."[30]

For Sister Madeleva both the poetry and the prose of Irish life seem to have unfolded before her in equal measures during her time in Donegal. Every day began with Mass. (The first day also included a visit to the grave of MacManus's wife, poet Ethna Carberry, who died young in 1902.) But every day was also "rich with the lived life of an enchanting and partly enchanted people."[31] Visiting the whitewashed thatch-roofed cottages of fishermen and their families, she absorbed many details: "The kitchen dresser with its literal sideboard of brown-figured or bright-colored cups, saucers, plates, the outshot bed by the fireplace, the wag-by-the-wall long pendulumed clock, the Saint Brigid's crosses tucked up among the rafters, the half-lofts—all became part of my home economics in Donegal."[32] She also appreciated the landscape she passed through with MacManus as her chauffeur and guide: "We came past rivers, atumble with waterfalls, to Lock Esk [*sic* Lough Eske or Eask], lying north and south among mountains with coves, wooded shores."[33]

Along the way she seems to have been entertained almost non-stop not only by her host half-chanting "tales from Fioin" [*sic* Fionn mac Cumhaill], a hero of the Fenian cycle of tales whose texts date to the fourteenth and fifteenth centuries, but also by local talent of various sorts. Admiring how MacManus responded to a farmer's story told in Gaelic with verses from James Clarence Mangan's poem "Woman of Three Cows," she muses: "Here I was among the singers and bards, children of the epic poets of the past, in a company and an art rare and all but lost in our Western world."[34] She was likewise touched by children she encountered in a village: "They greeted us half shyly. Upon our eager request, they buoyantly found themselves in reels and jigs, hands and arms motionless, free knees, ankles and toes, heads splendidly erect. All this they matched with Gaelic songs and their moving minor refrains like a cry."[35]

But she seems to have been most impressed by ninety-two-year old James McCahill who, greeting her from his rocking chair, his fingers entwined in his fifteen-decade rosary, proceeded to regale her with songs—"The Green Broom" (an English folksong also popular in Ireland) and a long ballad celebrating Napoleon Bonaparte (thought of, in the Irish folk imagination, as a possible liberator of Ireland from British rule). He also shared with her the names of his future pallbearers as well as the names of men forbidden from attending his wake because of political differences. "Never have I met a gayer spirit," Sister Madeleva declares.[36] And thus, notwithstanding her remark in her journals that she found the Irish people "dirty" and "disorderly," though also "happy,"[37] she would conclude with great warmth the chapter in *My First Seventy Years* that centers on her Irish experience: "I had known and lived with and shared deeply, the world, the culture, the spontaneous hospitality, the indigenous charm of a people that I love."[38]

Sister Madeleva's Hoosier Winter

And yet her Irish experience was not quite finished. Her original plan had her leaving Ireland from Cobh in County Cork on the ship *Scythia* of the Cunard–White Star Line. Instead, she took the train from Bundoran in Donegal to Galway City (thanks to MacManus, "the only first-class railway passage I had had in Europe"[39]) and intercepted the ship there on its final stop before Boston en route to New York. (She would be named the third president of Saint Mary's College on August 15th of 1934, just a couple of days after docking in Boston and taking the train to South Bend.) She thus spent her final forty-eight hours in Ireland in rainy Galway where the River Corrib flows into the body of water Bing Crosby would make immortal in 1947 with his recording of a moving composition penned by Arthur Colahan:

> If you ever go across the sea to Ireland,
> Then maybe at the closing of your day,
> You will sit and watch the moon rise over Claddagh,
> And see the sun go down on Galway Bay.[40]

In its own way, Sister Madeleva's lasting memory is just as specific: "All day long hundreds of white swans flew, crying from the river to the bay, from the bay to the river. I had never known that there were so many swans in the world."[41]

As she goes on to explain, she carried that memory intact to her new appointment at Saint Mary's. Obviously, she had spent winters in South Bend previously, during her undergraduate days at Saint Mary's and then again while studying for her M.A. at Notre Dame. But in 1935 her poet's mind and spirit were on full alert: "Winter that year brought us a strange, restless snowstorm with winds blowing and crying across the campus. For me the swans of Galway had returned. I wrote this much in a brief lyric, 'Snowstorm.'"[42] For its inclusion in a slim volume titled *Four Girls and Other Poems*, published in 1941, she would spell out the title in two words. Before that, as she happily reports in her memoir, the poem achieved a certain measure of distinction in 1939: "The World's Fair in New York City gave it first place among poems from Indiana. By birth, a loyal Wisconsin Badger, by transplanting a Utah Beehiver, I was now qualified as an Indiana Hoosier poet."[43]

Eminent American poet Robert Frost once remarked: "There are many things I have found myself saying about poetry, but the chiefest of these is that it is metaphor, saying one thing and meaning another, saying one thing in terms of another, the pleasure of ulteriority."[44] In seeing the swans of Galway in the blowing snow of northern Indiana, Sister Madeleva's poem is indeed a pleasing illustration of that principle as well as an enduring memory of her rich sojourn in Ireland:

Snow Storm

The air is white and winds are crying.
I think of swans in Galway flying.

Winds are wings; snow is a rover;
Swans of Galway are flying over.

Winds are birds; snow is a feather;
Wild white swans are wind and weather.

Wings drift downward; snow is falling;
Swans are wild winds crying, calling.

Winds are white with snow but alway
Mine are white with swans from Galway.[45]

Notes

1. Sister M. Madeleva, CSC, *My First Seventy Years* (New York: Macmillan, 1959), 87.

2. Madeleva, *My First Seventy Years*, 88.

3. Seamus MacManus, *Through the Turf Smoke: The Love, Lore and Laughter of Old Ireland* (New York: Doubleday & McClure, 1899), x.

4. Madeleva, *My First Seventy Years*, 57.

5. Madeleva, *My First Seventy Years*, 88.

6. Quoted in Gail Porter Mandell, *Madeleva: A Biography* (Albany: State University of New York Press, 1997), 111.

7. Madeleva, *My First Seventy Years*, 88.

8. W. B. Yeats, "To be carved on a Stone at Thoor Ballylee," in *The Collected Poems of W. B. Yeats, A New Edition*, ed. Richard J. Finneran (New York: Collier Books, 1989), 190.

9. W. B. Yeats, "Among School Children," in *The Collected Poems of W. B. Yeats*, 216.

10. W. B. Yeats, "Letter to Olivia Shakespear, 8 July 1932," in *The Letters of W. B. Yeats*, ed. Allan Wade (London: Rupert Hart-Davis, 1954), 799.

11. W. B. Yeats, "An Acre of Grass," in *The Collected Poems of W. B. Yeats*, 301.

12. Yeats, "Letter to Olivia Shakespear," 799.

13. See Mandell, *Madeleva*, 141.

14. Madeleva, *My First Seventy Years*, 88.

15. W. B. Yeats, "What Then?" in *The Collected Poems of W. B. Yeats*, 302.

16. Quoted in Mandell, *Madeleva*, 141.

17. W. B. Yeats, "Letter to John Quinn, 18 January 1904," in *The Collected Letters of W. B. Yeats*, vol. 3, ed. John Kelly and Ronald Schuchard (Oxford: Clarendon Press, 1994), 522.

18. Quoted in Mandell, *Madeleva*, 111.

19. Mandell, *Madeleva*, 141.

20. W. B. Yeats, "In Memory of Eva Gore-Booth and Con Markiewicz," in *The Collected Poems of W. B. Yeats*, 233.

21. W. B. Yeats, "Coole Park and Ballylee, 1931," in *The Collected Poems of W. B. Yeats*, 243–44.

22. Madeleva, *My First Seventy Years*, 89.

23. "No Second Troy," in *The Collected Poems of W. B. Yeats*, 91.

24. Ella Young, "The Rose of Heaven," in *At the Gates of Dawn: A Collection of Writings by Ella Young*, ed. John Matthews and Denise Sallee (Cheltenham: Skylight Press, 2011), 73.

25. Madeleva, *My First Seventy Years*, 89.

26. Charles L. O'Donnell, "A Shrine of Donegal," in *The Collected Poems of Charles L. O'Donnell* (Notre Dame, IN: University of Notre Dame Press, 1942), 27.

27. Alice Curtayne, *Lough Derg: St. Patrick's Purgatory* (Dublin: Burns Oates & Washbourne, 1944), 167.

28. Curtayne, *Lough Derg*, 167.

29. Madeleva, *My First Seventy Years*, 89.

30. Robert Lynd, "Introduction," in Peadar O'Donnell, *The Way It Was with Them* (New York: G. P. Putnam's Sons, 1928), xi–xii.

31. Madeleva, *My First Seventy Years*, 90.

32. Madeleva, *My First Seventy Years*, 90.

33. Madeleva, *My First Seventy Years*, 90.

34. Madeleva, *My First Seventy Years*, 90.

35. Madeleva, *My First Seventy Years*, 90.

36. Madeleva, *My First Seventy Years*, 91.

37. Quoted in Mandell, *Madeleva*, 141.

38. Madeleva, *My First Seventy Years*, 92.

39. Madeleva, *My First Seventy Years*, 91.

40. Arthur Colahan, "Galway Bay" (New York: Leeds Music Corporation, 1947), 1–2.

41. Madeleva, *My First Seventy Years*, 93.

42. Madeleva, *My First Seventy Years*, 93.

43. Madeleva, *My First Seventy Years*, 93.

44. Robert Frost, "The Constant Symbol," in *Robert Frost on Writing*, ed. Elaine Barry (New Brunswick, NJ: Rutgers University Press, 1973), 129.

45. Sister M. Madeleva, "Snow Storm," in *Four Girls and Other Poems* (Paterson, NJ: St. Anthony Guild Press, 1941), 3.

8

Madeleva's "Book of My Soul"

Eva Hooker, CSC

I
the song
I walk here.

"Modoc Song"[1]

1958, I am a first-year student at Saint Mary's. Sunday afternoon. Word from our big sisters: Listen up. She is a special person.

What I remember from her talk:

the call to the intellectual life

the call to contemplation

the call to poetry (necessary as water).

Madeleva may have said other things to us (such as welcome); all the rest is blur. She quoted Antonin Sertillanges's book *The Intellectual Life*.[2] I had never heard of the intellectual life. She said with a bit of a flourish and a light stomping of her foot: "Begin by creating within you a zone of silence, a habit of recollection, a will to renunciation and detachment which puts you entirely at the disposal of the work." This was probably my first big thought in my new collegial life.

I was taken by surprise. Then she said, "Every intellectual work begins by a moment of ecstasy; only in the second place does your talent…come into play." Big thought #2 had arrived. I knew about silence, recollection, and detachment. Or at least the words were familiar. I knew (more or less) how to "do" them. (They had something to do with Lent.) It wasn't at all clear to me how I was going to "get" any moments of ecstasy. Whatever ecstasy was, Madeleva made me want it. She had hooked me, and she had done it in a most surprising way. As I look back, I think making intellectual surprise was one of Madeleva's primary gifts. Sertillanges was not written for college students. Yet she dared to shift its argumentative ground and charge us with making that ground our own.

Note our dilemma: Here we were, a bunch of smart women, being told intellectual work begins with ecstasy. My recollection is that we were full of doubt. We had studied hard. No one had mentioned contemplation. No one had advised us to prepare for ecstasy *before* we could get around to the task of learning.

Madeleva played with our doubt. That was another of her strategies. She was, I think, fearlessly bold in the juxtaposition of ideas. (I didn't know this then, but I know this now: Much of what she said about strategies for learning came straight out of her study of the mystics.) To arrive at ecstasy, she suggested (although it sounded more like an order): first, consideration (sitting with the stars) and second, contemplation (just plain sitting with—). How were we to do that? *Sit in silence. Learn to look. Learn to listen. Be on the watch. Love solitude. Pay attention. Remember*. She used a lot of imperatives. Short, plain sentences. And a ton of charm. Charm and a well-worded series of imperatives: delivered oh so softly.

Wryly, she asked, "Who wants to be a seer, a singer? Who wants to be a poet?"[3] I sat in my good dress thinking me! me! me! I spent a lot of time trying to figure out how you can have all that mystery happen to you. *How* could you "get to" ecstasy? Was "get" even the right word?

And so to *now*. I think of this essay as a *shadow draft*. My task is to make as clear as I can: Madeleva, a woman called to leadership, a woman called to be a poet, a woman called to Presence. My evidence is her poetry. Within her small lyric spaces, Madeleva speaks most clearly:

~~~~~~~~~~~~~~~~~

I
the song
I walk here.

~~~~~~~~~~~~~~~~~

For days in late spring, I read and reread Madeleva's poetry. I tried to read as if I were a stranger, as if for the first time, I encountered her craft, her art. Our archives hold boxes and boxes of her letters, speeches, and essays. First drafts in her handwriting, barely legible now: stacks and stacks of notebooks. I scoured boxes for her presence. I felt like a soul thief.

Oddly, despite all her very public work, she felt absent. Even hidden. I was searching for the voice of Madeleva's poet-self. The fragile carbons seemed to hold a simultaneous veiling and unveiling. The paper on which her drafts were typed felt like it could disappear in my hands. It was fragile. So was the self I found there. I was stunned by that discovery. I felt constrained by what felt hidden and vulnerable. In a way, I also felt constrained by the history of the poet. Her public persona as president. Her public persona as religious woman. The fragility of the paper, the graying pages of published books, the formality of her letters: all of it seemed a mirror of vulnerability. I was startled. Here was someone strangely new. I have to admit that SHE, this new SHE made me nervous! Whatever was I to do with her?

In her autobiography, Madeleva describes her "hungry reading of poetry for beauty's sake, [her] constant, restive desire amounting to an imperative need to write, with no time, no leisure, no freedom from the pressure of persons and things."[4] In poignant detail, she describes the push and pull of work as she set about the creation of a college in Utah. There, she found work and more work, but she also found the mountains and their violent beauty:

> We watched wonder in the making: rivers of sand...canyon contours changed entirely as cloudbursts hurled mountainsides of shattered rock....We followed the silver path of the sun in its setting behind the mountains beyond Great Salt Lake. After its rose-colored afterglow, two firmaments awoke in the darkness: the stars above us and the twinkling lights of Salt Lake City.[5]

After, there was also this: "the moon a silver line, a quickly growing surface, a completed sphere. While watching this phenomenon of magnitude and splendor we caught something of our own dizzy daily journeying around and around."[6] In the desert and the mountains, she created a college. She says quietly at the end of this sun /moon paragraph, the Wasatch was school, home, convent: "It was my self."[7] I was stopped by that short sentence. Here, I found a shadow of her: "the moon a silver line" and the mountain. That silver line, and the Wasatch mountain, the college, as if one, were her self. Such a brief sentence slipped in after a long string of descriptors of natural beauty: "It was my self." The Wasatch, all of it, mountain and college! That simple sentence is the first shadow sentence of this essay.

Think of the way shadows work: They refract an image; they outline; they change as light changes; shadows change as the dark changes. They pick up the emotional resonance with which we receive them. I will explore three poems in which I find Madeleva shadow drafting. She uses her craft to define the essence of her self, her soul. On the slant, oblique, in a play of verbal light. And verbal shadow.

Tiya Miles, a scholar working on slave narratives, gave me a helpful methodology:

> When I hit a wall, I try to find ways around it, sometimes by moving backward or forward in time....When I encounter a gap, I try to understand the absence as information that can tell me about the circumstances of the production of the document....I imagine the enslaved person or family within the gap and try to fill in the space around them using other evidence until I can discern the shadow's shape.[8]

I had found a method! By shadow drafting, looking in the gaps within the poems, I hoped I could see more deeply into Madeleva's poetic art and self. The college was her self. (Let's remember that.) But so are the poems.

My gamble here is the hope that I might find or even imagine Madeleva within the gap(s) that her poems contain and/or shape. The gaps within her poems form the shadow, shape the shadow. Gap-work is the work of poetry. Gap-work reveals more clearly the poetic persona Madeleva so carefully made and perhaps also its relationship to her public persona as scholar and as president of Saint Mary's College. I can imagine her being really annoyed about such gap-work. So be it!

Thinking about poems as containers of gaps or silences may seem strange. It is a way of reading that makes it easier to find the speaker's silences and then to interpret them. Madeleva's silences change, move within, and shape the texture of our reading. My first example is a poem Madeleva clearly loved, "Design for a Stream-Lined Sunrise." We poets do have favorites in our own work even though we don't admit it. She chose to read this poem in several formal settings:

> If you must draw mere beauty,
> Subtend one third of the whole arc of heaven
> With a gray chord of cloud
> Stretched from the quick southeast to the still dubious west.
> Edge all the chord with white, bright mutable silver.
>
> Draw it on cloudlessness at daybreak,
> If you would draw mere beauty.
> But you cannot do this
> Because the artless air achieved this brief design for sunrise
> Once and forever,
> Today at dawn,
> And then this long line, cutting with sheer simplicity of silver
> The breathless, deep-blue arc of the south,
> Because, because of my beholding,
> Beyond potential beauty, beautiful.[9]

I have to confess I had read and passed over this poem many times. I don't quite know why. It was certainly beautiful. This time I got stopped in the poem. Perhaps because of its moon and sun imagery. I was also stopped by the word *subtend*. Who uses a word like that? To be honest, I did not know what it meant. As a verb, one meaning is: "to form at a particular point when straight lines that form its extremities are joined at that point."[10] Having looked the word up, I was not much wiser. What is clear is that lines are bent and joined. Madeleva is mildly ironic about the artist (or a mathematician?) who subtends. The tone of the stanza is different because of that word. Second question: who "subtends" in this stanza? Poet? Painter? Mathematician? Reader?

For the sake of argument, let's merge the who: poet, painter, mathematician. Madeleva isn't done. She adds the word *chord*. So, musician. The speaker could be all four: poet, artist, mathematician, musician.

All of this for the making of "mere beauty"! Look at that long line that describes the "gray chord": "Stretched from the quick southeast to the still dubious west." What kind of description is that? As reader, I first thought I could see something, but not quite: the west is "still dubious." An odd word, *dubious*. Thought moving through color, stopped. Made "dubious."

Then, Madeleva sneaks up on you. After all that work of imagining in full color and geometry, she says, "You can't do this"! Why? Because "artless air" has already "achieved this brief design." Another long line ("because the artless air"), then, two short lines, almost like teasers. Or those road signs you see in New England that say "Thickly Settled!" Two lines follow that convey that thickness and make the poem a painting: "cutting with sheer simplicity of silver / The breathless, deep-blue arc of the south." There's that silver color again, the moon over the Wasatch. And there is also that mysterious bending, the subtending action.

In those two lines, Madeleva paints with alliteration and color: ("simplicity of silver"; the "breathless deep-blue arc"). Here, I find the shadow: "because of my beholding," Madeleva makes shadow and beauty. Because of *her* beholding. Note all the lines that have to do with her /our making: "If YOU must," "If YOU would," "But YOU cannot...." However, let's recall again what happened earlier. The speaker makes beauty because of her beholding. Because she, too, makes that long line within the poem AND she, too, (a huge claim here), makes beauty. Like Keats, she will not be restrained. You can't do this, she implies, but I can! Poet triumphant.

I have to be very clear here. Madeleva was always a public champion of beauty. However, I see something more in this poem. Madeleva tells us clearly you "cannot do this." You cannot draw mere beauty. You cannot duplicate the "lines" of nature. However, and put "HOWEVER" in caps, "because of MY beholding" (caps mine), the "deep-blue arc of the south" becomes beautiful! She did that! Her shadow-self speaks: I, too, am beauty-maker. She, as her poem's title claims, has made a "breathless" design. Design exists because of her. (!!!) The gift of making design does not just belong to nature. It is also hers. She emphatically claims it. Perhaps her making is a version of Meister Eckhart's "The eye with which I see God is the eye with which God sees me."[11]

The pattern of the shadow: "If you must draw"; "If you would draw"; "But you cannot do this." A long line follows: "cutting with sheer sympathy of silver." The motion she constructs moves very quietly from

"If you must" to "If you would" to "But you cannot" to "AND THEN this long line" (caps mine). The pattern more than suggests the poetic power of her beholding. What she beholds she can make. She shadows that claim. Why? Its "sympathy" is daring. She loves making that line. That joy in poetic making is a cause for trouble. What kind? Such sympathetic daring can be the first step toward arrogance. A fault only avoided by "beholding." In "beholding" something, the seer honors it with a kind of presence. When you "behold," you pay deep attention. "Behold" also signals that the object of sight is significant. We don't say "Behold the street sign." Madeleva suggests very quietly her and our "deep attention," in this case, to nature itself. Attention makes the capacity for beauty. She suggests a poetic ecology. An ecology she makes. "Because," she says, "of MY beholding," that line in the sun gets made by her poetic self!

Gustav Sobin gives us another version of this poetic ecology:

The   poem happens
before us,   and we send it   across, in-
nocent and still,   hesitant,   instead of   us.[12]

Sobin's "instead" is significant. If we apply Sobin's statement to Madeleva's poem, her poem happens as a substitute, hesitant and bold, for herself. We have then a kind of circle in her poem that comes round and is fully present: to "subtend" is to make. In this case, with "sheer sympathy." As readers, we can see through the "sheer." And there, right there, Madeleva's poetic self is visible! Because of her beholding, shadow is no more.

~~~~~~~~~~~~~~~~~

I
the song
I walk here.

~~~~~~~~~~~~~~~~~

In "Jail Bird," Madeleva makes another very startling assertion:

I am a prisoner in a cell of trees;
Great walls of green
Close in about me, the attendant breeze
Fetches me fare
Of simple and sufficing air.
My pallet is the straight turf, hard and clean.

My leafy window bars
By day let in three slender beams of sun, by night three thousand
    stars.

It was the face
Of beauty brought me captive to this place
Where now I lie in indolent disgrace!
For who am I
To be in this wise made
Thrall to a sweet-faced glade,
I who am kin to mountain-top and cloud?
Why not deal cunningly, devise some tool
To freedom and escape from this adventureless school?
Why not break prison bonds and fly
Up, up to where
The high hills and the high heavens lie bare
With no tree nigh?
Beauty, outrivalled, may behold me there.
Aloof, austere, most inaccessible, most proud
To die,
A convict hooded in cerulean shroud
On mountain gallows by the hangman sky.

Now is my plot well laid!
Presently I shall pick these locks of shade,
Shall drug the gauntlet of belaying flowers,
And fugitive, shall run
Out to my mountain freedom and keen air,
Into the arms of the sun![13]

"Jail Bird" is one of Madeleva's clearest and most daring "shadow poems." She asserts, "I am a prisoner in a cell of trees." And "kin to mountain-top." She sleeps on a pallet of "turf, hard and clean." How did she get to this mean place? Here is her answer: "It was the face / Of beauty brought me captive to this place / Where now I lie in indolent disgrace." She asks bluntly, "For who am I / To be in this wise made / Thrall…?" In a bold almost-shout, she asks, "Why not break prison bonds and fly / Up, up to where / The high hills and the high heavens lie bare / With no tree nigh?" Yes. And yes. And yes! Exactly. Why not?

Because, then she can be "fugitive!" And run. To where? To her "mountain freedom" into "the arms of the sun!" The mountains, most likely her beloved Wasatch, are her refuge from the "cell of trees." The shadow here: the untold story. HOW did beauty make her captive to a place of "indolent disgrace"? Who or what made her "thrall"? Did she "deal cunningly" to escape her prison? In what way are mountains her place of freedom?

Three questions in the third stanza give us an opening into the shadow places, her deep questions in the poem:

> "For who am I / To be in this wise made / Thrall"
> "Why not deal cunningly, devise some tool / To freedom and escape"
> "Why not break prison bonds and fly / up, up…?"

Madeleva answers her own questions in truly haunting fashion: "Beauty, outrivalled, may behold me there, / Aloof, austere, most inaccessible, most proud / To die, / A convict hooded in cerulean shroud / On mountain gallows by the hangman sky." A convict on mountain gallows, she calls on beauty to be witness to this boldly imagined death. She escapes as "fugitive" running "Out to my mountain freedom and keen air." The shadows here are brave and, in their way, luminous acts of will. Within the poem's concluding lines, Madeleva constructs a plot for freedom. As speaker of the poem, she has an extravagant confidence: she will pick locks, drug the morning mist, dare the gauntlet, and run out to her mountain into the arms of the sun. Sun as lover! Who knew! All that wild, bold energy will construct the creative will to foil "indolent disgrace." (I am still wondering why she was made jail bird and by whom!) How does being jail bird affect her soul, her work, her poetic self, her praying poet self? Is being jail bird necessary to her art? To successful administration of a college? Why not "deal cunningly, devise some tool / To freedom"? Why not "fly, / up, up…?"

Another poem may lead us to the beginning of an answer: "—And So I Am Betrayed":

> You spoke of loneliness before I went;
> You knew that I would be too proud to show it,
> In which security I was content.
> You did not say the mocking-bird would know it.

Longing you mentioned in a casual way;
You thought the sea and mountain-trails might bring it;
Knowing you were too merciful to say
The mocking-bird, the mocking-bird would sing it.

Hunger and thirst and loneliness would come;
This wild, this poignant singing has unmade me;
It is not pride but longing holds me dumb.
The mocking-bird, beloved, has betrayed me.[14]

The title implies we begin in mid-narrative. It has a kind of nonchalance: "as if oh by the way" there is this too. "—And so" as if in the midst of things: "You spoke of loneliness." The details of "things" are missing. What are they? From the poem, we only know she is too proud to show it, to say it. Then, however, there is all that longing, only mentioned in a casual way: sea and mountain trails might bring it. Note the rhyming pairs: "show it," "know it," "bring it," "sing it." They make for a solemn lightness until the last stanza when the rhyming pairs signal a dark pain: "come," "dumb," and finally "unmade me," "betrayed me." The person addressed is called "beloved." That person receives the full story even as her "longing holds" [her] "dumb." There, just there, in the last line, the beloved!

And that person receives the poem's strange refrain: "the mocking-bird" knows and betrays her longing. I wonder who that person is: whoever she or he is knows her longing. And knows now that longing keeps her "dumb." Except, of course, when obviously it doesn't. Caught on the slant, as it were, in the swift iambic lines, is not the mocking-bird's song of betrayal but the fact that the song has "unmade" her: "longing holds [her] dumb." And yet, despite being dumb, she speaks. The poem is as much about silences as it is about what the mocking-bird knows and what the mocking-bird sings. And presumably, what the songs of the mocking-bird imitate and, therefore, mock. Who knew silence could get this complicated? Silence is in this poem a form of speech for longing. Longing is shadow. Shadow is longing. Longing "holds her dumb." From the place of "dumb," a prison, Madeleva, oh happy jail bird, sings! Her song makes her free. Small aside: perhaps this was one of the inner purposes of her writing. In some of her poems, she could speak and gain a deep inner freedom, absent, perhaps, from the rest of her life.

~~~~~~~~~~~~~~~~~

I
the song
I walk here.

~~~~~~~~~~~~~~~~~

Madeleva's "Ballade on Eschatology" is intended for "the Hero of the Habitually Relaxed Grasp." Who could that be? Some other miraculous person, but not, wry aside, "petty deities of clay"? Caught here in shadow is the speaker who says, "there are matters for a heart's relinquishings." I repeat: "matters for a heart's relinquishings"!

What "matters"? What "relinquishings"? Oh, how I wish I knew. We have only this:

Detachment is a virtue, teachers say.
Then let me practice it without regret.
What do I hold beyond this short today?
What cherish that I shall not soon forget?
These small things upon which my heart is set
Are matters for a heart's relinquishings.
One ultimate matter do I cleave to yet.
This, I shall not forget the four last things.

Remembrance, in a thief's unnoted way,
Filches from me with neither leave nor let
My thousand petty deities of clay.
Perhaps my eyes are still a little wet;
Perhaps my heart may still a little fret.
Detachment is the stuff of sunderings.
Time, so they tell me, is a brave asset.
And I shall not forget the four last things.

Your voice, your eyes,—or are they blue or grey?
The day we said good-bye, the day we met;
Hills we have walked, birds, flowers, our work, our play;—
Memory, how do you aid me and abet?

Time closes round me with impalpable net.
I'll not advert to clay or crowns or wings.
I have no thing to lose, all things to get,
For I shall not forget the four last things.

ENVOI

Lord, though by mortal tyrannies beset,
Immortal freedom in my wild heart sings.
A pauper comes to pay a pauper's debt.
God, I shall not forget the four last things.[15]

An important note: This poem was first published as the last poem in *American Twelfth Night*.[16] Madeleva made it the closing poem in *The Four Last Things*. Her decision gives the poem increased significance. She closes her book with a boldly proclaimed thematic: "One ultimate matter do I cleave to yet." What is that "ultimate matter"? She repeats her answer with variations at the end of each stanza: "…This, I shall not forget the four last things."

So, what are they, the four last things? Death, judgment, hell, and heaven. Oddly, Madeleva doesn't make explicit reference to them at all. Either she thinks we already know what they are. Or she, clever she, is making new ones. Madeleva, poet/theologian, shall not forget the four last things." HER four last things. And she will SING them in a ballade!

Not "ballad" but "ballade," a rather formal song about an event or person (Coleridge's "Ancient Mariner" is an example). Shadow questions: why should the speaker not forget the four last things? Why is the speaker clearly worried about memory? She says (or does she sing?) over and over, "I shall not forget." Almost a verbal imperative. Addressed to self. And to us. Is that memory only hers? Or is it also ours? Don't forget. Don't forget. Don't forget there is a real SHE here!

Each of the three stanzas has "heart ravishing knowledge": Madeleva's tough talk! Like another American poet, she will "tell all the truth, but tell it slant":[17]

These small things upon which my heart is set [from stanza one]
Are matters for a heart's relinquishings

Perhaps my heart may still a little fret. [from stanza two]
Detachment is the stuff of sunderings.

Memory, how do you aid me and abet? [from stanza three]
Time closes round me with impalpable net.

"Relinquishings." "Sunderings." "Impalpable net." "Small things." What small things? She doesn't say in the first stanza. Or the second. Although the second stanza has a few clues: wet eyes, a heart that "may a little fret." In the third stanza: "the day we said good-bye, the day we met;/ Hills we have walked, birds, flowers, our work, our play—." In sum, the whole nine yards of a particular memory! Given to us in four lines stuffed with that memory: voice, eyes, "the day we said good-bye, the day we met, / Hills we have walked, birds, flowers, our work, our play—." Her "wild heart sings": she will not forget the four last things. Even though she is "beset" by "mortal tyrannies," she will not forget all this stuff of memory: "I have no thing to lose." Madeleva will NOT forget THINGS. In this case, Madeleva "weird[s] the truth, re-arrange[s] it, re-present[s] it, cause[s] us to re-envision the past, to rememory... [her] own history."[18]

In this last poem in her collection, a book that contains "a heart's relinquishings" and the "stuff of sunderings" (your voice, your eyes), despite "the impalpable net" of time, Madeleva will remember it all. She comes to "pay a pauper's debt" with this astonishing closure poem. Making this poem was for her, I think, a vast aid to memory. And also a practice in radical detachment. When you write a poem and finish it, you let it go, its matter, its stuff of sunderings. Her radical net, the emotive stuff of the poem, is Madeleva's relinquishings. Her sunderings make her poet-self fully known. "Sundering" is such an odd word. We know it mostly from the Bible: "What God has joined together, let no man put asunder." In other settings, it means a violent tearing apart. Detachment is then the stuff of violent tearing. Her memory contains that tearing, that sundering. Somehow, a very BIG somehow, the poem HOLDS that truth-telling tumult. I wonder whether, as Madeleva made this poem, she wondered about the safety of placing these words on the page. Their shadows are luminous; they break privacy into shards of truth:

~~~~~~~~~~~~~~~~~

I
the song
I walk here.

~~~~~~~~~~~~~~~~~

Notes

1. "Modoc Song," in Brian Swann, ed., *Smoothing the Ground: Essays on Native American Oral Literature* (Berkeley: University of California Press, 1983), 28.

2. Antonin Sertillanges, *The Intellectual Life: Its Spirit, Conditions, Methods* (New York: McMullen, l952).

3. Madeleva Wolff, CSC, "Cassandra Speaks on Poetry," in *Conversations with Cassandra* (New York: Macmillan, 1961), 45.

4. Madeleva Wolff, CSC, *My First Seventy Years* (New York: Macmillan, 1959), 46.

5. Wolff, *My First Seventy Years*, 58–59.

6. Wolff, *My First Seventy Years*, 59.

7. Wolff, *My First Seventy Years*, 59.

8. Tiya Miles, "Shadow Drafting," *The New York Review of Books*, May 25, 2024, https://www.nybooks.com/online/2024/05/25/shadow-drafting-tiya-miles/#:~:text=I%20imagine%20the%20enslaved%20person,it%20represents%20into%20historical%20context.

9. Madeleva Wolff, CSC, "Design for a Stream-Lined Sunrise," in *The Four Last Things: Collected Poems* (New York: Macmillan, 1986), 164.

10. "Subtend," in *Oxford English Dictionary*, 2nd ed., 20 vols. (first published in 1989), continually updated at https://www.oed.com/dictionary/subtend_v?tab=meaning_and_use#20125437.

11. Meister Eckhart, "Sermon 57," in *The Complete Mystical Works of Meister Eckhart*, trans. M. O'C. Walshe (New York: Herder & Herder, 2009), 298.

12. Gustov Sobin, "Shadow Rattles," in *Collected Poems* (Northfield, MA: Talisman House, 2010), 125.

13. Madeleva Wolff, CSC, "Jail Bird," in *The Four Last Things*, 92.

14. Madeleva Wolff, CSC, "—And So I Am Betrayed," in *The Four Last Things*, 88–89.

15. Sister M. Madeleva, CSC, "Ballade on Eschatology," in *The Four Last Things*, 125.

16. Sister M. Madeleva, *American Twelfth Night and Other Poems* (New York: Macmillan, 1955).

17. Emily Dickinson, "Tell All the Truth, but Tell It Slant," in *Emily Dickinson's Poems as She Preserved Them*, ed. Christanne Miller (Cambridge, MA: The Belknap Press, 2016), 563.

18. Camille T. Dungy, "Tell it Slant," *The Poetry Foundation* (June 10, 2014), https://www.poetryfoundation.org/articles/70128/tell-it-slant.

9

"God Give Me Grace to Be a Fool!"

Francis of Assisi and the Spirituality of Sr. Madeleva Wolff

Daniel P. Horan

The person of Francis of Assisi (ca. 1182–1226) and the legacy of Franciscan spirituality haunt the pages of Madeleva's poetry and essays. In her memoir *My First Seventy Years*, Madeleva recounted the extraordinary adventure she embarked upon while visiting Oxford University in 1933. Looking back over the previous four months, she noted that she had the distinct privilege of visiting the shrines of her "predilect friends," which consisted of Dame Julian of Norwich and St. Francis of Assisi.[1] Later in life, after her formal retirement, Madeleva was commissioned by CBS to write a television script titled, "Praised Be My Lord," which was a biographical motion picture depicting St. Francis of Assisi and the story of the first Christmas creche in Greccio, Italy. The program was broadcast on Christmas Eve in 1963.[2]

It is also notable that a number of Madeleva's artifacts in the archives of Saint Mary's College contain explicit Franciscan themes or references. For example, at the time of this writing, there is a small ceramic dish on display in an exhibit in Madeleva Hall that belonged to Madeleva Wolff and contains the inscription: "*Laudato si', mi Signore, per sora luna e le stelle, in celu l'ai formate clarite e preziose e belle*" (Eng. trans. "Praise be you, my Lord, through sister moon and the stars, in heaven you formed them clear and precious and beautiful"). This is a direct quote of the fifth verse of St. Francis of Assisi's "Canticle of the Creatures."[3]

Even when neither Francis nor the tradition that followed him are mentioned explicitly, there are recognizable seeds of such inspiration buried in the soil of her foundational spirituality, many of which continued to grow and blossom in a variety of distinctive ways. There are other times when the specter of Francis and his spiritual legacy are more overtly present, such as in many of the poems contained in Madeleva's first published collection titled *Knights Errant*, which appeared in print in 1923.[4]

While there is so much that could be said about the broader spiritual outlook, life, and practices of someone like Sr. Madeleva Wolff, one essay could never exhaustively examine such depths. For this reason, a narrower focus had to be adopted and, in both wonderful coincidence and perhaps even divine providence, this significant aspect of Madeleva's life and legacy intersect with my own research interests and life experience. In addition to being a Franciscan scholar who has specialized in both medieval sources and contemporary appropriations of thirteenth-century thought, I spent two decades as a professed member of the Franciscan Order. To see this dimension of my own spiritual foundations come together in distinctive ways in Madeleva's life and writings has been nothing short of a joy. What follows is not a complete analysis of her Franciscan interests or appropriation of Franciscan spirituality, but what I hope is an interesting yet preliminary exploration of one spiritual thread that is woven together along with other sources of inspiration in the tapestry of her life and faith. I attend to these two aspects of the Franciscan spiritual influence on Madeleva's life and writing in respective sections. First, I want to say a bit about the general Franciscan spiritual disposition Madeleva embraced and embodied. And second, I will invite us to look at some of her early Franciscan poetry in *Knights Errant*.

Brother Sun, Sister Madeleva

Even those casually familiar with the life and legacy of Sr. Madeleva will observe her appreciation for and love of the more-than-human natural world. Throughout her memoir, she herself recounts the various ways she has been struck by the beauty of creation and lure of nature. From gardening to poetry, the natural world has been a preoccupation and place of creativity. In her later years, she remembers her advice regularly given out to students inquiring about what texts they ought to read to become better poets. Madeleva writes, "With no hesitation at all, I say, 'The Bible, the Oxford Dictionary, seed catalogues.' This is spoken in parable. Here are the words of God, of man [*sic*], of nature."[5] There is an Augustinian dimension to her appreciation for what the ancient Doctor of the Church would call the "book of nature," which can be read in a manner analogous to the "book of scripture"; both tell the "reader" something about the Creator and about us.[6] This sentiment is both reified and radicalized in the life and vision of Francis of Assisi, who remains perhaps Christianity's greatest nature mystic.[7] His was an intuitive understanding of the very real sense of kinship that exists within the created world. As later Franciscan theologians would explain in the High Middle Ages, everything that exists was created by God, sustained by God, comes from God; therefore, all that exists shares both a common source and goal, thereby affirming a community of interdependence and interrelatedness. This is known as a theology of emanation, which the thirteenth-century Franciscan theologian and Doctor of the Church St. Bonaventure expressed most clearly in an attempt to provide theological and philosophical structure to Francis's nature mysticism.[8]

For Francis of Assisi, this reality led to his loving and powerful affirmation of the intrinsic dignity and value of all creatures, something that has been subsequently overshadowed by anthropocentrism and hubristic assumptions of "human separateness" from the rest of creation in recent centuries. There are discrete times in Madeleva's writing that echo the medieval wisdom of Francis, such as when she talks about her early childhood and home. She writes, "My friends, the trees, dominated our entire domain."[9] Her affection for plants and animals, such as for the trees of her childhood, are not merely fanciful departures into naïve or romantic musings.[10] Instead, Madeleva shared a kindred intuition with Francis of Assisi for the truth of our kinship with all else that exists within creation. Elsewhere in her recollections, we read about Madeleva's memory of visiting a family farm in southern Wisconsin during her youth. She writes:

> On our last visit to the farm, when I was perhaps twelve, mother took me one late afternoon on a walk along the

> places dear to her childhood. We climbed the highest bluff and looked down at the tumultuous river fifty feet below. But between it and us, sheathed in a single leaf, a showy orchid, a lovely pink moccasin flower lifted its beauty for us to share. To me it was "beauty's self and beauty's giver."[11]

Following the categorization of Bernard McGinn, the renowned scholar of Christian mysticism, Madeleva can rightly be said to be a "vernacular Franciscan theologian."[12] While admittedly not a scholar of the Franciscan philosophical, theological, or historical sources in the strict sense, Madeleva nevertheless expressed her appreciation for and understanding of the natural world in accessible language and framing that resonates deeply with that of the Franciscan tradition. What Madeleva saw was more than mere beauty as an end in itself, but rather the gift of God's self in and through creation, which is a notably Franciscan perspective. As we will see shortly, this aspect of Franciscan spirituality, among other themes, is exhibited most clearly in her early poetry.

In addition to the manifold ways Madeleva's prose and verse exhibit a vernacular Franciscan theology and spirituality, there are a few biographical similarities between them that are also worth noting. For instance, the way she describes her early adult life and unlikeliness of becoming a religious sister is reminiscent of the way Francis of Assisi is remembered in his youth (especially when contrasted with his contemporary cofounder Clare of Assisi, the noblewoman). What is not often recalled by those with only a passing familiarity with the life and legacy of Francis of Assisi is that his earliest interest was to enter into the lower noble class as a successful knight in battle. This aspiration was never realized. During his first significant foray into battle, in the intercommune disputes of the region and time, he was captured swiftly and held for ransom as a prisoner of war for more than a year in the city of Perugia.[13] There was little in Francis's early life up to the time he formally "left the world," as he put it in his *Testament*, that would signal a budding religious vocation or interest in formal ecclesiastical ministry.[14] These two individuals—Francis and Madeleva—separated by centuries and social locations, nevertheless rise to become towering figures in their own contexts, which is another resonance shared between them.

Madeleva's own appreciation for and developing understanding of evangelical poverty—what she sometimes referred to in terms of her now well-known expression, the "relaxed grasp"—likewise echoes that of the Franciscan commitment to the divestment of those things, material and nonmaterial alike, that get in the way of relationship with others, oneself, and God. This is another underappreciated aspect of Franciscan spirituality that can be identified in Madeleva's life and writings. For while the caricature of Franciscan poverty reduces it to the pursuit of abject poverty, the principle within the tradition is more complex. For example, Francis and Clare of Assisi saw poverty not as an end in itself but as a means toward deepening relationships. Following the model of Christ in the gospels, who theologically divested himself of all divine possession through the incarnation (see Phil 2:5–11) and all material possessions through his earthly itinerant lifestyle, Francis and Clare sought to divest themselves of those material and nonmaterial barriers to relationship with others. This was especially true when it came to the most precarious people in society and those most marginalized by the Church. Perhaps there was something to this complexity in approaching religious life that spoke to Madeleva during her own discernment and spiritual journey, even if she never articulated it in such a manner.

It is clear that Madeleva had the highest respect for Francis and the spiritual tradition that followed him. But for all the ways Madeleva personally reflected the Franciscan spiritual tradition, we can see in her poetry a more concentrated source of this inspiration. This ought not be surprising in the case of the poet Madeleva Wolff, who in the preface to the 1959 edition of her collected poems noted: "Poetry is a distillation, not a diffusion; a high concentrate, not an atomizer."[15] What may have been diffuse in her personal and prayer life became crystalized in her versification. And so, now let us turn to her Franciscan poetry.

The "Unmistakably Franciscan" Poetry of Sr. Madeleva

In her description of Madeleva's first published collection of poetry, *Knights Errant*, biographer Gail Porter Mandell writes: "As its title suggests, *Knights Errant* is medieval in spirit, and in its spiritual approach to nature, unmistakably Franciscan."[16] Even those not well versed in the Franciscan tradition, its history, or its medieval founder might recognize some recurring themes in this collection of poetry. The first, as Mandell notes, is Madeleva's particular view of the so-called natural world. There is perhaps nothing more recognizably Franciscan than an appreciation for the whole of creation and humanity's distinctive yet interconnected place within this divine community. There are at least two poems in *Knights Errant* that not only reflect Madeleva's nascent vernacular-Franciscan ecospirituality but also echo St. Francis's most famous extant text, the "Canticle of the Creatures."[17] Within the "Canticle": Francis depicts a dynamic world in which all creatures—sentient and otherwise—exhibit agency and relate to the rest of the community as subjects. Using familial language—brother, sister, mother—Francis addresses both God and the more than human world from a stance of awe, humility, and profound appreciation for relationship. Commonly misunderstood, Francis's "Canticle": is not a prayer of praise to God, at least not in a superficial or plain sense. Instead, this prayer and theological vision set in proto-Italian Umbrian verse celebrates the diverse manner in which all created elements of the cosmos *give praise to God* by being what it is that God created them to be: Brother Sun by shining light and giving us the day; Sister Water by being pure and refreshing; Mother Earth by providing us with a home and all vegetation. It is humanity that is the creature who regularly fails to do and be what God created us for—namely, being creatures that love, reconcile, forgive, and bear difficulty in peace.

There are two poems in this collection that not only celebrate the goodness of creation but also convey the familial relationship inherent in a Franciscan view of the cosmos. These poems are titled "The Pepper Tree" and "The Quest." The resonances are striking. For example, in both poems, nonhuman elements of the created order exhibit agency and subjectivity. "The Pepper Tree" opens with the stanza: "On a night the sun and the earth and the weather/And their brother, the wind, all slept together."[18] Each element of creation awakes having had a dream that is shared with the other sibling creatures. In "The Quest," Madeleva returns to the sibling elements and the theme of dreaming. The narrator in this instance inquires of the elements, beckoning their perspective, insights, and dreams. The poem opens:

> Wind of the west, wistful wings, tireless feet,—where are you
> going,
> Hastening, blowing?
> When will you rest?
> Is there no place you will bide, all your journeying over,

Wanderer, rover,
Wind of the west?

Mountains,—what thoughts in your heart lie a-sleeping,
        wishful and
    tender,
Wrapped in cloud splendor?
What is your dream?
River,—say, whose are your singing and all of your joy? say,
        what shall
    come after
Such dreams and such laughter,
Mountain and stream?[19]

Additional elements appear in the poem, such as the myriad stars of the sky and a river. They are queried and respond, joining the lively chorus of the cosmic community. Famously, the last stanza of Francis's "Canticle": which was composed close to the saint's own *transitus*—or death, a passing from this life to the next—centers on another figure: Sister Death. Francis's spirituality of death was not one of fire and brimstone, fear and terror, but continuity and naturalness with the created order.[20] Francis referred to death as "our Sister Bodily Death," signaling his recognition that death was as much a part of the divine order for creation as life itself.

This brings us to a second major Franciscan theme present in the thought and writing of Madeleva: death. Noting the prominence of death as a theme in Madeleva's writing, Mandell explains: "She contemplated death in her poetry and, one presumes, in her prayers; spoke and wrote of it often; and always idealized it. To imagine death, she borrowed the familiar terms of Saint Francis of Assisi; death became 'Sister Death.'"[21] It is perhaps not an exaggeration to say that Madeleva wrote about death more than any other subject over the course of her literary career. It is a theme that appears in a variety of settings, sometimes the centerpiece of a poem or the focal point of a reflection, at other times it appears like a shadow cast over Madeleva's other work. A fuller examination of the theme of death across her writings would be a worthwhile and formidable project. But for our purposes, it is worth looking again at her earliest poetry, which carries the clearest marks of the influence of Franciscan spirituality on her reflections about death.

The titular poem from her collection *Knights Errant* addresses the subject of death head-on, signaling the spectral presence of this inescapable facet of creaturely life. The poem begins: "Death is no foeman, we were born together; / He dwells between the places of my breath."[22] In much of Madeleva's creative reflections on death, there is also often an association with life; not life generally speaking, but creaturely life, earthly life, life that is formed from the "dust" or "clay" or, as she repeatedly says, the "clod" of the ground. Such is the case in the next poem in her first collection, titled "Surrender." She addresses human persons, considering that God made us from the "dust of the earth" (*ha-adamah* in the original Hebrew of Genesis), she describes us as "cousin to the clod" and brings together our kinship with the rest of the earth, the proximity of death, and the hope of the next life to come all in just two stanzas.

These intersecting themes of death and earthly, creaturely life appear in the aptly titled poem "Of Dust," in which Madeleva personifies the narrator's physical human body in dialogue with her soul. The closing line brings these Franciscan preoccupations of Madeleva's together in a striking, if lengthy, line: "And this clay will pass from me, and life, aye, and death, like a vapor; I shall rise at His word, light as light, quick as thought, swift as wing; For though dust, soul of mine, even dust in the hands of its Shaper is a glorified thing."[23]

It is in the poem simply titled "Sister Death" that the fullness of Madeleva's Franciscan view of death comes to the fore in a dialogue between the narrator and death personified herself.

> Doff your mourning robe, my Sister; I have for you raiment new,
> The very stuff of glory, golden and white and blue.
> Your darling feet in sorrow no longer shall go shod;
> Here are shoon of divine impatience for trafficking with God.
> Your hands, my little Sister, are very young and cold;
> See, I bring my life's one blossom for their still, white strength
>   to hold.
> Such eyes you have are strangers to tears of sorrowing—
> Let me grow sick with longing—for they gaze upon the King!
> I wait at your quiet doorway, beneath love's architrave;
> Unloose its bolts and lead me into the golden grave.
> Lovely my Death, constrain me, I would be comforted;
> My sweetest Sister, kiss me,—whisper that I am dead.[24]

While there is much here to unpack (too much for our limited space), it is worth noting that, from the outset, Madeleva embraces the Franciscan emphasis on the fact that death is not to be feared nor is it a cause for sadness (hence the reference to the "mourning robe" to be taken off).

The last Franciscan theme we will explore here is that of the figure of St. Francis himself. Although Madeleva will return to the figure of Francis in her later poetry, such as in "Things to Be Loved" and "Sentries at Umbrian Farms," which were both published in the collection *Four Girls, and Other Poems*, we will stay focused on the earlier works due to the limitations of space here.[25] In *Knights Errant*, Madeleva includes two poems that either address or describe the medieval saint himself (although, it is worth noting that allusions to the *poverello* also occur in other passages, often in passing).

The first of these poems is titled "Roses for My King" with the parenthetical note "(The Stigmata of St. Francis)."[26] Here Madeleva composes an allegory in which the stigmatic wounds of Francis are described as a bouquet of five of the fairest roses gathered and presented as a gift to God ("my King"). It is an interesting take on the stigmata of Francis, which is widely recognized as the first recorded instance of such a miracle in the Christian tradition. Traditional theological interpretation suggests that the physical wounds that appeared on the body of Francis of Assisi were an external manifestation of the *a priori* internal conformity to Christ Francis cultivated by his life of virtue and pursuit of the *vita evangelica* ("Gospel Life").[27] Madeleva's rendering of the miracle is one that reflects a view of the stigmata that is both gift and sacrifice. It is framed as a presentation to God of the wounds or "roses" that are also reminiscent of Juan Diego's presentation of the *tilma* containing the icon of Our Lady of Guadalupe in the Americas. This particular approach to the theme of the stigmata is a distinctively Madelevan interpretation, revealing something of Madeleva's own appropriation and interpretation of the Franciscan tradition.

While this first poem clearly centers the distinctive experience of Francis and reception of the stigmata, signaling a clear interest in and appreciation for the *poverello*, it is her poem "I Go to School" that shines the brightest light on Francis as her would-be spiritual guide and aspirational exemplar. She opens the poem with the line, "I seek a teacher and a rule, / Dear Brother Francis, and a school / Where I can learn to be a fool."[28] Before continuing, it is important to observe a few details here from the outset. First, the fact that Madeleva, for whom education was her vocation and focus of life, frames her (or her narrator's) own quest for a teacher and a rule (we might translate the medieval *regula* into the modern "syllabus" or "curriculum"), speaks volumes of her love and admiration for Francis, as well as his importance in her own thinking. This is particularly striking given Francis's own ambivalence about higher education and the ostensible danger of self-aggrandizement or immodesty among the learned.[29] Second, her use of *fool* in reference to herself is a nod to Francis's own self-reference as a "fool for Christ," which is a play both on the virtue of *minoritas* in the Franciscan tradition and the Pauline spirituality of the wisdom or logic of God perceived as foolish by the worldly and educated (see 1 Cor 1:15–31). The phrase "God's Fool" is also a title that was made popular later in the twentieth century by the acclaimed French novelist Julien Green in his biography titled *God's Fool: The Life of Francis of Assisi*.[30] Returning to Madeleva's text, the poem continues:

> The world is erudite to-day;
> The folk of Gubbio and your gray
> Brother Wolf are dead, they say.
> Sweet friend of Christ, yourself shall be
> My book of gentle courtesy.
>
> A single purse, a single cloak
> Do scarce suffice for modern folk;
> Such foolishness as once you spoke
> About your Lady Poverty,
> That, poverello, tell to me.
>
> Bird songs in Umbria were sweet,
> Or else, mayhap, your quaint conceit
> Found meanings now quite obsolete.
> God's little one, please share with me
> Your sister birds' sweet psaltery.
>
> Stars nebular and wise, indeed,
> Above Averno shared your creed
> Of Pierced heart and wounds that bleed.
> Enamored Knight of Calvary,
> Teach me love's madmost ecstasy.

Behold my teacher and my rule;
Yourself, St. Francis, are my school;
God give me grace to be a fool![31]

This poem is full of deeply significant Franciscan spiritual imagery, with multiple allusions to the well-known stories of Francis and his followers, which were likely conveyed to Madeleva through an edition of the so-called *Little Flowers of Saint Francis*, a late fourteenth-century text that contains both early stories and historically spurious accounts of the life of Francis.[32] This source would have been Madeleva's primary Franciscan reference at the time. She mentions the Wolf of Gubbio, personified Lady Poverty, birds (with an apparent allusion to the famous scenes of Francis preaching to birds), a reference to Mt. Alvernia (here "Alverno") where Francis both composed the first part of the "Canticle of the Creatures" and later received the stigmata, and she makes passing reference to his short-lived military career and aspirations to knighthood. What is impressive is not only the familiarity but especially the fluency with which she is able to speak a Franciscan idiom.

While there is much more to say about the Franciscan spiritual valences in the poetry and other writings of Madeleva, suffice it to say that her interest in the tradition and the figure of Francis himself was more than passing. The degree to which she was able to incorporate distinctively Franciscan spiritual and historical themes into her creative work points to a level of study and commitment to the tradition that may have rivaled even professed Franciscans of her generation. And although there is more work to be done excavating this area of her life and work, it is my hope that these considerations—originally presented on the Feast of St. Francis of Assisi, no less—have invited further interest in the Franciscan spiritual themes in her life and writings.[33]

Notes

1. Sister M. Madeleva, *My First Seventy Years* (New York: Macmillan, 1959), 86. Gail Porter Mandell, *Madeleva: A Biography* (Albany: SUNY Press, 1997), 134.

2. Mandell, *Madeleva*, 248.

3. Francis of Assisi, "The Canticle of the Creatures," in *Francis of Assisi: Early Documents*, ed. Regis Armstrong et al., 3 vols. (New York: New City Press, 1999–2001), 1:114–15.

4. The edition of *Knights Errant* I will reference appears in the first part of Madeleva's "Collected Poems," titled *The Four Last Things: Collected Poems* (Notre Dame, IN: Saint Mary's College, 1986), 2–40.

5. Madeleva, *My First Seventy Years*, 148.

6. For example, see Oskari Juurikkala, "The Two Books of God: The Metaphor of the Book of Nature in Augustine," *Augustinianum* 61 (2021): 479–98.

7. For example, see Roger D. Sorrell, *St. Francis of Assisi and Nature: Tradition and Innovation in Western Christian Attitudes toward the Environment* (New York: Oxford University Press, 1988).

8. See Daniel P. Horan, *All God's Creatures: A Theology of Creation* (Lanham, MD: Lexington Books, 2018), esp. 143–79.

9. Madeleva, *My First Seventy Years*, 9.

10. For more on Madeleva's relationship to trees, see Sally Geislar's contribution to this volume.

11. Madeleva, *My First Seventy Years*, 12.

12. For more, see Bernard McGinn, "Meister Eckhart and the Beguines in the Context of Vernacular Theology," in *Meister Eckhart and the Beguine Mystics: Hadewijch of Brabant, Mechthild of Magdeburg, and Marguerite Porete*, ed. Bernard McGinn (New York: Continuum, 1994), 4–14; Dominic V. Monti, "Francis as Vernacular Theologian: A Link to the Franciscan Intellectual Tradition?," in *The Franciscan Intellectual Tradition*, ed. Elise Saggau (St. Bonaventure: Franciscan Institute Publications, 2002), 21–42; and Daniel P. Horan, "Thomas Merton's Vernacular Franciscan Theology," *The Merton Journal* 16 (2009): 26–36.

13. For a concise summary of this period in Francis's early life and its long-term consequences, see Paul Moses, *The Saint and the Sultan: The Crusades, Islam, and Francis of Assisi's Pilgrimage of Peace* (New York: Image Books, 2009).

14. See Francis of Assisi, "Testament," no. 3, in *Francis of Assisi*, 1:124.

15. Madeleva, *The Four Last Things*, iv.

16. Mandell, *Madeleva*, 77.

17. See Francis of Assisi, "The Canticle of the Creatures," in *Francis of Assisi*, 1:114–15. Also, see Horan, *All God's Creatures*.

18. Sister M. Madeleva, CSC, "The Pepper Tree," in *The Four Last Things*, 14.

19. Sister M. Madeleva, CSC, "The Quest," in *The Four Last Things*, 36.

20. See Daniel P. Horan, "Embracing Sister Death: The Fraternal Worldview of Francis of Assisi as Source for Christian Eschatological Hope," *The Other Journal* 14 (January 2009).

21. Mandell, *Madeleva*, xiv.

22. Sister M. Madeleva, CSC, "Knights Errant," in *The Four Last Things*, 3.

23. Sister M. Madeleva, CSC, "Of Dust," in *The Four Last Things*, 6.

24. Sister M. Madeleva, CSC, "Sister Death," in *The Four Last Things*, 10.

25. An interesting historical coincidence worth noting here is that this book of poetry, published in 1941, was published by a Franciscan publisher in Paterson, NJ, titled St. Anthony Guild Press, which was the publishing house of my own former Franciscan community, Holy Name Province (1901–2023). This Franciscan publishing house also published her volumes: *A Question of Lovers and Other Poems* (1935); *The Happy Christmas Wind and Other Poems* (1936); *Christmas Eve and Other Poems* (1938); *Addressed to Youth* (1944); and *A Song of Bedlam Inn, and Other Poems* (1946).

26. Sister M. Madeleva, CSC, "Roses for My King," in *The Four Last*, 16–17.

27. See Jacques Dalarun, Michael F. Cusato, and Carla Salvati, eds., *The Stigmata of Francis of Assisi: New Studies, New Perspectives* (St. Bonaventure, NY: Franciscan Institute Publications, 2006).

28. Sister M. Madeleva, CSC, "I Go to School," in *The Four Last Things*, 8.

29. See Neslihan Senocak, *The Poor and the Perfect: The Rise of Learning in the Franciscan Order, 1209–1310* (Ithaca, NY: Cornell University Press, 2012).

30. Julien Green, *God's Fool: The Life of Francis of Assisi*, trans. Peter Heinegg (New York: Crossroad, 1985).

31. Madeleva, "I Go to School," 9.

32. The critical English edition of this collection is "The Little Flowers of Saint Francis," in *Francis of Assisi*, 3:566–660.

33. The conference at which an earlier version of this chapter was presented took place on October 4, 2024, and was hosted by the Center for the Study of Spirituality at Saint Mary's College.

PART 3

MADELEVA'S LEGACY AS AN EDUCATOR AND ADMINISTRATOR

10

"'Lackademic' Freedom"

Madeleva on Students, Teachers, and the Work of Holy Cross Education

David A. Clairmont

In 1944, Sr. Madeleva Wolff, CSC (1887–1964) published *Addressed to Youth*, a collection of speeches originally given as commencement addresses to Saint Mary's College students. In the essay titled "Student Defense," Madeleva says,

> We are in college to learn to think quickly and clearly, to judge honestly and fearlessly, to act bravely and unselfishly, to work tirelessly and uncomplainingly, to live nobly and holily. This life of the mind is a holy thing. It is an experience in immortality. It is all that will survive these brief and troubled years.[1]

She had been leading Saint Mary's College (1934–1961) for about ten years when she revised those words for publication, and it is difficult not to hear with the ear of one receiving a prophecy: in our time too, the "life of the mind is a holy thing" and it may be "all that will survive these brief and troubled years."

This essay explores the life of the mind in the context of academic communities, specifically in the life of a faith-imprinted academic community such as Saint Mary's College, one whose imprint has the shape and topography of the Holy Cross educational heritage. The Holy Cross religious family, which was born from the ministries of the Sisters of Providence (1806/1831) and the Brothers of Saint Joseph (1820)—communities whose ministry Fr. Jacques-François Dujarié (1767–1838) coordinated and nurtured in the years after the French Revolution—and the Auxiliary Priests of the Diocese of Le Mans whose ministry Fr. Basil Moreau (1799–1873) advanced and expanded into an international Catholic religious community, has been living a faith-imprinted educational vision for more than two hundred years. One of the distinctive aspects of that educational vision is the challenge of cultivating the life of the mind in a community of persons, where each person travels a unique path toward a shared educational horizon, one variously colored by the sunrises and the sunsets of each life of faith.

To present Sr. Madeleva Wolff's distinctive mediation and advance of this educational vision, I explore her approach to education in conversation with other religious and secular educational models that were live options at the beginning of her Saint Mary's presidency in 1934. Each educational model depended on an understanding of the relationship between the person and society in light of a wider educational horizon, that is, an account of education's proximate and ultimate purpose. Each approach was tested against the strong pull of national interest. Madeleva's approach, I suggest, understood not only the proper place of religion in human life but also the dynamics of intersecting religious lives in the context of an academic community. I argue that this approach to education suggests one of the strongest expressions of Madeleva as a Holy Cross educator, of one who was not afraid to accompany her students into their deepest questions about faith, personal integrity, changing social roles, and the great contesting ideologies of her time.

I begin by offering a brief overview of the educational context that Madeleva faced when she began her presidency of Saint Mary's in 1934, discussing in turn the religious (in particular the Catholic) context and also the secular educational debates of this period. I then turn in the second section to a sketch of Madeleva's educational model, drawn primarily from two sources: *Addressed to Youth* (1944) and *Conversations with Cassandra: Who Believes in Education?* (1961).[2] In the third and final section, I offer some brief comments on what today are recognized as certain characteristic elements of the Holy Cross philosophy of education, drawn from Basil Moreau's Circular Letter 36 (1849)[3] and his book on "Christian Education" (1856).[4] I conclude with some thoughts on how Madeleva's approach to education relates both to the secular educational debates of her day and to the Holy Cross approach to education that preceded and followed her. Madeleva's most significant development of Holy Cross spirituality for education is signaled by the intriguing locution "lackademic freedom," which names the ongoing relationship between teachers and students as God-directed truth seekers whose time together in the classroom marks the beginning rather than the end of their academic friendship.

Historical Context of Madeleva's Approach to Education

Madeleva's work as an educator coincided with some significant developments in education in the first half of the twentieth century. This was a time of profound change, not only because of international military conflicts that occurred during Madeleva's lifetime (1887–1964) in the First (1914–1918) and Second (1939–1945) World Wars but also because of the changes in the places, purposes, and approaches to education.[5] In the United States, for example, the places of education changed as land grant universities were relatively new, created through the Morrill Acts of 1862 and 1890 that gave rise to seventy-six new educational institutions focusing especially on the development of agricultural and technical competencies. The purposes of education were also under scrutiny, and Catholic higher education was growing in availability and stature with the establishment of the Association of Catholic Colleges and Universities in 1899 and of the National Catholic Educational Association in 1904.[6]

Historian of education Michael Rizzi divides Catholic education into five periods: "the Frontier Period (1789–1862), the [Morrill Act/] Land Grant Period (1862–1920), the Interwar Period (1920–1945), the GI Bill Period (1945–1967), and the Land O'Lakes Period (1967–present)."[7] The period of Madeleva's presidency of Saint Mary's College (1934–1961) bridges the Interwar Period and the GI Bill Period, and Rizzi notes some of the significant curricular changes that took place during these periods. The traditional *Ratio Studiorum*[8] ("method of studies") of the Society of Jesus (developed from its original 1599 model and adapted to a six-year period of study) moved during the Interwar

Period from a six-year model to a four-year curriculum, including remnants of the Jesuit approach but with a focus on the philosophy of Thomas Aquinas as the most trustworthy resource for establishing a solid metaphysical foundation to withstand the swelling storms of modern philosophy.[9] The GI Bill period—which included the second half of Madeleva's presidency—saw the transition of the Catholic college curricula through the organization into academic departments to better reflect conformity to emerging national standards. The national standards were not, however, without some disputation of their own. Among the most important issues for debate during that period was the meaning of the liberal arts and the balance between lecture-style teaching and seminar-style teaching.

One of the most important such experiments in the liberal arts took place at the University of Chicago under Robert Maynard Hutchins (1899–1977), who served as Chicago's president from 1929 to 1951. The Great Books initiative, initially developed by John Erskine at Columbia,[10] was institutionalized in a seminar initiative by Hutchins and his Chicago colleague Mortimer Adler (1902–2001) and was an important national topic of conversation. At the beginning of her presidency, Madeleva invited Adler to give a lecture at Saint Mary's in 1935 on the topic "Metaphysics and the Liberal Arts," which Madeleva hoped would provide some inspiration for how to integrate elements of this new movement with the traditional medieval study of the liberal arts and the restoration of the philosophy of Thomas Aquinas advocated by Leo XIII.[11]

These periods of Catholic education also relate to developments and debates in secular and religiously informed philosophies of education in the late nineteenth and early twentieth centuries, which in turn mirror developments in modern philosophy more generally. Historians of education usually identify five competing approaches to philosophy of education during this period, although the specifics of curriculum and approaches to pedagogy differ and, in some cases, overlap. The five approaches are:

1. Idealism
2. Progressive (Experimentalism)
3. Classical Humanism
4. Essentialism
5. Existentialism

The first, Idealism, is often associated with the writings of Herman Horne (1874–1946), who taught at Dartmouth College and then at New York University. For Horne, as for other idealists, what was most "real" in the world was the working of the mind, and this meant that education was a process of bringing the mind to an awareness of its own process and purpose. "Education is adjustment," wrote Horne. "We shall not be far wrong in considering true education as the process of becoming ever better adjusted, inwardly and outwardly, that is to say, in our relation with ourselves, our fellows, with nature, and with God."[12] Horne's main opponent in the early twentieth-century education debates was John Dewey (1859–1952), who taught at the University of Michigan and the University of Chicago before moving to Teacher's College at Columbia University for the remainder of his academic career.

The approach to education developed by Dewey was called variously Progressive, Experimentalist, Pragmatic, or Instrumentalist.[13] Dewey's approach begins with the reality of social groups and of the survival of biological organisms within groups. "Education," Dewey writes, "is thus a fostering, a nurturing, a cultivating, process. All of these words mean that it implies attention to the conditions of growth."[14] Linking those conditions of growth to social cohesion, Dewey continues, "we speak of education as shaping, forming, molding activity...the *way* in which a social group brings up its immature members into its own social form."[15] In this way, the progressive approach assumed no final religious goal of education, nor did it require a metaphysical foundation, but rather found its goal in the continuation of the social group and of the individual members of that group. An important aspect of progressive education was a focus on the individual experience of the one learning, which meant for Dewey that "what is required is a transformation of the quality of experience till it partakes in the interests, purposes, and ideas current in the social group."[16]

The Idealists were not the only ones who disagreed with Dewey on the purpose of education. The Classical Humanist approach, often identified with the aforementioned Chicago pair of Hutchins and Adler (although Dewey also taught at Chicago and had founded its influential Laboratory School), was concerned that Dewey's approach did not strike the right balance between the teacher and the students in the process of learning. The Great Books initiative, which became the heart of the core curriculum at the University of Chicago and which occasioned Madeleva's invitation to Adler, was based on the conviction that, as

Hutchins had said, "The best education for the best is the best education for all." The "best education" was one that introduced all people to the best ideas that human thinking had yet produced and invited students into a conversation about those ideas. Much later in his life, Adler wrote two small volumes titled *The Paideia Proposal* and *The Paideia Program*, outlining the method and content of an education in and for humanity (with *humanitas* being the Latin equivalent to the Greek word *paideia*, which Adler translated as "general, unspecialized, untechnical human learning" but also in the sense of a discipline or training).[17] In an article explaining the need for the Paideia Program, Adler identified five challenges facing education. I quote at length from Adler's article since it both helps us understand his differences from Dewey and explains why Madeleva might have found him a worthy lecturer at Saint Mary's.[18]

> The first error is to think that only some children are educable, even though all have a right to aspire to become truly educated human beings.
>
> The second error is to suppose that the process of education is completed in our educational institutions during the years of basic schooling or even during the years of advanced schooling after that. Nothing could be further from the truth. Education never is completed in the school. Youth and immaturity are insuperable obstacles to becoming educated.
>
> The third error is to suppose that teachers are the sole, primary, or principal causes of the learning that occurs in students. That is not the case. The primary cause of all learning—unless it be rote memory, which is not learning at all—is the activity of the student's mind. The best that the best teacher can do is to assist that activity.
>
> The fourth error is probably at the heart of the matter, and the correction of this error is at the heart of The Paideia Proposal: the error is to suppose that there is only one kind of teaching and one kind of learning, the kind that consists in the teacher lecturing, or telling, and the students learning what they hear said or what they find in textbooks. That's the least important kind of learning and teaching. There are two much more important kinds of learning and teaching ["Development of Intellectual Skills—Skills of Learning" and

> "Enlarged Understanding of Ideas and Values"], and all three must be in basic schooling, from kindergarten through the twelfth grade.
>
> Finally, there is the error of supposing that schooling—basic or advanced—is primarily a preparation for earning a living, and that it will not hold the attention of students unless that is manifestly so. Obviously one of the objectives of schooling is to prepare the young to earn a living, but that is the least important objective. One of the great troubles with our schools is that both teachers and parents make the mistake of thinking that job preparation is the primary objective.[19]

Now there were two additional groups of educational critics worth noting. The first was the Essentialists, associated with the work of William C. Bagley (1874–1946), who taught at the University of Illinois and then at Columbia. Bagley himself noted a series of important differences between the Essentialists and the Progressives (Dewey's group): whereas the former (the Essentialists) focused on student effort in light of established subject matter, the latter focused on student interest; whereas the former focused on teacher initiative for learning, the latter focused on student initiative; whereas the former focused on the historical experience of the social group, the latter focused on the experience of the individual; whereas the former focused on the clarification of the subject matter, the latter focused on classroom activities; whereas the former sought a logical organization of course content and classroom plans, the latter focused on the psychological impact of material and pedagogical strategies.[20] The second was the Existentialists, whose chief advocates were Van Cleve Morris of Rutgers University and George Kneller of UCLA. As Morris explained it, education means "awakened awareness in the learner—existential awareness of himself as single subjectivity present in the world." The aim of education, therefore, is "to provide the occasions and circumstances for the awakening and intensification of that awareness."[21]

So we have, at Madeleva's time, not only a change in Catholic education from the Jesuit *Ratio Studiorum* to a generally Thomistic model guided by Leo XIII's and Pius XI's interventions, we also have a secular debate about the purposes of education, its content, its processes, and the relation between teacher and student. How did Madeleva negotiate these changes and what was distinctive about her approach?

Dr. Sr. Madeleva's Diagnosis and Prescription for Educational Ailments

Madeleva was aware of the secular education debates of her time and also of the changes that were coming to Catholic education. In her chapter titled "That Not Impossible She" from *Conversations with Cassandra*, she charges recent graduates of Catholic colleges like Saint Mary's with "...the responsibility [both] of a faithful love of truth and a loving concern for those who are seeking it."[22] Those seekers are, she said, those from "Traditional Christian Protestantism" who, like prodigal sons, are "returning to their father's house," having "fed on the husks of Hegel [1770–1831] and Freud [1856–1939], [having] lived behavioristically with Dewey [1859–1952] and Keynes [1883–1946]."[23] As she describes the challenge of working one's way through college, she reminds the women she leads that "our proper work is study. Study has been described as a prayer to truth. As college students and teachers we are consecrated to truth. We are lovers of truth as philosophers are lovers of wisdom."[24] In "The Right to Truth in Education," she goes on to say that "the right to teach supernatural truth is our greatest human right in education. To exercise that right we must have proper training." Considering recent changes in education, she recalls how in earlier days "education itself, without the dazzling material perfections of modern plant equipment and the relentless application of standardized theories, had somehow managed to attend to first things. What validity there is in our present intellectual life testifies in a large measure to the correctness, the soundness of our pre-Dewey training."[25] A Christian approach to education proceeds from the conviction that "our three greatest privileges are birth, baptism, and death. Once we are successfully born our biggest business is to make a perfect success of dying. All that fills the interval called life is some form of education."[26] This conviction extends from the earliest days of education through to its most advanced forms, including graduate education in theology.[27]

Now one might be tempted to think that Madeleva is simply relating the classic insights of a Catholic approach to Christian education in light of rival secular approaches current at her time, but this would be to understate the extent of her intervention. She was aware especially that the women of Saint Mary's from the 1930s through the 1960s confronted new social and cultural challenges that earlier expressions of Christian education did not anticipate. Among the most profound changes that most concerned Madeleva, two were especially important: what she labels "standardization" and "security," both of which she explains as specific forms of idolatry. Standardization itself has several expressions, whether in standards of beauty or social utility, against which "the college girl today must fight the difficult fight of keeping her independence, of being simply and completely herself."[28] Security also has a social component, but for Madeleva the Saint Mary's student must resist two different forms of idolatry expressed in the desire for security. The first form she shares with all who look to the government to keep them safe from threats to a secure and comfortable way of life (for Madeleva, it is the communist threat that pervades national consciousness). The second form of security as threat is the one that is "bound round with such companionship as will save one from being alone or dependent on one's own social expedients for a moment."[29] She concludes, "We must educate our daughters to the fact that we are secure only when we can stand everything that can happen to us."[30]

So how is the Saint Mary's student to become one who loves truth, prepares throughout life for a good death by growing in love of God and service to neighbor and by resisting the most prevalent forms of twentieth-century idolatry in standardization and security? Here is the point at which Madeleva turns to the relationship between teachers and students and, with a mind equally attuned to classic and modern images, channels her poetic imagination to comment on the social imagination of her time, thinking now about human dreaming of the stars. In her essay "The Beginning of Work," she says,

> College is a space world for a space age, a world of metaphysical rockets, jets, satellites. During four years the college takes its students into the world of intellectual space, into ballistic exploration of deep space. How often in her courses in theology or philosophy or science, has the student's mind been projected beyond the farthest sun, into the Infinity in which we live and move and have our being? How many have brought back communicable records from such projections?

> Our Courier, our Discoverer, our Echo are slow-moving imitators of the majestic speed and instancy with which our minds reach deep into outer space and report back from infinity in the intellectual order. Do not think that this space age is foreign to us. It is our promised land, our homeland. Infinity is our proper dimension.[31]

We might add that, for Madeleva, there is nothing standardized or secure about space exploration, either intellectual or astronomical.

Lackademic Freedom: The Interpersonal Christocentric Paideia of Sr. Madeleva

Yet this exploration of intellectual space, of flights through the infinities of the spirit, is not without companionship, and it is here, I suggest, that we see Madeleva touching on some of the most important themes in Holy Cross education but adapting them to her own time and her own community. By way of conclusion, let me propose two ways to view Madeleva as a Holy Cross educator, although there are certainly many more.

First, Madeleva focused on Christian education for better times. In his 1856 work titled "Christian Education," Basil Moreau wrote extensively about the relationship between teachers and students. He explored the virtues of good teachers, and he explored the different kinds of challenging students that he expected teachers in Holy Cross schools would encounter and must prepare themselves to teach.[32] Moreau identifies a series of virtues that he thinks are required, or at least should be developed over time, by those who discern a true vocation to teaching in Holy Cross: faithfulness, knowledge, zeal, vigilance, seriousness, gentleness, patience, prudence, and firmness. He thinks that these virtues are required because the work of teaching is not easy, and the challenges that students face are great and complex. Education, he says, is a "work of resurrection," by which he means that it is work that changes a person from a glimpse of the goodness of which they are capable to a full expression of that goodness, a conformity to the person of Jesus both in outward actions and in inner dispositions.[33] But it is important, he says, that Christian educators are "preparing the world for better times than our own" and that "these children who today attend your school are the parents of the future and the parents of future generations."[34] In her commencement address titled "Guidance with a Capital G," Madeleva, though not quoting Moreau directly, says something similar:

> Guidance, like education, rests upon the two facts that every student has a future and every student has capacities.... Guidance may be defined as the collaboration of the teacher with the student toward the finding and developing of his best potencies, his best self...all forming and informing of minds is done under the influence of His Holy Spirit.[35]

Second, Madeleva understood education as a cooperative activity between teachers and students. In his Circular Letter 36 (April 15, 1849—so roughly seven years before he writes "Christian Education"), Moreau discusses the ideals of Catholic education and the relationship between teachers and students. He states,

> We wish to accept science without prejudice and in a manner adapted to the needs of our times. We do not want our students to be ignorant of anything they should know. To this end, we shall shrink from no sacrifice. But we shall never forget that virtue, as Bacon [1561–1626] puts it, is the spice which preserves science. We shall always place education side by side with instruction; the mind will not be cultivated at the expense of the heart. While we prepare useful citizens for society, we shall likewise do our utmost to prepare citizens for heaven.[36]

As if addressing Moreau's admonition a hundred years later, Madeleva responds in a mid-twentieth-century key:

> This means fitting ourselves for work, a bilateral activity.... As students you do not demand enough work of your teachers. You do not begin to ask from them all that they have and want to give you. They are much brighter than you may think they are....They represent a very large, rich, ballistic world.

> Use them as ballistic stations from which the mysteries of knowledge and the knowledge of mysteries can be radioed back, telephoned back, bounced back to you.[37]

A Holy Cross approach to education places both teachers and students under the same teacher: Jesus, the teacher of the heart and of the mysteries of the universe. This means that teachers and students have a capacity for a religious and intellectual friendship that comes with struggling through these mysteries together. As Madeleva puts it,

> Use [your teachers] as friends. In four years, or sooner, the academic distinction between teacher and student will no longer exist. Anticipate that happy day of "lackademic" freedom. Put down deep roots in this common ground of common allegiances to the best values and the best years of your lives....We do not give you objectives big enough, assignments hard enough, motives exalted enough. The Dean's list is one-dimensional. It is the least we can ask. Add a second, a third, a fourth dimension in richness of readings, art perceptions, versatility, the qualities of mercy, the sublimated arts of friendship. Never again, and nowhere else will you be so surrounded with opportunities for all these.[38]

Madeleva, no less than Moreau, recognized that there would be practical challenges to this intellectual and spiritual friendship. Today we might caution against any form of friendship between teachers and students that transgresses appropriate personal boundaries and blurs necessary social distinctions in the classroom. Yet Madeleva's central point remains, I suggest, since the only real boundary between teachers and students in the search for intellectual and spiritual truth is experience—the time spent in reading, writing, and conversation about what is most important in life. For a Holy Cross educator, we are all equal as we sit engaged in the Seminar on the Mount.

Now there are certainly many other events in Madeleva's life and many more of her writings that would need to be examined to make a compelling argument for the resonance between Madeleva's approach to education and Moreau's. This essay has provided an initial picture of Madeleva as both an educator in the Holy Cross tradition and as one responsive to the debates of her times and the needs of her community.

Madeleva's legacy, and the educational vision and work of Saint Mary's College today, provide an apt conclusion to this introduction to Madeleva as a Holy Cross educator.

By 1844, the sisters started a school that would become Saint Mary's College. The sisters' story reveals one of the most distinctive features of Holy Cross: "a commitment to respond to the needs of the time....[1] Seek an education of the mind and heart. [2] Respond to the needs of the time. [3] Prepare the world for better times than now."[39]

Madeleva's approach to education recalls, reframes, and renews this Holy Cross educational mission today.

Notes

1. Sister M. Madeleva, CSC, *Addressed to Youth* (Paterson, NJ: Saint Anthony Guild Press, 1944), 16.

2. Madeleva, *Addressed to Youth*; Sister M. Madeleva, CSC, *Conversations with Cassandra: Who Believes in Education?* (New York: Macmillan, 1961).

3. Basil Moreau, "Circular Letter 36," in *Basil Moreau, Essential Writings*, ed. Kevin Grove, CSC, and Andrew Gawrych, CSC (Notre Dame, IN: Ave Maria Press, 2014), 415–23.

4. Basil Moreau, "Christian Education," in Grove and Gawrych, *Basil Moreau, Essential Writings*, 329–76.

5. See Michael T. Rizzi, "We've Been Here Before: A Brief History of Catholic Higher Education in America," *Journal of Catholic Higher Education* 37, no. 2 (2018): 153–74.

6. "About NCEA," National Catholic Education Association, accessed February 8, 2025, https://www.ncea.org/NCEA/NCEA/Who_We_Are/About_NCEA/About_Us.aspx?hkey=5470d2fe-6f67-4aae-8b5b-4385a9a39082.

7. Rizzi, "We've Been Here Before," 154.

8. Allan P. Farrell, SJ, *The Jesuit Ratio Studiorum of 1599* (Washington, DC: Conference of Major Superiors of the Jesuits, 1970), "*Ratio atque Institutio Studiorum Societatis Jesu*," that is, "Method and System of the Studies of the Society of Jesus."

9. The restoration of writings of Thomas Aquinas to the Catholic curricula was most clearly presented in Pope Leo XIII's commendation of Thomas Aquinas in *Aeterni Patris* (On the Restoration of Christian

Philosophy, 1879) and in Pope Pius XI's *Divini Illius Magistri* (On Christian Education, 1929). Yet these letters by Leo and Pius carry forward a growing concern on the part of church leaders that a philosophy of education without a solid metaphysical foundation was bound to lead to confusion, especially on the capacities and limits of human reason apart from faith.

10. Thomas E. Blantz, CSC, *The University of Notre Dame: A History* (Notre Dame, IN: University of Notre Dame Press, 2020), 356.

11. On Madeleva's invitation to Adler, see Gail Porter Mandell, *Madeleva: A Biography* (Albany: SUNY Press, 1997), 150–51. See also Sister Miriam Joseph Rauh, CSC, *The Trivium: The Liberal Arts of Logic, Grammar, and Rhetoric: Understanding the Nature and Function of Language*, ed. Marguerite McGlinn (Philadelphia: Paul Dry Books, 2002 [1937]), 3. The *trivium* included grammar, logic, and rhetoric ("the three arts of language pertaining to the mind") and the *quadrivium* included arithmetic, music, geometry, and astronomy ("the four arts of quantity pertaining to matter" with the first two focusing on discrete quantity/number and the second two focusing on continuous quantity/space), 3–11.

12. Herman Harrell Horne, *This New Education* (New York: Abingdon Press, 1931), 125.

13. Joe Park, "Philosophy of Education in Twentieth Century America," *The High School Journal* 50, no. 1 (1966): 1–7.

14. John Dewey, *Democracy and Education: An Introduction to the Philosophy of Education* (Monee, IL: Myers Education Press, 2018 [2016]), 13.

15. Dewey, *Democracy and Education*, 13.

16. Dewey, *Democracy and Education*, 14.

17. Mortimer J. Adler, "The Reform of Public Schools," *The Center Magazine*, Center for the Study of Democratic Institutions, 1983, https://cooperative-individualism.org/adler-mortimer_reform-of-public-schools-1983.htm.

18. Adler's formulation was continuous with, although a much later iteration of, the curriculum and its rationale that Madeleva would have encountered in the aforementioned lecture.

19. Adler, "The Reform of Public Schools."

20. Park, "Philosophy of Education in Twentieth Century America," 2.

21. Park, "Philosophy of Education in Twentieth Century America," 2.

22. Madeleva, *Conversations with Cassandra*, 56.

23. Madeleva, *Conversations with Cassandra*, 56–57.

24. Madeleva, *Conversations with Cassandra*, 71.

25. Madeleva, *Conversations with Cassandra*, 72.

26. Madeleva, *Conversations with Cassandra*, 80.

27. In the chapter titled "The Idea of the University" (drawn from John Henry Newman's book of the same title), in her published reminiscence *My First Seventy Years*, Madeleva relates the following story. "In spite of the war, with shattered enrollments, accelerated programs in the men's colleges, the Problems Committee of the National Catholic Education Association in 1942 decided that the preparation of teachers of religion in college constituted our biggest problem. The task of investigating possibilities and solutions was assigned to me." With Bishop Edwin O'Hara's support but with no institutions volunteering their campuses or faculty services, Madeleva recounts how, "with that strange impulse outside my will, I stood up and said: 'I do not know how we will do it, but this summer we will offer at Saint Mary's a six-weeks graduate program in Theology, without tuition and without credit. I regret that we shall have to make a nominal charge for maintenance. We will send you details in a fortnight.'" Sister M. Madeleva, CSC, *My First Seventy Years* (New York: Macmillan, 1959), 115.

28. Madeleva, *Conversations with Cassandra*, 19.

29. Madeleva, *Conversations with Cassandra*, 19.

30. Madeleva, *Conversations with Cassandra*, 19.

31. Madeleva, *Conversations with Cassandra*, 10.

32. Moreau, "Christian Education."

33. Moreau's focus on the person of Christ, including especially imagining the inner dispositions in the heart of Jesus, was important to Moreau, although not unique to him. Perhaps the most significant version of this pedagogical inspiration comes from the thinkers of the French School, especially Jean-Jacques Olier, "Introduction to the Christian Life and Virtues," in *Bérulle and the French School: Selected Writings* (New York/Mahwah, NJ: Paulist Press, 1989), 217–76.

34. Moreau, "Christian Education," 376.
35. Madeleva, *Addressed to Youth*, 26.
36. Moreau, "Circular Letter 36," 417.
37. Madeleva, *Conversations with Cassandra*, 10–11.
38. Madeleva, *Conversations with Cassandra*, 11.
39. "The History of Holy Cross Education," Saint Mary's College, https://www.saintmarys.edu/spiritual-life/holy-cross-education/history.

11

Reflections on Madeleva's Promise

Grappling with Discovery

Susan Mancino

Sister M. Madeleva Wolff, CSC, is celebrated as Saint Mary's College's poet-president. She regularly integrated her training and eloquence as a poet into her rhetorical style and leadership practices. This quality has imbued her words with a staying power that continues to resonate with the college community today. One regularly encounters Madeleva's words in quotes by administrators, her persona in marketing campaigns, her image visually depicted, and her name on a campus building; her legacy maintains organizational power. Discursive engagements with organizational communication inform an institution's culture, identity, decision-making, and coordination; this perspective specifically examines where and how power is (re)produced. Inspired by the poststructuralist work of Michel Foucault, organizational communication occurs through capital-*D* Discourses (formalized communication in official institutional policies and by organizational leaders) and lower-case-*d* discourses (the language used in the daily interactions of organizational constituents).[1] In other words, how an organization communicates results in material and symbolic consequences that coordinate daily life for its constituents and surrounding communities.

Discursive communication's critical lens calls for examining sources of power to understand how organizational knowledge is constructed, represented, and controlled. Within the context of Saint Mary's College, Madeleva's discursive legacy is a prime site for analysis. In this essay, I turn to Madeleva's well-known promise of discovery from her 1939 address: "We promise you discovery, the discovery of yourselves, the discovery of the universe, and your place in it."[2] These words are commonplace on campus with a specific presence in the college's formal Discourse. Madeleva's promise has been printed on a T-shirt included in the student welcome packet for several years, appeared on the cover of the twelfth Presidential Search Profile,[3] and referenced in online donor-relations and -appreciation videos.[4] More broadly, metaphors of discovery guide summaries of student and faculty research[5] and directives for student discernment.[6] The Mission Division's website describes the promise of discovery as more than "a marketing tagline."[7] Anecdotally, during class discussions about Madeleva's discovery quote, students respond with quick familiarity, often sharing how her promise relates to their experiences. From its presence on a wall of the former Campus Welcome Center[8] to its use as a rationale in the college's Public Speaker Policy,[9] this quote has quiet but wide-reaching material and symbolic consequences for the college's various constituents.

"Tomorrow, and Tomorrow, and Tomorrow": Madeleva's Promise

Madeleva's address, "Tomorrow, and Tomorrow, and Tomorrow," delivered just five years into her tenure as president in 1939, appears in a collection of essays published for Saint Mary's College's centennial anniversary.[10] Despite the address's direct reference to *Macbeth* in its title and a later allusion to *Hamlet*,[11] Madeleva makes no mention of Shakespeare; rather, she discusses *The Book of Christopher Columbus*, a play written by the French poet and dramatist Paul Claudel.[12] In short, Claudel's lyrical drama positions Columbus as a spectator to his life as recorded in his diary.

Madeleva celebrates both the play and Columbus as its subject. She notes the "prophetic value" of Claudel's drama for her audience of teachers and students.[13] Her primary emphasis is the metaphor of discovery as an expression of God's will. She describes the explorer as "literally the Christ-bearer and the dove" whose "greatest and most devastating adventure was his continuing discovery of the will of God."[14] Madeleva offers unwavering support of Columbus, crediting him with expanding the reach of Christianity and Western values to North America. Her address persistently relies on a rhetoric that connects Columbus's exhibition to the will of God.

Throughout the address, Madeleva aligns Columbus's story with the lives of her students. Like her illustrations of Columbus, she describes her students as "Christ-bearers," "bearers of peace and the dove."[15] She sees their futures as quests of discovery in fulfillment of God's will.[16] Alluding to both *Macbeth* and *Hamlet*, she writes: "Tomorrow, and tomorrow, and tomorrow lie before you and your undiscovered worlds."[17] She makes use of a rhetoric of colonization, stating: "Most of all you are discoverers, in quest of your native land, which is the will of God."[18] For Madeleva, the will of God manifests in vocational expression, beyond the bounds of a career. The notion of vocation has powerful connotations ingrained with a sense of purpose and an underlying assumption of dedication. For Madeleva, a vocation has spiritual meaning that equips her students with tools to navigate a world of uncertainty.

Preparation for an uncertain world, according to Madeleva, is part of her promise of discovery. In fact, she positions her promise in opposition to happiness or security, writing:

> We will not promise you happiness. We will not wish you security. For we remember that "security is the mortal's chiefest enemy." And we know that you can be secure only when you can stand everything that can happen to you. If your school has prepared you for this, it has been a good school.[19]

Directly following this statement, which clarifies what the college will *not* guarantee, Madeleva offers her promise of discovery. She believes that true security comes from God rather than the self, a machine, or even a school. Rather, the school is tasked with providing a space for spiritual training as a means for discovery.

The often excerpted promise does not highlight this spiritual component prominently; instead, the phrasing centers discovery. Not only does the quote begin by explicitly stating, "We promise you discovery," but the subsequent amplification of this metaphor—repeated three times—advances this notion even further. Madeleva's use of Claudel's drama and the mythic legacy of Columbus contextualizes discovery as not only the focus of her promise but also her essay. In so doing, the outcomes of her promise—the self, universe, and one's situatedness within it—are overshadowed by the metaphor of discovery. However, the sentences immediately following Madeleva's assurance incrementally shift the focus. She states,

> We promise that you will find these [self, universe, and situatedness in it] marked by the Cross, that you will take possession of them in the name of the Holy Cross, our legacy and your birthright. Tomorrow, and tomorrow, and tomorrow we pray for your ultimate and complete discovery of the will of God for you. It will lead you beyond the farthest limit of happiness. For in that will is your peace.[20]

These sentences, which conclude the address, push the reader's attention beyond a principal focus on discovery, revealing that what is uncovered matters just as much as the act of discovery.

Throughout this address, Madeleva makes no reference to the colonizing and violent legacy of Columbus, perhaps unsurprisingly, since it was not prominent in dominant public memory narratives at the time. Madeleva's assessment is more in line with many Christian groups' celebration of Columbus for bringing Christianity to the "New World." This perspective positioned Columbus as not only a national hero but also one within Christian traditions. Following the formalization of Columbus Day as a federal holiday in 1968, criticism of Columbus became more prominent, countering the prevailing mythic persona.[21]

Madeleva's honorific references to discovery, inspired by Columbus, persist throughout her writings and are even the focus of one of her poems. Columbus, again characterized as "the Christ-bearer" and "the Dove," appears in a poem titled "American Twelfth Night." Here, Madeleva associates Columbus with the three wise men traveling to see the infant Jesus, marking the Feast of the Epiphany.[22] In "American Twelfth Night," Madeleva unites imagery of Christmas with notions of American patriotism—connections that are articulated in the essays that together comprise her 1961 book, *Conversations with Cassandra: Who Believes in Education?*

Conversations with Cassandra: Discovery in Education

Published in 1961 shortly after Madeleva retired from her presidency, *Conversations with Cassandra* outlines her educational philosophy. The book's dustcover identifies its aim to explore the distinctiveness of women's Catholic education attentive to the value of these specifications. Throughout the text, Madeleva revisits the metaphor of discovery alongside other persistent themes emerging in "Tomorrow, and Tomorrow, and Tomorrow," including security, vocation, and preparation for "everything that can happen to you." These themes stress underlying connections to Catholic spirituality and American patriotism in ways that affirm discovery and defense as driving forces in women's education.

Madeleva saw education generally and women's Catholic education specifically to be in need of defense. She recalls attending a meeting of the American Council on Education that explicitly placed women's colleges as the lowest priority for funding; Madeleva undoubtedly considered institutions like Saint Mary's as among "the last and the least supported" but nonetheless worthy of funding and defense.[23] Against these threats, she calls upon the persona of the Greek prophetess Cassandra, whose warnings of impending crisis and disaster during the Trojan War were left unheeded despite their accuracy.

Madeleva illustrates these issues using militant language that activates national, patriotic interests and reflects broader trends in Catholic rhetoric in the mid-twentieth century. In fact, the book's preface opens with a description of education as "militant" and the contention that any teacher of "genuine dimensions subscribes to the militancy of his [*sic*] vocation."[24] Madeleva situates the challenges facing women's Catholic education with phrasing from her earlier comments about security and preparation. She writes, "We are said to be secure when we can stand everything that can happen to us. If this is the test we are on a fair way to security in education."[25] She compared her teachers to "officers" and her students to "armies," both called to act in service rather than security.[26] Seeking expressions of defense and service, Madeleva offers Cassandra as a guide imbued with belief in education and a "natural endowment" of faith.[27]

These themes appear throughout the text alongside references to discovery. For instance, in a chapter that asks why we educate "our daughters," Madeleva yet again refers to *Hamlet* by positioning students "at the mysterious frontier of existence, the undiscovered country of her own potential womanhood."[28] Set against an "obsession" with security as a "trap of the devil," Madeleva reiterates that, in the midst of such uncertainties, "we are secure only when we can stand everything that can happen to us."[29] Madeleva emphasizes preparation tied to spiritual and theological training as a distinctive cornerstone of Catholic women's education.

She continues this point in a chapter titled "The Time Is Now," which republishes her promise and content on Claudel from "Tomorrow, and Tomorrow, and Tomorrow." In this expanded essay, Madeleva expresses concern about the machine age and a prevailing assumption that technological devices can satisfy spiritual needs. Particularly, she cautions that these presuppositions direct attention toward scientific and technological developments rather than religious practices such as prayer. Within this context, Madeleva's promise of discovery extends one's attention beyond the machine age. While still accompanied by references to Columbus and Claudel's play, Madeleva adds reflections associating discovery with spiritual exploration. In this text, the lines directly following her promise read: "With these unguessed, untried potencies you begin your lifetime enterprise of exploration into God. Affairs are now and always, for you, soul-size."[30] Although Madeleva repeats her promise of discovery verbatim, her concerns with the machine age emphasize a spiritual need to explore God's world set against the technocratic impulses of the machine age.

In line with this discussion, Madeleva relies on a metaphor of discovery for the space age. She conceptualizes of college as "a space world for a space age."[31] She views space exploration as a defining historical moment of her students' lives. She again compares them to Columbus with a "destiny" of discovery, but this time cautions of the temptations of "greed and exploitation" that so often accompany moments of exploration and expansion.[32] She anticipates that the space age will change the question "How far can we go?" into "Where shall we stop?"[33] She references explorations into the sky and the sea, offering an invitation to wonder that might counterbalance her promise of discovery. This time referring to a poem by William Davies, Madeleva writes, "I invite you to a life of wonder, a life of thinking, a life in which often and often we will take time to stand and stare."[34] This invitation to wonder can inform her promise of discovery, especially when placed within her reflections on poetry.

Madeleva aligns the contemplative life with a poetic attentiveness that enlivens creativity and spirituality. Madeleva conceptualizes "supernatural contemplation" as "our vocation as persons."[35] This perspective is informed by the philosophical work of her friend and correspondent Jacques Maritan. Here, the metaphor of discovery resurfaces as she contends that supernatural contemplation yields discovery in need of poetic translation through "the language of beauty."[36] Madeleva associates the work of the poet with that of an "artist" and the philosopher with "discoverer," where the poet creates beauty and the philosopher defines truth. For Madeleva, art and philosophy are deeply related; she writes, "The poet is the architect of the house of words in which truth may dwell."[37] Her promise of discovery directs students' engagement with spirituality, contemplation, and poetry in search of God's truth.

Throughout *Conversations with Cassandra*, Madeleva broadly contextualizes her educational philosophy, providing important insights that give meaning to her promise of discovery. For instance, she contends that colleges offer spaces of hope—of *spes unica*, the motto for the Congregation of Holy Cross and for Saint Mary's College.[38] Madeleva describes the college experience as an act of making, of personal creation emerging as a byproduct of every class and every teacher. For Madeleva, this training helps students recognize their likeness to God as the "prime poet."[39] Simultaneously, she describes how institutions like Saint Mary's instill notions of womanhood, largely defined by motherhood. In fact, she suggests that in pursuing women's education, a student chooses "to be educated as women with an existential major and minor in womanhood"[40] and later explicitly states that her students' "vocation is motherhood."[41] This perception, despite the limitations and pressures that it pressed upon her students, was a longstanding assumption of the college prior to and during Madeleva's presidency. Alongside this assessment, she was a strong advocate for educational opportunities for women generally and women religious specifically. This commitment led to the School of Sacred Theology at Saint Mary's College, which expanded opportunities for theological study for women and other lay people.[42]

Behind this work was Madeleva's concern for teacher education during a time when Saint Mary's relied most heavily upon the Sisters of the Holy Cross for its faculty—a theme she also addresses in *Conversations with Cassandra*. Madeleva recognizes that teachers require not only "skills and technics" but also education "in the great world of ideas and ideals, the abiding values of life."[43] For Madeleva, this meant that teachers must be developed as persons, not just as teachers. She suggests that such an education can "begin very simply with wild flowers, birds, trees."[44] Madeleva shares a personal experience riding a train across the Northern Rockies when she observed a bald eagle sweep across the landscape and land on a pine tree; she writes:

> Perhaps no one in all the world saw this lone king on his stark throne except myself. Perhaps I have no sense of values. But for me this is one of the great moments of my life, one with which Bestor, or Highet, or Livingstone cannot compete. We find our great teachers and our great lessons everywhere, even from a train window.[45]

Beyond what could be gained from reading or formal training, Madeleva positions experiences in nature as an illustration of God's creation that develops teachers as persons. She describes moments such these as a "richer, more unforgettable experience than one finds in libraries or professional books on education."[46] This sense of nature's role in personal development perhaps lies at the intersection of Madeleva's reflections on education, her invitation to wonder, and her promise of discovery.

Final Reflections

As I reflect upon Madeleva's writings on discovery and education, the derivative nature of her promise emerges most prominently. When she speaks of discovering the self, the universe, and one's place in it, her reference is not to a hypermodern, individualistic, or self-sovereign notion of *my* self, *my* world, or *my* will. Instead, Madeleva understood that all of these belong to God—she promises the discovery of God's world, of a self created by and in the image of God, and of a life comprised of talents, gifts, and purpose coming from and directed by the will of God. Madeleva's faith was a cornerstone of her writing and surfaces as one of the most (if not the most) significant theme across her poetry, scholarship, and public addresses. Separating this context from interpretations of her work misses a key aspect of her writing.

Madeleva believed that a broad liberal arts education helps to reach this goal. She offered several essays advocating for the practical value of theology, literature, and poetry. She advocated for ongoing formation and development for instructors as an enduring educational value. Specifically, she describes poetry's ability to translate discoveries so they can be made meaningful and shared with others. She contends that poetry "is seeing things from God's point of view."[47] Madeleva saw poetry as a form of prayer that attends to the interplay between the self and God's world. Poetry's perspective-altering abilities allow it to translate discovery and demonstrate the derivative nature of her promise.

For Madeleva, the notions of self, universe, and one's placement within it are what is to be discovered from Catholic higher education. Unlike the machine age that sought a sense of certainty, omnipotence, and omnipresence, Madeleva's educational promise was aimed toward satisfying spiritual needs while forgoing what she saw as society's obsession with security and happiness, which she explicitly excluded from her guarantee. Instead, she offered and later reiterated connections between discovery and a sense of preparation. For Madeleva, any true sense of security and certainty came from God and spirituality offered a path for preparation. Madeleva's goal for a Saint Mary's College education was for students to understand these distinctions.

The derivative nature of Madeleva's promise becomes clear as themes of spirituality, faith, and supernatural contemplation persist. These components were central to her educational philosophy as well as her reflections on aesthetics and nature.[48] Underlying connections to discovery are likewise present throughout these discussions, as illustrated in *Conversations with Cassandra* and *Addressed to Youth*. Although the excerpted quote emphasizes discovery so prominently, it fails to capture Madeleva's broader focus. Organizational discourses empower discovery as an institutional value, but perhaps this framing is too narrow as it overshadows the focus on self, universe, and one's placement within it. Undoubtedly, discovery was a paramount good for Madeleva but so too are the byproducts of her promise. Critical considerations of Madeleva's promise acknowledge the limitations and deficiencies of discovery while opening space to explore the byproducts of her guarantee. In examining self, universe, and one's place in it, broader conceptions of Madeleva's view of education and its relationship to spirituality come to the forefront. Grappling with discovery repositions the focus of her promise and continues discussions about the value and outcomes of a Saint Mary's

College education. As part of this consideration, ongoing conversation can uncover the relationships between discovery and other discursive outlets for organizational identity. As organizational members answer these questions, they discursively constitute its identity, culture, decision-making, and coordination. Questioning D/discourses facilitates reflexive engagements that empower organizational members to activate answers to who Saint Mary's College is, how it meets the world's most urgent needs, and what is its relationship to broader communities. Participating in these discursive engagements will contribute to organizational life at Saint Mary's College within and beyond Madeleva's promise of discovery.

Discovery is an undoubtable site of organizational power at the college. This Discourse is far reaching, cutting across all constituent groups; not only do discursive descriptions of discovery guide administrative rhetoric, marketing campaigns, and college policies, but also every incoming student, at least for the past several years, has been welcomed with a shirt bearing this promise. Contemporary Discourse about this quote reproduces organizational power and knowledge stemming from Madeleva's vision of a Saint Mary's education. Broader contextualization of this promise quickly reveals an explicit connection between the metaphor of discovery and the legacy of Christopher Columbus. The destructive consequences of Columbus's colonizing actions, although not prominent in public memory narratives at Madeleva's time, produce concern and caution. Grappling with this legacy, however, can guide the college's discursive practices about Madeleva's promise within and beyond discovery's limitations and deficiencies.

The implications of this pervasive organizational good are not value neutral. Discovery is in need of further examination. The metaphor of discovery, particularly when inspired by Columbus, carries forth underlying ties to colonization; Discourse that reproduces this site of power requires critical engagement. Not only do discursive communication strategies produce more thoughtful institutions, but they also give voice to members as they constitute organizational identity and culture. Furthermore, discursive engagement that situates Madeleva's promise within the broader scope of her writing will guide critical consideration of its implications for the college today.

Notes

1. See François Cooren, *Organizational Discourse: Communication and Constitution* (Cambridge: Polity, 2015); Mats Alvesson and Dan Kärreman, "Varieties of Discourse: On the Study of Organizations through Discourse Analysis," *Human Relations* 53, no. 9 (2000): 1125–49, https://doi.org/ 10.1177/0018726700539002.

2. Sister M. Madeleva, *Addressed to Youth* (Paterson, NJ: St. Anthony Guild Press, 1944), 44.

3. Saint Mary's College, "Presidential Search Profile" (Notre Dame, IN: Saint Mary's College, 2015), https://www.saintmarys.edu/files/Saint-Marys-Presidential-Profile.pdf.

4. For example, see "How is Saint Mary's keeping Sister Madeleva's 'promise of discovery' today?," Saint Mary's College, moderated by Gail Porter Mandell, recorded panel, 2012, https://www.saintmarys.edu/giving/donor-appreciation/video-highlights.

5. For examples, see "When Discovery Meets Innovation," Saint Mary's College, accessed July 14, 2024, https://www.saintmarys.edu/news/when-discovery-meets-innovation-and-stem, and "Research and Discovery in the Sciences and the Arts," Saint Mary's College, accessed July 14, 2024, https://www.saintmarys.edu/discovery-in-sciences-and-arts.

6. "Use This Time to Explore," Saint Mary's College, accessed July 14, 2024, https://www.saintmarys.edu/explore-your-options.

7. "Mission," Saint Mary's College, accessed July 14, 2024, https://www.saintmarys.edu/spiritual-life/holy-cross-education/mission.

8. This building is currently being renovated to welcome guests to the Heritage and Research Center for the archival collections of nine women's religious congregations, including the Sisters of the Holy Cross.

9. "Public Speaker Policy," Saint Mary's College, accessed July 14, 2024, https://www.saintmarys.edu/public-speaker-policy.

10. Madeleva, *Addressed to Youth*.

11. William Shakespeare, *Macbeth*, ed. David Bevington and David Scott Kastan (New York: Bantam Classic, 2005), 5.5.16–27; *Hamlet, Prince of Denmark*, ed. David Bevington and David Scott Kastan (New York: Bantam Classic, 2005), 3.1.78–83.

12. Paul Claudel, *The Book of Christopher Columbus* (New Haven, CT: Yale University Press, 1930).

13. Madeleva, *Addressed to Youth*, 42.

14. Madeleva, *Addressed to Youth*, 42.

15. Madeleva, *Addressed to Youth*, 43.

16. Madeleva, *Addressed to Youth*, 43.

17. Madeleva, *Addressed to Youth*, 43.

18. Madeleva, *Addressed to Youth*, 43.

19. Madeleva, *Addressed to Youth*, 43–44.

20. Madeleva, *Addressed to Youth*, 44.

21. Amy Corning and Howard Schuman, *Generations and Collective Memory* (Chicago: University of Chicago Press, 2015); Howard Schuman, Barry Schwartz, and Hannah D'Arcy, "Elite Revisionists and Popular Beliefs: Christopher Columbus, Hero or Villain?," *Public Opinion Quarterly* 69, no. 1 (2005): 2–29, https://doi.org/10.1093/poq/nfi001.

22. Sister M. Madeleva Wolff, CSC, *American Twelfth Night and Other Poems* (New York: Macmillan, 1955), xix.

23. Sister M. Madeleva Wolff, CSC, *Conversations with Cassandra: Who Believes in Education?* (New York: McMillan, 1955), 52.

24. Madeleva, *Conversations with Cassandra*, vii.

25. Madeleva, *Conversations with Cassandra*, vii.

26. Madeleva, *Conversations with Cassandra*, viii.

27. Madeleva, *Conversations with Cassandra*, vii–viii.

28. Madeleva, *Conversations with Cassandra*, 19.

29. Madeleva, *Conversations with Cassandra*, 19.

30. Madeleva, *Conversations with Cassandra*, 38.

31. Madeleva, *Conversations with Cassandra*, 10.

32. Madeleva, *Conversations with Cassandra*, 84, 92.

33. Madeleva, *Conversations with Cassandra*, 93.

34. Madeleva, *Conversations with Cassandra*, 95.

35. Madeleva, *Conversations with Cassandra*, 45.

36. Madeleva, *Conversations with Cassandra*, 46.

37. Madeleva, *Conversations with Cassandra*, 46.

38. Madeleva, *Conversations with Cassandra*, 14. The motto of the Congregations of Holy Cross (including its Sisters, Brothers, and Priests) is *Ave Crux Spes Unica* (Hail to the Cross, Our Only Hope). Saint Mary's College associates the challenge of education with the transformative power of hope through its motto, *Spes Unica* (Our Only Hope).

For more information on the motto, see "Meaning of Spes Unica," Saint Mary's College, accessed January 14, 2025, https://www.saintmarys.edu/meaning-of-spes-unica.

39. Madeleva, *Conversations with Cassandra*, 41–42.
40. Madeleva, *Conversations with Cassandra*, 49.
41. Madeleva, *Conversations with Cassandra*, 63.
42. See Sandra Yocum's chapter in this volume.
43. Madeleva, *Conversations with Cassandra*, 98.
44. Madeleva, *Conversations with Cassandra*, 104.
45. Madeleva, *Conversations with Cassandra*, 107.
46. Madeleva, *Conversations with Cassandra*, 104.
47. Madeleva, *Conversations with Cassandra*, 95.
48. See this volume's chapters by Molly Gower and Sally Geisler.

12

Madeleva's Legacy in the Landscape

Sally Geislar

"Let me teach you to wonder."[1] In 1956, Sister Madeleva Wolff, CSC, extended this invitation to students gathered for the school year's first convocation at Saint Mary's College, where she served as president. These words so stirred a young first-year student, Marilyn Kraemer Kiep, that she would include them years later in a collection of alumnae memories to honor the late leader. Whereas "wonder" often represents a naive quality, Madeleva revered a sense of wonder as something to be valued, preserved, and even taught. Wonder toward nature featured prominently in Madeleva's life: through her own engagement with the natural world, with the divine; through her pedagogy; and through her curation of the college grounds.

In this chapter, I consider the curation of wonder among Madeleva's many legacies in the landscape at Saint Mary's College. Beyond mere aesthetic appreciation or provincial import, Madeleva's vision for the landscape conjured wonder as a virtue, echoing that of her contemporary nature writers. Moreover, her engagement with the natural world anticipated modern place-based pedagogies, among others. Here, I explore how Madeleva evolved in her regard for nature as an epistemic object to regarding it as a site for reflection, as the embodiment of the divine spirit, and as a canvas for her own creation to "honor the Creator."

What Is a Legacy?

To understand Madeleva's legacy, I first ground a conceptualization of legacy in the extant literature. Diverse fields have sought to define *legacy*, including scholars of postcommunism, aging, and those examining "mega-events" such as the Olympics. While debate remains over how to measure a legacy and establish its causality,[2] a shared language emerges even across such diverse disciplines. In studying postcommunist Europe, Jason Wittenberg defines legacies as the persistence of a phenomenon or order.[3] Similarly, Jacques Rogge, the president of the International Olympic Committee, referred to the legacy of the games in their host cities as the "lasting outcomes of our efforts."[4] Others clarify the legacy of mega-events as outcomes that affect people and/or space."[5] In aging studies, legacy is understood as a "meaningful… continued existence…after death."[6]

Further, both the aging and mega-events literature consider the "story" as constitutive of legacy. For one to have a legacy, it is not enough to cause a lasting change in the world; the story of your efforts must survive alongside the outputs of those efforts. At the human scale, people want to be remembered and to shape how they are remembered.[7] Mega-events are similarly concerned with image maintenance regarding how host communities remember the impacts of the games. By telling and retelling the story of the actor's efforts, the lasting outputs thereof become part of their legacy. For my purposes then, a legacy is not only the lasting outcomes of an actor's efforts but also the story that connects the actor to those outputs. In the absence of such a story, an heirloom walking stick[8] becomes just another useful, lonely object waiting by the door. Likewise, if the story of the campus grounds omits Madeleva's efforts in shaping them, her legacy in the landscape will have been forgotten even as the sycamores still shade your way.

Before recounting the story of Madeleva's legacy in the landscape, I present a typology of legacies that I adopt from the aging literature to help frame our understanding of the lasting outputs of Madeleva's efforts. Elizabeth Hunter and Graham Rowles developed a typology using a grounded theory approach to analyze interviews with participants near death. Three "distinct but overlapping" themes emerged in how people understood their own legacies: biological, material, and values-based.[9]

Biological legacies referred to passing on respondents' genetic traits or biological matter. In the current essay, biological legacies will pertain to cultivated biological communities rather than a genetic inheritance.

Material legacies include heirlooms, possessions, and symbols. While heirlooms are objects imbued with an "explicit obligation for both the giver and the recipient," possessions are passed on for their usefulness but "do not carry the responsibility associated with an heirloom."[10] Symbols are the third type of material legacies and pertain to "the transmission of the self through the creation of a lasting, public testament to one's existence."[11] While symbols might seem incongruent with a materially centered theme, its focus is on the physical object that represents or honors the deceased as in a statue of the honoree or a building in their name.

Finally, one's values were also seen as being transmitted beyond death. Interviewees discussed the importance of value transmission at both the personal and social levels. On the one hand, respondents hoped to pass on their personal values, such as in education or in being unique. Others emphasized a commitment to social justice and a social responsibility to the community.

In the next section, I explore Madeleva's regard for the natural world, her efforts to beautify the grounds of Saint Mary's College, and how her works persist. I then use Hunter and Rowles's typology to understand different dimensions of Madeleva's legacy in the landscape.

Nature's Teachings

To understand Madeleva's legacy in cultivating the landscape of Saint Mary's College, it is instructive to explore how she regarded natural beauty during her life. Through biographical and autobiographical texts, her poetry, archival materials, and interviews with those who worked to beautify the grounds, we see that Madeleva regarded the natural world as an object to be known, a site for reflection, a teacher, and as revelatory of the divine.

In her extensive biographical work on Madeleva's life, Gail Porter Mandell conjures an image of young Eva Wolff growing up in rural, Northern Wisconsin. On long Sunday rides by horse and carriage, she and her siblings learned to identify the plants around them. Madeleva writes in her autobiography that she "tended her mother's asparagus bed and strawberry patch and…knew and marked the seasons accurately. We watched the continuing mystery of creation."[12] She not only knew the plants and seasons but learned to "see beauty in the woods and wildflowers and to listen for the music in the cries of orioles and deer."[13] From a young age, Madeleva was curating a knowledge about and appreciation for nature.

Madeleva's engagement with the natural world would take a contemplative form while serving as president of St. Mary of the Wasatch near Ogden, Utah. In her autobiography, she paints a stunning picture of the last glowing embers of the day gradually growing dim behind the Wasatch range and the moon's nightly journey. "While watching this phenomenon of magnitude and splendor, we caught something of our own dizzy daily journeyings around and around."[14] Observations of the natural world were no longer merely informative, but a mirror through which to reflect on our own "dizzy daily journeyings."

In her time at the Wasatch, Madeleva would extend this contemplative regard for nature to her students. Each summer during what Madeleva would revere as the "happiest years of her life,"[15] she would take students to one of the great parks of the West. "What an exchange of campus, classrooms and books! Yellowstone, the very fulfillment of Scriptural text: Wisdom playing in the world…we found ourselves at school in the original and best sense of the word: at leisure to learn and to be taught."[16] Nature is both a place of learning and itself a teacher, if one is attentive to its teachings. Still, important differences emerge in this transition from recognizing plants to grasping a deeper sort of knowledge about the universe and our place in it.

For Madeleva, the natural world was not only a site for reflection and a teacher but was revelatory of God. It was an invitation to the divine and immanent thereof. The idea that beauty reveals God's presence was a regular refrain throughout her poetry and autobiography. Madeleva wrote that "of the trinity—goodness, truth, and beauty, each an equation for God—beauty is the most palpable, the most irresistible."[17] In her later writings, Mandell argues that, more than revealing the existence of God or calling to communion through its "irresistibility," the Spirit was immanent in the very materiality of the natural world. Mandell draws on an excerpt from "Mirrors" to demonstrate.[18] "Can I not find you in all the winds that blow, / In the wild loneliness of lark and plover, / In slender shadow trees upon the snow?"[19] The wind is not merely revelatory of God's existence, it is *of* God; the lark, the plover and the trees' own shadow are more than messengers, they are the message.

Finally, Madeleva became a creator of beauty herself. Mandell recounts Madeleva's drive to create beauty on the grounds after her parents died. Madeleva would refer to her work as an "apostolate of Beauty."[20] She increasingly understood her work in "build[ing] a home for beauty"[21] as sacred, imitating God's creation as a form of honoring the creator.[22] Indeed, Madeleva wanted not only to curate beauty as a gift to "beauty's giver," but to inspire her students as well.

> I even want students who know trees by their first names, who love them better in winter than in summer....I should like them to watch for the unfurling of oak leaves in dubious greens, coral pinks and creams, delicate as the details of some old French tapestries; beech buds unfolding like small, perfect fans in the sun. I want them...to open their arms, their eyes, their lives wide to the universe, to understand palpably that "Underneath are the everlasting arms."[23]

Madeleva understood that curating beauty in the landscape and curating certain kinds of knowledge were intertwined projects. "God's visibility" was also an invitation to know God as manifest in nature (for example, in the unfurling of oak leaves) and an invitation to God's love (that is, the everlasting arms).

Giving Beauty Back

When Madeleva was abruptly called to serve as president of Saint Mary's College, she took on the unusual responsibility of beautifying the grounds. "Madeleva concerned herself with landscaping as well as with curriculum; from her travels, she brought home seeds and cuttings and planted them herself."[24] While the college had been in its location for decades by the time Madeleva returned to her alma mater as its leader, it was very much still a place among the plains. Even the grandest of buildings at the time, Le Mans Hall and Haggar College, were surrounded by farm fields on three sides with few trees dotting the landscape. Lake Marion's island, now a centerpiece of beauty adorned with towering beeches and draped in sweeping willow boughs, was all but denuded save for a manicured hedge on the perimeter.

Yet Madeleva was not working on a blank canvas. Indeed, one of the founding directors of the college, Mother Angela Gillespie, worked with her stepfather, William Phelan, to plant some of the first trees on the grounds. Having facilitated the relocation of the college from its original site in Bertrand, Michigan in 1855, Mother Angela planted many of the now revered maples and sycamores lining the Avenue that inspired Madeleva's poem "Old Soldiers." Lesser-known trees also carried a deeper history. In the June 1913 *Chimes*, Mrs. Ella Ewing Brown, an alumna of the class of 1870, remarked,

> More than 100 years ago, a willow slip was planted and grew in the town of Lancaster, Ohio…at the doorstep of her home by a young bride, who had carried it…from her father's house in Western Pennsylvania.…Thirty or forty years later, a slip from it was planted beside the grave of another daughter.… From [her great-grand aunt's] tree, at the request of Mother Angela, a slip was cut and sent to her.…that self-same slip, now a magnificent tree, is the pride and beauty of St. Mary's.[25]

So began a tradition carried on by Madeleva and others of multigenerational seedling transplanting on the grounds.

Just fifteen years later, an article in the *Courier* announced the formation of the Joyce Kilmer Club, named after the poet famed for his ode to trees. The club's president, Rose McCollough Sullivan, indicated that one need only buy a tree to become a member, beseeching her peers and alumnae that "Alma Mater does not need our poems—which possibly is fortunate for her—but she does need the trees."[26] An optional memorial was offered with the tree planting, though record of such memorials has yet to emerge among the college archives.

After decades of curating the college's landscape, smuggling seedlings from her journeys, and planting them on her own time, Madeleva found a partner in manifesting her vision of beauty on the grounds. In 1954, she hired Joe Bonadies, a formally trained horticulturist and master gardener. Bonadies said that when he arrived, the campus was very much an unfinished project.[27] With no landscaping budget, Bonadies grew all flowers on the grounds from seed and cuttings in the college greenhouse.[28]

Bonadies proved himself a ready comrade. "Wherever I went, I stole cuttings. One day I went over to Potawatomi Park. I had my knife with me. I knew the guy in charge. I was halfway through the greenhouse when he said, 'Help yourself Joe.' I never told him I already had two pockets full."[29] Madeleva continued to return with seedlings as well. After a trip to Boston in the 1950s, she brought Bonadies a set of beech seedlings which are now great trees on the west side of Lake Marion, just north of the bridge. These same trees sprouted seedlings of their own, which now stand just north of Spes Unica Hall.[30] So continues the tradition of multigenerational seedling transplanting.

Together, Madeleva and Bonadies worked with a mostly shared vision, though apparently, they had their disagreements. Bonadies revealed that "[s]he'd introduce me this way: 'we don't agree on everything, but we're friends.'"[31] Mark Kubacki, the current director of grounds, recounted three key values that continue to inform decisions on the grounds today.[32] Long before the narrative of native plants took hold in western landscaping, Madeleva and Bonadies knew that putting the right plants in the right place reduced their maintenance. Here, they considered both regional acclimation and the social uses of the space. Second, at a time when campuses around the country looked like a cordoned off English garden—untouchable, immaculately manicured—the two wanted the campus to look as natural as possible. Bonadies would boast that "the wild look is no accident."[33] Finally, they wanted the students to feel at home on the grounds; students should walk on and lie on the grass and even pick the flowers.[34]

Madeleva's favorite trees would soon populate the campus; American beech around Lake Marion, and pin oaks and sycamores on the south and east sides of campus. But Madeleva and Bonadies also sought trees that would ignite the senses and adorn the campus with blooms for special occasions: hemlocks to touch and Douglas firs to smell. In late spring, the dogwood, crabapple, and viburnum blooms would greet the graduates and their families, though Kubacki indicated that the blooms have already started arriving sooner with the warming climate.[35]

The beautification of the grounds is never really a finished project. But it is one to which Madeleva dedicated some of her precious final years. While she lamented in her autobiography that she daily "bur[ies] so many deceased projects, so much of what I have had to let die and must bury without regret,"[36] the work of beautification would not die. Instead, it would continue to grow and change. So, while other unfinished projects she let go without regret, she held onto this work with some longing. In the last paragraph of her autobiography, Madeleva shares her few remaining desires in this life. Among them, she still has another book or two she would like to write, some songs she would like to chew on, and she wrote, "I should like to watch my seedling oaks and beeches grow into great trees."[37] Indeed, they have.

Persistence

In the time since Madeleva's passing, a remarkable continuity of vision has unfolded. Joe Bonadies served as the first grounds director and hired his only successor to date, Mark Kubacki, in 1975. Few colleges can boast only two grounds directors across seventy years. One can trace a direct line from the significant changes to the grounds during that time to Madeleva's early works and regard for nature. Bonadies completed the rock garden to the west of Lake Marion in the late 1980s as a place of respite, inviting contemplation. The two-mile-long nature trail completed in 1970 facilitates both education and enjoyment of natural beauty.[38] More recently, the sustainable farm has grown into a vibrant space for learning, camaraderie, and connecting with nature.

Toward the end of her tenure as president, Madeleva initiated a new tradition of dedicating trees. While there is some evidence of tree dedication as early as the late 1920s, the earliest documented dedications are two oaks planted on the south side of Le Mans Hall by Sister Madeleva herself in 1959. The first, a burr oak, was to her friend and colleague Sister Maria Pieta, and the second, a pin oak, was to commemorate her own twenty-fifth year as president and fiftieth year as alumna. She held the planting ceremony on her birthday for full effect. Nearly twenty years passed before then President Duggan formalized a tree dedication program. In May 1977, Duggan wrote a letter to Bonadies that they ought to "develop a policy of planting Memorial trees in honor of deceased individuals who have made significant contributions to the College."[39] The next summer, the inaugural tree dedication honored the Golden Jubilee of the class of 1928.[40] It is only fitting that this is the same cohort that initiated the Joyce Kilmer Club.

After its formalization, a flurry of dedications in the 1980s and 90s grew the program from a few dozen to more than six hundred dedicated trees representing more than fifty species. Each of these trees has come to represent a person connected to the college in some way. Many are staff, faculty, and alumnae or members of their families. Some are entire classes, departments, or in one case, Justice. Addie Cashore, who graduated from the college in 1970, began managing the dedicated tree program in the Development office in 1998. In a recent interview, she explained that in part, it appealed to donors to "make a tangible contribution to the campus."[41] More than that was the deep symbolism the dedicated trees carried. In her view, the trees were "a way that the person lives on."[42] Cashore showed her mettle and compassion in assisting with tearful ceremonies and regular returns to the trees, especially over reunion weekend. "I can't tell you how much it means to people. It's part of the grieving process."[43]

Over the past two years, the dedicated trees have also served as the basis for place-based pedagogy and research. Dr. Susan Mancino and I have led the Campus Canopy Consortium, a collection of faculty-student research teams from multiple disciplines. We engage with the grounds and the dedicated trees as a living laboratory to apply knowledge gained in the classroom. In the first project, I worked with a student to map the environmental benefits of the dedicated trees using iTreeEco, a tool from the USDA. We geocoded each tree to create the foundation for a dynamic, interactive map that could integrate future projects in the consortium. Next, Dr. Mancino's team used oral history and archival methods to tell the stories of the honorees. In another project, Dr. Joel Ralston led a team using ornithological methods to map the birdsong soundscape across different campus land uses (such as nature area, sustainable farm, main campus). In a nascent project, Dr. Marelys Valencia will guide Spanish heritage speakers in developing their own multilingual ecopoetry in which students will express their own relationship to the natural world and their place in it. Each of these projects will become "layers" on the interactive map, showcasing the multidimensional relationship between humans and their environment.

Recently, the Sisters of the Holy Cross and the college began the process of establishing our shared grounds as the region's first arboretum. In addition to aligning with our goals of teaching, research, and connecting with the community, an arboretum also honors the vision of Madeleva and the dedicated staff who have carried out her vision over the last seventy years. The fertile ground for inquiry, discovery, and reflection that Madeleva cultivated continues to bear fruit through the development of the campus grounds as a place for new questions to be explored and new ideas to take root.

Legacy in the Landscape

In telling Madeleva's story, we can better connect the lasting outcomes of her efforts to the many dimensions of her legacy. First, I extend Hunter and Rowles's biological legacy[44] to the biological communities that persist from Madeleva's efforts. Madeleva's seedlings have grown into great trees, as have their seedlings. The curation of human-designed and natural green spaces and the more-than-human creatures that are helped or hindered by their management represent Madeleva's biological legacy. This legacy bestows countless and sometimes hidden benefits. The maturation of the trees better sequesters carbon, filters water, and saves energy (for example, when shading the southern side of buildings). The trees and the broader green spaces also provide social (that is, memorialization) and physical health benefits.

Madeleva's material legacy is rich in heirlooms and symbols. The beautification of the landscape is not merely useful to the recipients but also comes with an "explicit obligation" to each subsequent generation. As such, the landscape represents an heirloom of sorts. The care for this heirloom is both formal as in the grounds director's charge, and informal as in the sense of responsibility with which some alumnae, staff, and faculty regard the grounds. Indeed, by dedicating trees over the decades, new generations have, in effect, indicated their interest in continuing the project of beautifying the grounds and preserving the meaning that their dedications imbue in the landscape.

Symbolic legacies are those "lasting public testaments to one's existence." No doubt that this edited volume is but a thread in the tapestry of Madeleva's symbolic legacy. Indeed, a tree and a building both bear her name. However, insofar as Addie Cashore's perception is right, that most alumnae and others do not fully grasp Madeleva's role in beautifying the grounds,[45] Madeleva's symbolic legacy of the campus landscape has not yet been woven. If the arboretum effort is successful, whether adorned with Madeleva's name or not, the story of her efforts would be better preserved, thereby constituting the grounds as part of her legacy. Moreover, the symbolic legacy that each dedicated tree represents for the honorees would be better preserved.

The final type of legacy is values-based. As a groundbreaking and revered leader of a college for thirty years, Madeleva communicated her values, both personal and social, in a multitude of venues. As her regard for the natural world and the cultivation of the grounds blossomed, some values were made explicit, others can only be inferred. Some of the most enduring values evident in the landscape were made explicit by both Madeleva and Bonadies: to create a campus with plants in the right place with a natural or even wild feel where students feel at home.

Among Madeleva's values in the landscape that we can only infer are those related to knowledge and wonder. In many ways, Madeleva's engagement with nature as a site for learning and nature itself as a teacher anticipated Western pedagogies of place-based learning[46] while echoing this long-standing tradition in indigenous communities. Since Madeleva's passing, several developments on the grounds reflect these values: the nature trail, the sustainable farm, the Campus Canopy Consortium, and the hoped-for arboretum. Each provides for learning in, about, and from the place in which the students and educators are.[47] Embodying Madeleva's regard for nature as revelatory and even immanent of God, the places of quiet beauty for contemplation and reflection offer the attentive an opportunity for wonder and awe. Places such as Bonadies's rock garden, the nature trail, or the gardens around Reidinger House offer spaces in which the community can pause from the frenetic pulse of modern life.

It's fitting that opportunities for wonder should abound in a landscape tended by Madeleva's sure hand. Still, wonder as a value may seem contradictory to the purpose of a college. Where one might argue that formal education is the pursuit of knowledge, wonder seems to stand in blissful, childlike ignorance by contrast. However, I argue that Madeleva saw wonder and the pursuit of knowledge as intertwined, and that each carries an innate value. In the summer before Madeleva promised to teach her willing students how to wonder, Rachel Carson published an essay extolling its value. In *The Sense of Wonder*, Carson not only encourages adults to preserve children's innate sense of wonder, she argues that wisdom needs wonder. Carson writes, "Once emotions have been aroused—a sense of the beautiful, the excitement of the new and unknown, a feeling of sympathy, pity, or love—then we wish for knowledge about the object of our emotional response."[48] Indeed, Madeleva demonstrated that this relationship is cyclical in nature; as one learns more about something, there emerge new opportunities to love and wonder at it.

But why should students need to be taught to wonder given Carson's account that the young have a "true instinct"[49] for it? Just as Carson's audience was adult parents who had lost their sense of wonder, Madeleva knew that for many arriving on campus, the joy and awe of the world may have already dimmed. Indeed, there is likely a greater need among today's students to rediscover a sense of wonder. As tangible and visible as beauty may be among the trinity, in the modern world of infinite distractions at one's fingertips, the beauty of the natural world, especially in the place where you are, may remain invisible to the inattentive. In her writings, Madeleva was enamored, not by distant Instagrammable places of world renown, but by the places in which she dwelled. The plants and animals and even the moon's passage were known in their place. What wonders she uncovered simply by being attentive to where she was? How lost is the practice and spontaneity of wonder if our attention is stolen away from where we are?

Importantly, Madeleva conceives of wonder not only as something to be retained through childhood or "rediscovered" in adulthood, as Carson puts it, but as something that could and should be taught. That something should be taught indicates not only that it has value, but also that it can be improved upon in oneself. Wonder becomes a practice, a skill, a means, and an end. For Carson, "those who dwell among the beauty and mysteries of the earth are never alone or weary of life…[they are] able to find inner contentment and renewed excitement for living."[50] Madeleva, as though harmonizing with Carson's vision, wanted students to know the names of trees, to love all forms of their beauty, and to "understand palpably that 'Underneath are the everlasting arms.'"[51]

Notes

1. Center for Spirituality, *Alumnae Memories of Sister M. Madeleva Wolff '09, CSC (1887–1964)* (Notre Dame, IN: Saint Mary's College, 2014), 22.

2. Jody LaPorte and Danielle N. Lussier, "What Is the Leninist Legacy? Assessing Twenty Years of Scholarship," *Slavic Review* 70, no. 3 (2011): 641–42, https://doi.org/10.5612/slavicreview.70.3.0637.

3. Jason Wittenberg, "What Is a Historical Legacy?," *American Political Science Association Annual Meeting* (2013), 18, https://ssrn.com/abstract=2303391.

4. Richard Cashman and John Horne, "Managing Legacy," in *Managing the Olympics*, ed. Stephen Frawley and Daryl Adair (London: Palgrave Macmillan, 2013), 54, https://doi.org/10.1057/9780230389588_4.

5. Holger Preuss, "Event Legacy Framework and Measurement," *International Journal of Sport Policy and Politics* 11, no. 1 (2019): 106, https://doi.org/10.1080/19406940.2018.1490336.

6. Elizabeth G. Hunter and Graham D. Rowles, "Leaving a Legacy: Toward a Typology," *Journal of Aging Studies* 19 (2005): 328, http://dx.doi.org/10.1016/j.jaging.2004.08.002.

7. Hunter and Rowles, "Leaving a Legacy," 330–31.

8. On Madeleva's many journeys, she collected walking sticks that are now preserved in the college archives. Each president of Saint Mary's College now chooses one to lead the college's annual commencement and shares Madeleva's story as part of the ceremony. See "Sister Madeleva's Walking Stick," Saint Mary's College Commencement Program (May 14, 2022), 21.

9. Hunter and Rowles, "Leaving a Legacy," 335.

10. Hunter and Rowles, "Leaving a Legacy," 335.

11. Hunter and Rowles, "Leaving a Legacy," 338.

12. Sister M. Madeleva, *My First Seventy Years* (New York: Macmillan, 1959), 10.

13. Gail Porter Mandell, *Madeleva: A Biography* (Albany: State University of New York Press, 1997), 12–13.

14. Madeleva, *My First Seventy Years*, 59.

15. Madeleva, *My First Seventy Years*, 59.

16. Madeleva, *My First Seventy Years*, 59.

17. Madeleva, *My First Seventy Years*, 104.

18. Gail Porter Mandell, *Madeleva, One Woman's Life* (Mahwah, NJ: Paulist Press, 1994), 54.

19. Madeleva, *The Four Last Things* (New York: Macmillan, 1959), 163–64.

20. Mandell, *A Biography*, 230.

21. Madeleva, *My First Seventy Years*, 104.

22. Mandell, *A Biography*, 233.

23. Madeleva, *My First Seventy Years*, 108–9.

24. Mandell, *One Woman's Life*, 54.

25. Ella Ewing Brown, "A Treasured Landmark." *Chimes* (Notre Dame, IN: Saint Mary's College, June 1913), 190.

26. Rose McCollough Sullivan, "Joyce Kilmer Club," *Courier* (Notre Dame: Saint Mary's College, May 1928), 21.

27. Shari Overdorf, "Joe Bonadies: The Man with a Thousand Plants," *Courier* (Fall 1989), 11.

28. Mark Kubacki, interview by Sally Geislar, August 20, 2024.

29. Overdorf, "Joe Bonadies," 11.

30. Kubacki, interview.

31. Overdorf, "Joe Bonadies," 11.

32. Kubacki, interview.

33. Overdorf, "Joe Bonadies," 11.

34. Kubacki, interview.

35. Kubacki, interview.

36. Madeleva, *My First Seventy Years*, 172.

37. Madeleva, *My First Seventy Years*, 172.

38. Courier, "A Saved Environment: For Study, for Research, for Enjoyment," *Courier* (Spring 1970), 2.

39. John M. Duggan, Inter-office Memo to Bonadies from Jason D. Lindower Jr. Secretary to Duggan. College Archives, Saint Mary's College, May 13, 1977.

40. John M. Duggan, Inter-office memo to Katharine Dooley Alumnae Office. College Archives, Saint Mary's College, June 19, 1978.

41. Addie Cashore, interview by Sally Geislar, August 12, 2024.

42. Cashore, interview.

43. Cashore, interview.

44. Hunter and Rowles, "Leaving a Legacy," 335.

45. Cashore, interview.

46. Miri Yemini et al., "Place-Based Education: A Systematic Review of Literature," *Educational Review* (2023): 1, https://doi.org/10.1080/00131911.2023.2177260.

47. Yemini, "Place-Based Education," 2.

48. Rachel Carson, *The Sense of Wonder: A Celebration of Nature for Parents and Children* (New York: Harper Perennial, 2017), 49–50.

49. Carson, *Sense of Wonder*, 44.

50. Carson, *Sense of Wonder*, 98.

51. Madeleva, *My First Seventy Years*, 108–9.

13

The Leadership Lessons of Sister Madeleva Wolff, CSC

Reflections from a College President

Katie Conboy

There have been several significant personalities in the leadership of Saint Mary's College over its nearly two centuries. At the very beginning, four French Sisters answered a call from Father Edward Sorin in 1843 and traveled for forty days over sea and rough land to remote Northwest Indiana, where they would assist the priests who had founded the University of Notre Dame just a year earlier. Father Sorin had ideas for the Sisters, and they had ideas of their own. Within twelve months, the Sisters had opened an academy for girls that would eventually evolve to become Saint Mary's College. These four sisters—Sisters Mary of the Heart of Jesus, Mary of Calvary, Mary of Nazareth, and Mary of Bethlehem—might be called the *framers* of all that Saint Mary's would, over time, become.[1]

A decade later Mother Angela Gillespie—a big personality in our institutional history—served as both the director of studies at Saint Mary's Academy and the leader of the convent. She came to the Sisters of the Holy Cross quite by accident. When she was still the young Eliza Gillespie, she and her mother stopped at Notre Dame on the way to the convent of the Sisters of Mercy in Chicago, where she intended to enter religious life. But after meeting Father Sorin and spending a short time with the Sisters of the Holy Cross in Bertrand, Michigan, "she was simply convinced that this was where God wanted her."[2] While the Academy was still in Bertrand, she deepened the curriculum and was ultimately responsible for moving the convent and the academy (buildings and all!) from their original location in Michigan to the current location of Saint Mary's College—adjacent to the University of Notre Dame. She might be considered our *trailblazer*.

Mother Pauline O'Neill was also a notable personality in the history of Saint Mary's. During her term as the college's first president, from 1895 to 1931, she transitioned the Academy to its legal and accredited status as a college, and she conferred the first collegiate degree in 1898. She was known as "the builder," and her infrastructure legacy includes the extraordinary gothic centerpiece of the campus, Le Mans Hall. Mother Pauline had the audacity to construct this enormous building in 1925, when the student body numbered fewer than three hundred. The construction allowed for "the college to separate completely from the academy, to break away from a shared dining room and kitchen, even classrooms and dormitory space" and to become "a first-rate women's college."[3] She was one of many big thinkers in the history of Saint Mary's.

The four framers, Angela the trailblazer, and Pauline the builder—each of these leaders left a mark on the college. But if you ask anyone to name the single figure most associated with the life—the vital identity—of the college, they will probably say Sister M. Madeleva Wolff, CSC, the third president, who served from 1934 to 1961. In her twenty-seven years leading the college, Madeleva faced some of the greatest challenges of the twentieth century: she began in the dark heart of the Great Depression, and she later saw the full length of World War II, the spread of communism, the Cold War, the Korean War, and the early years of the Civil Rights and Women's Rights movements. She inherited a college saddled with debt from the infrastructure decisions of her predecessors. Yet, throughout her time, she continually inspired others to a greater vision for Saint Mary's as a distinguished and truly rigorous liberal arts college. Indeed, she is often credited with transforming Catholic women's higher education in the United States. She was not only a visionary academic leader; she was also a poet, an essayist, and a memoir writer.

When she took the role of president—a role she did not want and that she had been promised she would not have to fill—she did it as an obedience.[4] She modestly claimed that her best qualifications for the position were her "ability to work" and her "capacity to dream."[5] She obviously brought many more qualifications than these. Madeleva always wore the distinctive habit of the Sisters of the Holy Cross, which unmistakably marked her as a professed religious, but she was also worldly and sophisticated: She earned her PhD at the University of California, Berkeley, undertook further studies at Oxford University, traveled extensively in the United States and beyond, and enjoyed the company of other prominent Catholic intellectuals. She also had extensive leadership experience, having built another college from scratch—the College of Saint Mary's-of-the-Wasatch in Utah. She brought all this study, investigation, and experience to an institution of higher learning that needed enlarged perspectives and new ambitions if it was to meet the changing needs of the world.

Leadership with a "Relaxed Grasp"

Through her writing and her recorded leadership decisions at Saint Mary's, Sister Madeleva left many enduring lessons that remain generally relevant for college and university decision-makers today. One of these is the concept of the "relaxed grasp," which she borrowed from Louise Imogene Guiney's description of Saint Ignatius of Loyola.[6] On a personal level, Madeleva embraced the Ignatian concept of "indifference" and holy poverty, which she interpreted as a kind of openhandedness that liberated her from a clutching hold on "friends, pupils, places, things."[7] In her role at the college, this manifested as an openness to change and a fearlessness in letting go of practices that no longer worked. She courageously pushed Saint Mary's College in new directions, and I believe her overarching message of a relaxed grasp has guided many of those who have followed in her footsteps. In our current paradigm shift for American higher education, where so much change is required, it certainly guides my own leadership as the fourteenth president of Saint Mary's College.

The relaxed grasp provides a metaphor for understanding many elements of Sister Madeleva's presidency. One example is her attention to organizational structure. When she started at the college, every decision fell to the president. The faculty could not even move furniture without her permission. She reviewed the reference texts they used in their courses and the content they described on their syllabi. Over time, she loosened her tight hold on many areas of the college, building an administrative team that had real delegated powers. She learned that she needed to save her efforts for the things *only she could do*—such as identifying the themes that would become the legacy of her presidency, which included leadership, excellence, and "the responsibility to teach 'our daughters to think ethically, honestly, morally about civil rights, about segregation, about the sacredness of human life, about power, wealth, truth.'"[8] She needed a strong and able team to execute the rest of the work.

Moreover, although she was herself a graduate of Saint Mary's College, she did not maintain a nostalgic grip on the past or assume that the education that had served her so well would necessarily be best for a contemporary student. She understood that students had changed over the quarter-century since she had attended college, and she encouraged them to be the cocreators of an educational environment in which they would thrive. A believer in what we might today call self-governance, Sister Madeleva, in the words of her biographer, Gail Mandell, "relaxed the strict convent-like rules that had governed most aspects of student life" and encouraged students to develop their own governance systems. Mandell notes that Madeleva's administration "welcomed Notre Dame men to campus, encouraging not only a more active social exchange between the two campuses but also intercollegiate drama, music, and debate."[9]

Operating in an environment of traditionalism, she also encouraged a relaxed grasp by opening up the long-standing undergraduate curriculum. Perhaps because she had been educated in multiple institutions or perhaps because she had made a practice of attending national meetings with other college administrators, Madeleva rejected insularity. She eagerly sought the best advice she could find for the undergraduate curriculum at Saint Mary's, at one point consulting Robert Hutchins—the young, brilliant, and charismatic president of the University of Chicago—and his colleague, Chicago law professor and philosopher Mortimer Adler. In fact, she assembled a team of Sisters on the faculty who spent five weeks building the program on visits to Professor Adler's Chicago apartment—something we might have to try hard to imagine: five earnest Sisters, clothed in the habit, studiously collaborating with these young secular leaders from a major research institution.

The result was a reimagined curriculum that was widely copied by other colleges and that stayed in place at Saint Mary's for twenty-five years.[10]

In addition to innovating the undergraduate curriculum, Sister Madeleva encouraged the development of adult education, primarily for intellectual enrichment. She once said:

> Christian education began with adult education....The first Christian college numbered twelve men students between the ages of 20 and 40, probably. They had the best possible teacher, Jesus of Nazareth. One of them not only left school but betrayed his teacher. Three went to sleep during a supreme hour in human history. All but one failed their comprehensive examinations....They received their degrees only after years of self-effacing work, suffering, martyrdom.[11]

Not only did she move Saint Mary's to offer this form of adult education, but she also led the college into the realm of graduate education. She established, in 1943, the Graduate School of Sacred Theology—the first program in the world that gave women access to full-time graduate education in Catholic theology. She understood that for women, advanced education in theology would have the beneficial outcome of preparing them to teach in Catholic elementary and secondary schools, and she relished the fact that Saint Mary's would have this kind of broad impact on Catholic education. Clearly, Sister Madeleva could open her hand to seize an opportunity, even if that opportunity changed the primarily undergraduate focus of the college.

And clearly those opportunities also put Saint Mary's on the educational map in new ways. The impact of the Graduate School for Sacred Theology cannot be underestimated. In her biography, Gail Mandell makes this abundantly clear:

> Within a decade, after close consultation with the faculty of the School of Sacred Theology, the Vatican set up its own graduate school of theology for women at Regina Mundi in Rome, patterning it on the Saint Mary's program. At the request of the Holy Father, Madeleva turned over all of the documents pertaining to the School, including its curricular plan, to his representatives. Furthermore, Saint Mary's agreed to validate the credits of graduates from the United

> States who completed their studies at Regina Mundi. Only after more and more Catholic universities began to admit women to their theology programs was the decision made, in 1966, to phase out the school.[12]

Paradoxically, phasing out the Graduate School of Sacred Theology could be seen as a declaration of victory by Saint Mary's: after all, the goal of educating women in theology was now widely embraced. This can also be seen as the relaxed grasp: the ability to hold and then to let go—or really to let *grow*—something immensely important. Twenty-four years, 76 doctorates, and 354 masters degrees are some measures of the School's success. But the chance to lead international change in opportunities for women was the ultimate victory. As Gail Mandell writes, "When Notre Dame and the Catholic University finally designed graduate programs in theology for lay people, Bishop O'Hara commented wryly that they were only following a suit that Madeleva had already played."[13]

The relaxed grasp may help us understand Sister Madeleva's presidency, but it is also a leadership lesson for today's Catholic colleges and universities. For many of us, our missions and our founding documents can make change difficult rather than enable it. We get so attached to fixed notions of our institutional identity that we are unable to ask whether our curriculum and supporting cocurriculum continue to speak to the longings and the aspirations of a new generation of students and faculty alike. Instead of exploring how we can maintain a core identity while remaining open to new ideas, we sometimes double down on what we think students need and want, rather than seeing how the past gives way to the possibilities of the future. In the institutions founded by the sisters, priests, and brothers of the Congregation of Holy Cross, we are fortunate to have a charism that embraces adaptability.

Sister Madeleva leaned into that spirit of adaptability throughout her leadership era. And others followed. Even in the late years of her presidency, Sister Madeleva watched as the Sisters of the Holy Cross saw their vocations beginning to dwindle. A few decades later, as they considered the future of Saint Mary's, the Sisters also practiced a version of the relaxed grasp—loosening their control of the college and welcoming even deeper collaborations with lay leaders as they transitioned from a Board of Regents to a two-tier, primarily lay Board of Trustees. And today, as the Saint Mary's faculty and staff devise a new signature experience,[14] a new general education program, and a new model for residential life, community, and engagement, we return frequently to the title of our strategic plan for inspiration: "Revere and Revise."[15] When we wrote the plan, I had not thought of the title as a version of the relaxed grasp, but, of course, it is.

"Taking the Blame for Things"

There are other leadership lessons from Sister Madeleva. One would be her concept of "Taking the Blame for Things." In her memoir, *My First Seventy Years*, Sister Madeleva recounts an amusing conversation she heard on a boat from Buffalo to Detroit. A man is observing to his wife that the captain of the boat does nothing:

> Wife: Oh! But he must do something.
> Husband: No, he doesn't. He doesn't do a thing.
> Wife: Who does the work?
> Husband: The crew. You'll see. The crew does the work. He sits in his office. He doesn't do anything.
> Wife: (still unconvinced) Well, I suppose there has to be someone to take the blame for things.[16]

Sister Madeleva came to think of "taking the blame" as a parable for her presidency, and as a portal to the imperative that governed her work: "first things must come first."[17] In this chapter of her memoir recounting her early years as president of Saint Mary's, she considers a number of "first things" she took on, ranging from reorganizing the college bulletin to ensuring the best advanced degrees for members of the faculty, from starting a nursing program to maintaining family-style meals and robust discourse in the dining room. But the chapter's culmination details her decision, in 1941, to integrate the college racially. Archbishop (later Cardinal) Stritch backed her all the way, even supporting her as she responded to "enraged letters" from Southern parents. She was willing to take the blame because, when she was asked if she would admit Black students, she said, "I knew only one answer, the right one."[18]

Taking the blame is another leadership lesson for our times. Almost eight decades after Madeleva's decision to admit the first Black student, Saint Mary's is still not as diverse as *all* our students deserve it to be. On my very first day as president, June 1, 2020, the United States was facing a racial reckoning. George Floyd was the most recent Black person to be murdered at the hands of law enforcement officers, and the resulting protests—often violent—were underway across the country. I knew I had to make a statement—and that I had to *do* something that mattered in the context of our campus community. At that time, I knew nothing of Sister Madeleva's integration decision in 1941. But for some reason, I walked over to the Sisters' cemetery on campus and stood by her grave in a kind of supplication. I said out loud: "Well, what would *you* do?"

Hard to believe, but true: I walked back to my office and picked up a copy of *My First Seventy Years*. I ran my thumb across the pages and stopped randomly, looking for some sign. I had opened to the very pages where she decided to integrate the college. In a number of decisions I have made during my first five years as President of Saint Mary's, including deciding how to respond to alumnae of color who told me during my earliest weeks of their difficult experiences at the college, I have taken to heart her words: "I knew only one answer, the right one." Of course, I have also discovered, in painful ways, that the social media environment we live in today produces a much different speed and force of reaction to a leader's decisions than Madeleva had to deal with in her era. But the result is the same. You take the blame.

Beyond Madeleva's Imagination

I could add more lessons from Sister Madeleva Wolff, a woman of capacious imagination—a remarkable personality. One of them is the ability to be still and to practice a kind of deep listening that is needed more than ever in our contemporary world. But I think it might also be important to say a few words about what Madeleva *did not* or *could not* imagine. Her writings, even when they grow solemn about the perceived threats of communism, about a world marked by continuous violence, or about illness or personal loss, have an overarching optimism.

In the penultimate essay in *Conversations with Cassandra*—an essay called "The Catholic College Changes Its Mind"—she brings that optimism to bear on the future of women's education, and on Catholic women's education in particular. In 1961, hearing a prediction by "distinguished educators" that "no more than ten of the hundred and more women's colleges now in existence will be functioning in 2061," she wrote: "All this is possible. I think it is neither necessary nor inevitable. Speaking for the Catholic college for women, I think that it will not happen."[19] In fact, the "hundred and more women's colleges" that Sister Madeleva referred to in 1961 were actually more than 230 women's colleges.

But here we are, in 2025, with only thirty-six years left on that prediction for 2061, and there are just thirty women's colleges left in the U.S. Only eight are Catholic women's colleges, and some of those eight are experiencing financial precarity. Some of the lost two hundred merged with other colleges. Others closed. Sister Madeleva's optimism certainly seems to have been misplaced. In her essay she celebrates the fact that the Catholic college had "changed its mind to meet the exigencies of the past forty years, even of every past year, and it will change it to meet present and future demands, contingencies, emergencies."[20] But she simply *could not* have imagined the dramatic speed of other changes to her contemporary Catholic world when she wrote of her Holy Cross sisterhood: "A body of women possessing both such stability and such adaptability is not likely to be destroyed by any intransigencies attributed to it or by its helplessness to survive the civilizations of the future."[21]

The decline in vocations across all Catholic religious groups, the priest sexual abuse crisis, the exodus from organized religion in general, even the fact that not one Sister of the Holy Cross is in employment today at her beloved Saint Mary's—all this would have been beyond the scope of Madeleva's imagination. She did not have what we might today call the catastrophic imagination—either the ability or the constitutional inclination to imagine the worst things that might happen. To do so might have destroyed those two gifts she brought to the role: the ability to work and the capacity to dream.

Nor, I believe, could she have imagined the level of career aspiration that college students bring to Saint Mary's today. Although she wrote so much about the importance of a liberal arts education, Sister Madeleva was more focused on it being "an avenue to eternity" or an "education for immortality" than an education for economic and social empowerment.[22] She wanted women to have a deep appreciation for the arts, sciences, and humanities, but she considered their primary roles to be as mothers who educated their children. I sometimes try to imagine her response to our current admission materials and what they promise as central elements of a Saint Mary's education—or her amazement at the extraordinary accomplishments of the graduates we honor each year at reunion. Many of our students today may still want to be mothers, but they also yearn to have their education contribute to a true professional fulfillment.

Sister Madeleva Wolff was a dreamer and a doer, a poet and a prophet, a preserver of the past and an architect of the future. She had big ambitions for a small college, and she was bold in both thought and action. She understood that everything must evolve if it is to survive, and she was unafraid to help the Catholic college change its mind. It is no wonder that Saint Mary's remains one of the eight Catholic women's colleges in America and is still thriving today. Sister Madeleva made changes in her era that positioned our college for the future. Today, even as we are clear-eyed about the headwinds facing American higher education, we honor her legacy—and the legacy of all our big-thinking forebears—as we work together to position the college for further tomorrows.

Notes

1. Sister Mary Immaculata Creek, *A Panorama: 1844–1977* (Notre Dame, IN: Saint Mary's College, 1977), 8–9.

2. Creek, *Panorama*, 21.

3. Creek, *Panorama*, 67.

4. Sister M. Madeleva, *My First Seventy Years* (New York: Macmillan, 1959), 93.

5. Gail Porter Mandell, *Madeleva: A Biography* (Albany: State University of New York Press, 1997), 146.

6. Madeleva, *My First Seventy Years*, 169–70.

7. Madeleva, *My First Seventy Years*, 170.

8. Mandell, *Madeleva*, 182.

9. Mandell, *Madeleva*, 149.

10. Mandell, *Madeleva*, 151.

11. Sister M. Madeleva, *Horizons: Reflections on a Liberal Education* (Notre Dame, IN: Saint Mary's College, 1981), 15.

12. Mandell, *Madeleva*, 187–88.

13. Mandell, *Madeleva*, 188.

14. "The Avenue Experience," Saint Mary's College, https://www.saintmarys.edu/avenue-experience.

15. Katie Conboy, "Revere and Revise: Saint Mary's College 2030," Saint Mary's College, January 2021, https://www.saintmarys.edu/files/2021/01/SMC%20Strategic%20Plan%202021%20%281%29.pdf.

16. Madeleva, *My First Seventy Years*, 94.

17. Madeleva, *My First Seventy Years*, 95.

18. Madeleva, *My First Seventy Years*, 98.

19. Sister M. Madeleva, *Conversations with Cassandra: Who Believes in Education?* (New York: Macmillan, 1961), 115.

20. Madeleva, *Conversations with Cassandra*, 115.

21. Madeleva, *Conversations with Cassandra*, 117.

22. Sister M. Madeleva, "Education for Immortality," in *A College Goes to School: Centennial Lectures* (Notre Dame, IN: Saint Mary's College, 1945), 167.

Contributors

Katie Ann-Marie Bugyis, PhD is the Rev. John A. O'Brien Associate Professor of the Program of Liberal Studies at the University of Notre Dame. A historian of Christian theology, liturgical practice, and material culture, she is particularly interested in reconstructing the lived experiences of religious women in the Middle Ages through their documents for practice and other material remains. She is the author of *The Care of Nuns: Benedictine Women's Ministries in England during the Central Middle Ages* and the coeditor of *Women Intellectuals and Leaders in the Middle Ages*, and *Medieval Cantors and Their Craft: Music, Liturgy, and the Shaping of History*. Dr. Bugyis is currently working on her second monograph, *Sibyl de Felton, Pastix of Barking Abbey*, and, in collaboration with Margot Fassler, developing a website on teaching and researching the medieval liturgy.

David A. Clairmont, PhD is an associate professor in the Department of Theology at the University of Notre Dame, where he studies comparative religious ethics, particularly the moral thought of Roman Catholicism and Theravada Buddhism; issues of method in Catholic moral theology; and the connection between ethics and spirituality. He is the author of *Moral Struggle and Religious Ethics: On the Person as Classic in Comparative Theological Contexts*, *Religious Ethics: Meaning and Method* (with William Schweiker), and coeditor (with Maria Antonaccio, Elizabeth Bucar, and William Schweiker) of the *Encyclopedia of Religious Ethics*.

Jessica Coblentz, PhD is an associate professor in the Department of Religious Studies and Theology at Saint Mary's College in Notre Dame, Indiana, where her teaching and research focus on Catholic systematic theology, feminist and queer theologies, and mental health in theological perspective. She is the author of *Dust in the Blood: A Theology of Life with Depression* and coeditor of two other volumes: *The Human in a Dehumanizing World: Reexamining Theological Anthropology and Its Implications* and *Women Responding to the Spirit: Selections from the Madeleva Lectures.*

Katie Conboy, PhD is the fourteenth president of Saint Mary's College. She has more than three decades of experience in Catholic higher education and a deep belief in the value of women's colleges and liberal arts education. Prior to Saint Mary's, Conboy served for seven years as provost and senior vice president at Simmons University, a women's college in Boston. Before that, she spent twenty-six years at Stonehill College in Massachusetts, serving first as a professor of English and then as the college's first provost. Dr. Conboy is an award-winning teacher and an active scholar. She earned her doctoral degree in English literature from the University of Notre Dame and her BA from the University of Kansas.

Sally Geislar, PhD is Assistant Professor of Environmental Studies at Saint Mary's College. An interdisciplinary scholar, Geislar uses theories and concepts from social sciences to investigate the environmental sustainability and social equity of policy outcomes. Her primary research focuses on sustainable food and waste systems with two driving lines of inquiry: how new efforts toward circular food systems can ameliorate rather than compound historical social disparities and ecological degradation, and how new understandings of the food-energy-water nexus (behavioral, institutional, and material) can improve decision-making in environmental policy and urban planning.

Molly M. Gower, PhD is Vice President for Mission and an associate professor in the Department of Religious Studies and Theology at Saint Mary's College, Notre Dame, Indiana. She is also Regional Fellow at the Medieval Institute and Faculty Affiliate at the Ansari Institute for Global Engagement with Religion at the University of Notre Dame. In spring 2025, Dr. Gower was Visiting Scholar at the Royal Institute for Inter-Faith Studies in Amman, Jordan. Her research and teaching interests include medieval Christian theology and spirituality, religious reflection on friendship, and the common good. She has published in *Religion & Literature* and the *Journal of Ecumenical Studies.*

Margaret Eletta Guider, OSF, STL, ThD is *professora ordinaria* of the Ecclesiastical Faculty of the Boston College Clough School of Theology and Ministry. Her teaching and research interests focus on ecclesiology, world mission studies, and religious life. Some of her publications include *The Grace of Medellín: History, Theology and Legacy* and *Daughters of Rahab: Prostitution and the Church of Liberation in Brazil*. She is past president of the American Society of Missiology and the Association of Professors of Mission. Sr. Guider is a Sister of Saint Francis of Mary Immaculate and a trustee of the University of Saint Francis in Joliet, Illinois.

Eva Hooker, CSC, PhD was Professor of English and Writer in Residence at Saint Mary's College until her retirement in 2022. Prior to that she was Regents Professor of Poetry at Saint John's University, Collegeville, Minnesota. In her long career, Sr. Hooker taught courses such as "Words of Love," "Twentieth-century Poetry," "Poetry Writing," "Renaissance Literature," "Shakespeare," and "Emily Dickinson." In *Godwit*, her first book, she traced the migration patterns of a bird, collected wildflowers for semblances, and explored the testimony of women mystics. Her second manuscript, *Portion*, explores the compass of the world in Margaret Cavendish's seventeenth-century voice. Chapiteau Press published two chapbooks, *The Winter Keeper* (finalist for the Minnesota Book Award) and *Notes for Survival in the Wilderness*.

Daniel P. Horan, PhD is a professor in the departments of Philosophy and Religious Studies and Theology at Saint Mary's College in Notre Dame, Indiana. A columnist for the *National Catholic Reporter*, he is the author or editor of sixteen books. His most recent books are *Engaging Thomas Merton: Spirituality, Justice, and Racism* and *Fear and Faith: Hope and Wholeness in a Fractured World*.

Susan Mancino, PhD is an associate professor of Communication Studies at Saint Mary's College in Notre Dame, Indiana. Her research focuses on public memory, semiotics, philosophy of communication, and communication ethics. Her research has appeared in *Review of Communication*, *The Journal of Dialogic Ethics*, *The Atlantic Journal of Communication*, *Versus*, and *Empedocles: The European Journal for the Philosophy of Communication*, among other outlets. She recently received Villanova University's Waterhouse Family Institute for the Study of Communication and Society Research

Grant and completed an editorship of *Journal of Communication and Religion*.

Gail Porter Mandell, PhD was hired to teach two English courses in 1971, when Saint Mary's College was in the process of merging with the University of Notre Dame. Merger negotiations fell through, and that part-time job eventually led to a forty-year career in the Humanistic Studies Program, where she is professor and Schlesinger Chair Emerita. Among other things, she has published a biography of Sister Madeleva and a memoir, *Angel Creek*. Best of all, she says, she has explored the lives, times, minds, and imaginations of some of the world's greatest writers with several generations of Saint Mary's students.

Thomas O'Grady, PhD is Professor Emeritus of English at the University of Massachusetts Boston, where he was Director of Irish Studies from 1984 to 2019. He has published widely on Irish matters in journals such as *New Hibernia Review*, *James Joyce Quarterly*, and *Irish University Review*. He is also the author of three books of poems, including *Coming Ashore: New & Selected Poems*. He is currently Scholar-in-Residence at Saint Mary's College.

Sandra Yocum, PhD is University Professor of Faith and Culture and Professor of Religious Studies at the University of Dayton. Her teaching includes courses on prayer, art-making in faith traditions, and the relationship between historiography and theology. Her publications include a history of U.S. Catholic theology in the last half of the twentieth century, an edited volume on clerical sexual abuse, and, most recently, an edited volume featuring the work of U.S. Catholic laywomen in the twentieth century. She is currently working on a history of Saint Mary's Graduate School of Sacred Theology and a book on prayer.